Noble to our View

Canada Council   Conseil des Arts   Newfoundland
for the Arts   du Canada   Labrador

We gratefully acknowledge the financial support of The Canada Council for
the Arts, The Government of Canada through the Book Publishing Industry
Development Program (BPIDP), and the Government of Newfoundland and Labrador
through the Department of Tourism, Culture and Recreation
for our publishing program.

Layout by Joanne Snook-Hann
Printed on acid-free paper

Published by
CREATIVE PUBLISHERS
an imprint of CREATIVE BOOK PUBLISHING
a division of Transcontinental Media
P.O. Box 1815, Stn. C, St. John's, Newfoundland and Labrador A1C 5P9

First Edition
Printed in Canada by:
TRANSCONTINENTAL PRINT

Library and Archives Canada Cataloguing in Publication

Darcy, J. B., 1920-
    Noble to our view : the saga of St. Bonaventure's College / J.B. Darcy.

ISBN 978-1-897174-11-1

    1. St. Bonaventure's College (St. John's, N.L.)--History. I. Title.

LE5.S325D37 2007   378.718'1   C2007-900618-3

Noble to our View

The Saga of
St. Bonaventure's College

St. John's, Newfoundland
and Labrador, Canada

The first 150 years
1856 - 2006

Brother Joseph B. Darcy

CREATIVE PUBLISHERS

St. John's, Newfoundland and Labrador
2007

Presidents/Principals of St. Bonaventure's College, 1856-2006

1856-1863	Father Enrico Carfagnini, O.S.F.	First President
1863-1868	Father Michael Walsh	Second President
1868-1869	Father Thomas McGrath	Third President
1869-1872	Father J. R. Lovejoy	Fourth President
1872-1877	Father P. A. Slattery, O.S.F.	Fifth President
1877-1881	Father William Fitzpatrick	Sixth President
1881-1888	Father William Fitzgerald	Seventh President
1888-1889	Father William Ahern	Eighth President
1889-1896	Brother J. L. Slattery, C.F.C.	Ninth President
1896	Brother J. J. Crehan, C.F.C.	Tenth President
1896-1901	Brother G. B. Lavelle, C.F.C.	Eleventh President
1901-1903	Brother J. J. Downey, C.F.C.	Twelfth President
1903-1912	Brother P. J. Culhane, C.F.C.	Thirteenth President
1912-1921	Brother J. B. Ryan, C.F.C.	Fourteenth President
1921-1927	Brother J. E. Ryan, C.F.C.	Fifteenth President
1927-1928	Brother P. B. Doyle, C.F.C.	Sixteenth President
1928-1931	Brother M. C. Ahern, C.F.C.	Seventeenth President
1931-1937	Brother J. V. Birmingham, C.F.C.	Eighteenth President
1937-1942	Brother W. K. O'Connell, C.F.C.	Nineteenth President
1942-1945	Brother J. V. Birmingham, C.F.C.	Twentieth President
1945-1947	Brother A. M. Knight, C.F.C.	Twenty-first President
1947-1953	Brother P. C. Fleming, C.F.C.	Twenty-second President
1953-1956	Brother H. P. Tarrant, C. F. C.	Twenty-third President
1956-1960	Brother J. B. Darcy, C.F.C.	Twenty-fourth President
1960-1962	Brother J. J. Enright, C.F.C.	Twenty-fifth President
1962-1966	Brother J. J. Enright, C.F.C.	First Principal
1966-1969	Brother J. M. McHugh, C.F.C.	Second Principal
1969-1974	Brother R. B. Lynch, C.F.C.	Third Principal
1974-1978	Brother J. I. Gale, C.F.C.	Fourth Principal
1978-1982	Brother R. A. White, C.F.C.	Fifth Principal
1982-1984	Brother A. R. Estrada,. C.F. C.	Sixth Principal
1984-1988	Brother D. M. Vaughan, C.F.C.	Seventh Principal
1988-1990	Mister Ronald Kieley	Eighth Principal
1990-1995	Mister Patrick Hogan	Ninth Principal
1995-1998	Mrs. Nina Beresford	Tenth Principal
1999-2003	Father Winston Rye, S.J.	Twenty-sixth President
2003 -	Father Vernon Boyd, S.J.	Twenty-seventh President
2006 -	Mister Cecil Critch	Eleventh Principal

Dedication

To the memory of
Bishop John Thomas Mullock, O.S.F.,
Who conceived this College;
To
His clerical colleagues,
Both Franciscan and Diocesan,
Who originated it;
To
The numerous
Teachers and students
Who have added to its lustre
Throughout its history;
To the dedicated Christian Brothers
Who directed its fortunes for ninety-nine years;
And especially
To
The intrepid Catholic laity who,
Together with the Jesuit Fathers and Brothers,
Refused to accept its demise
But, like a phoenix,
Caused it to rise from its ashes –
This work is respectfully
Dedicated.

TABLE OF CONTENTS

Foreword

There is a certain uniqueness about the history of St. Bonaventure's College (St. Bon's, as it is usually called.) It is rare for a religious institution, dealing mainly with primary and secondary education, to have such a deep and pervasive influence on the multi-denominational society in which it is situated. It is rarer still for such a history to be so richly documented as is that of St. Bonaventure's. Besides the House Annals of St. Bon's and of Mount St. Francis Monastery, and the scrapbooks of newspaper articles which the house archivists faithfully preserved, there are both the *Christian Brothers Education Record*, an annual publication valuable, particularly for our purposes, for its accounts of the lives of individual Christian Brothers, and *The Slattery Papers*, a series of over 450 letters written by the pioneer Christian Brothers in Newfoundland to their Superiors in Ireland. Above all, there is *The Adelphian*, the school magazine which has recorded in depth the life of the College from 1904 to the present. While all this information makes possible a rich insight into the life of the College, it also presents an author with an embarrassing wealth of material and the difficult task of selecting what should, or should not, be included.

For their assistance in meeting this challenge, I am grateful for the expert and sympathetic assistance of Donna Francis and her staff at Creative Publishing and in particular, of my editor, Don Morgan, who brought his great experience to the task. I am grateful, also, to Brothers P. J. Batterton, and J. G. Shea, as well as to Mr. James Greene Q.C., for their careful proof-reading of the manuscript and their insightful suggestions for its improvement. To Brother G. R. Bellows, who devoted so much of his time, energy and expertise to ensuring its accuracy, I am particularly indebted. To Rev. Father Vernon Boyd, S.J., present President of St. Bonaventure's College, I am especially grateful for his enthusiastic and practical support of this project.

The later history of many of those who figure prominently in the story of St. Bonaventure's College is readily available in the public record. For others, however, this is not the case and, for those readers who may be interested, a short summary of the later history of such individuals, particularly of the Presidents of the College, is given in a biographical section at the back of the book. To indicate which individuals are included, their names are given in **bold font** the first time they are encountered with a following asterisk. Please note that only deceased figures are so included.

While every effort has been made to ensure accuracy, in an account such as this, which includes so many names, facts, and dates, mistakes are inevitable. I accept full responsibility for this and would be happy to receive correction.

Statue of St. Bonaventure.

Chapter 1
THE GENESIS OF A COLLEGE

It is quite deplorable that many of the children of the respectable inhabitants should go for their instructions across the ocean, and, what is still more to be lamented, to the United States of America.

– John Nova Scotia[1]

hat possible connection could there be between the catastrophic revolutions of the eighteenth century in America and France and the founding of a small College in the remote island of Newfoundland? Strangely, the former events led almost directly to the latter. These revolutions had consequences far beyond the immediate boundaries of the countries involved. In England, for example, where the French Revolution caused the future of the monarchy to be balanced on a knife edge,[2] the Establishment viewed with dismay the radical ideas being introduced into the schools. Even such a far-off colony as Newfoundland was affected by this issue as evidenced by the above complaint of the Anglican Bishop of Nova Scotia to Sir Thomas Cochrane, Governor of Newfoundland (1825-34), over which island the Bishop had spiritual jurisdiction. The various Governors of the Colony were equally worried and therefore pressed that a classical school be opened in St. John's to keep the affluent youth safely at home and away from the influence of such heretical theories. Governor Cochrane, for example, complained to the British Government that some parents were sending their sons to the United States "there to imbibe republican principles with which to return and disseminate them in a monarchical government."[3]

However, the governor had more altruistic motives as well. Since the vast majority of the young people in Newfoundland received no higher education at all, the Governor repeatedly urged the people to establish a higher school, but the people did not respond, and he was not prepared to recommend that the British Government undertake the considerable expense involved in setting one up. His successor, Governor Prescott (1834-41), in his address to the Assembly in January 1836, noted that "the foundation of a public seminary for the higher branches of learning, and useful and elegant accomplishments, would do honour to our society; and spare its wealthier and middle classes the painful necessity of parting from their children at an age when parental care and supervision are supremely requisite."[4]

---

[1] Letter of Bishop John Inglis (1777-1850), Anglican Bishop of Nova Scotia, to Governor Cochrane of Newfoundland; quoted in F. W. Rowe, *The Development of Education in Newfoundland,* Ryerson, Toronto, 1964, p. 54. Bishop Inglis had jurisdiction over Newfoundland and made a lengthy visitation of the Island in 1827.

[2] cf. Paul Johnson, *The Birth of the Modern World Society, 1815-30,* Chap. 5, p. 362ff. Weidenfeld & Nelson, London, 1991.

[3] Appendix to the Acts of Legislature of 1850, PANL.

[4] *JHA,* 1836, PANL.

Bishop John T. Mullock, O.S.F.
Founder of
St. Bonaventure's College

The original College Building, opened 1857.

When Representative Government was established in the Colony in 1832, the Assembly became more actively involved in the educational process.[5] Following a committee report in 1836, it divided the Island into nine educational districts with school boards to oversee each, and increased the meager financial grants to the schools. The report also recommended that "Grammar Schools be instituted and schools even of a higher order to succeed them."

It took seven years to implement this recommendation, but finally, in 1843, an Act was introduced into the Assembly providing for the establishment in St. John's of "two Colleges, one for Protestant students and one for Roman Catholic."[6] The Assembly may have thought that this would please all parties, but it was a time of great political and religious turmoil, and the Act aroused much opposition. The Roman Catholic Bishop, Michael A. Fleming, O.S.F., objected that the Act made no provision for the Bishop to be on the Roman Catholic School Board, although the Anglican Bishop was to be a member the Protestant Board, nor to have any control over the appointment of teachers.[7] While these objections could be rectified, for the Wesleyans and other "dissident" Protestants, the very structure of the system was unacceptable. They presented a petition to the Assembly demanding that one educational institution, "totally free from all religious tests,"[8] be set up, and that the Churches not be given the right to appoint teachers. Several attempts to resolve these differences failed and the Bill was temporarily shelved.

In the following year, 1844, Governor Harvey (1841-46), in his speech at the opening of the Assembly, continued to press for such a school. He expressed his belief that no greater boon could be conferred on the Colony than a useful education based upon sound principles of religion and morality. He hoped that Newfoundland would not long be without the advantage of a "Collegiate or Academic Institution."[9] The Assembly responded with a flurry of activity. Two Grammar Schools[10] were established, one in Harbour Grace and the other in Carbonear, both undenominational.[11] The question of a similar institution for St. John's was reopened; the Wesleyans won the day, and an Act was introduced to establish a single non-denominational Academy in the town.

As might be expected, this Act also met with determined opposition. Bishop Fleming still objected to his having no say in the selection of teachers. But the

---

[5] Bishop M. F. Howley contended that this interest was stimulated by the great ferment in education in England which the Oxford movement generated. cf. "Address to the Old Boys of St. Bonaventure's College" as reported in *The Evening Telegram* of July 19, 1911.

[6] Act of Establishment of the St. John's Academy, JHA, 1843.

[7] Among other objections, he stated that the Ordinary of a R. C. diocese is automatically the superior of every R. C. College within his jurisdiction but that the Act provided otherwise.

[8] JHA, 1843, pp. 71-2, 113, PANL.

[9] JHA,1844, p. 13, PANL.

[10] The term *Grammar School* here refers, as in England, to élite secondary schools, not, as in North America, to elementary schools.

[11] Thomas Talbot claimed that it was at his instigation that this Act was passed. cf. *Newfoundland: or a Letter Addressed to a Friend in Ireland in Relation to the Condition and Circumstances of the Island of Newfoundland, with an Especial View to Emigration*, p. 39, S. Low, London, 1882.

Newfoundland School Society (Anglican) had more fundamental objections. It asserted that every Christian child had an undoubted right to "that early instruction in the faith and fear of the Lord which is only to be found in the Scriptures."[12]

However, it was the newly appointed Anglican Bishop Feild who was the Act's most determined opponent. Bishop Feild had already established his reputation in England as a distinguished educator (some English schools are still named after him). Even before arriving in Newfoundland, he declared that "education cannot be carried on without religion,"[13] and he set out to subvert the Assembly's intention. His declared purpose was "to prevent or mitigate the evil of a public Academy."[14] He had no sooner landed in St. John's than he established his own Classical School for Boys at *Avalon*, a large house on Forest Road, later to be the site of the Anglican Seminary. He appointed as Principal the Reverend Charles D. Newman, M.A. Oxon., whom he had engaged before leaving England. The Reverend Newman's passage to Newfoundland was by no means an uneventful one. Bishop Feild describes his voyage in a letter he wrote to a friend in England:[15]

> *Mr. Newman refused a passage by ye Hawk[16] that he might make ye voyage more quickly and thought he had taken the best and most certain method, by crossing over to Cork from Plymouth. That passage occupied 24 hours, he was detained a week in Ireland, and was then three weeks in crossing from Cork to St. John's .... My Hawk sailed almost from his own door in sixteen days.*

In spite of the opposition from so many sources, however, the Act was passed, with the munificent sum of £3,000 being allocated for the erection of a suitable building and the equipping of a library. Hoping to avoid controversy, the Assembly reserved the appointment of teachers to itself. The Senior Master was to have a salary of £300 a year and the Junior Master £250 — this compared with the £30 which was considered a reasonable salary for the teachers in the ordinary schools. The temptation of such a large salary may have proved too much for the Reverend Newman for he promptly applied for and received the post of Senior Master. The post of Junior Master was given to J. Valentine Nugent who had been a leading member of the Assembly before his appointment as first Inspector of Schools in 1844.

While waiting for a suitable building to be erected, a large private home, called *Castle Rennie*, on Signal Hill Road, was rented to provide temporary accommoda-

[12] JHA 1844, Petition of Reverend Bridge et al., p.109, PANL.

[13] Quoted in Paul O'Neill, *A Seaport Legacy*, p.779, Porcepic, Erin, On, 1976.

[14] Quoted in Vincent P. Burke, "Education in Newfoundland," *The Book of Newfoundland,* Vol. 1.

[15] *Feild Papers,* letter #10, AASJ, St. John's.

[16] The *Hawk* was the Bishop's sea-going yacht which had been given to him by a wealthy clerical friend in England for his visitations of the coast of Newfoundland.

THE ACADEMY OF ST. JOHN'S

Visitor; His Excellency the Governor
Directors: The Hon. Chief Justice, the Hon. James Crowdy, the Hon.
William Thomas, the Hon. Patrick Morris, the Hon. Robert Job, the
Hon. John Kent, John Rochford, Esq., John Stuart, Esq.
Senior Master: Charles Dunford Newman, Esq. M.A., Oxon.
Junior Master: John Valentine Nugent, Esq.

Will open Monday 29th Inst. at 9 o'clock, A.M.

The general course of instruction will embrace the Greek and Latin
Classics, French, Mathematics, Navigation, Book Keeping and the
usual branches of an English education. The annual fee will be 8
pounds currency, payable by half-yearly instalments in advance.
Spanish and other modern languages, excluding French, considered
as extras and charged for accordingly.

Each student is required to be eight years of age, or upwards, and
no pupil can be admitted until one or other of their Masters shall
have certified upon examination to the Secretary to be qualified for
admission to the academy.

The hours of attendance will be in the winter months from 9 1/2
a.m. to 3 p.m.; and in the summer months from 9 a.m. to 3 p.m. An
interval of half an hour being allowed at 1 p.m. for recreation.

The Board of Directors, as soon as necessary arrangements shall
have been completed, will be prepared to supply Books and
Stationary at reasonable charges; and Prizes will be awarded to the
Students for proficiency in their studies.

Such Parents and Guardians as may be desirous of entering the
names of the Children under their care upon the roll of the
Academy, will please signify their intention to the Secretary on or
before Saturday 27th inst.

By order
                    Harcourt Mooney Secretary

*This advertisement appeared in the local newspapers during
September 1845, announcing the opening of the Academy.*

tion for the Academy. *Castle Rennie* had been the home of the Honorable John Dunscomb who had recently left Newfoundland after his business premises were destroyed by fire. Under the name *St. John's Academy*, the school opened on September 29, 1845, with the full panoply of government support. The Governor himself was the Visitor. The Board of Directors was formed from the most prominent citizens of St. John's, including five members of the Legislature. During the course of its first year, Thomas Talbot was added to the staff as Writing Master. Talbot was later to establish himself not only as a prominent member of the Assembly, but also as an outstanding classical scholar, having several learned books to his credit, among others, a translation in verse of the Greek philosopher Epictetus. Archbishop Howley's four elder brothers became students there and, although he himself was too young to be admitted, he would sometimes be permitted to sit in on classes. Many years later, he described life in this Academy:

> *I was privileged many a time to peep into, and even take a seat on a form (a long desk) in the great schoolroom which to my juvenile eyes and imagination assumed gigantic and overawing proportions...Although the standard of education, especially in the Greek and Latin classics, was at that time of a very high grade, still things were done in a more free and informal manner, and, if you will, in a less business-like manner than nowadays.... It was surrounded by an atmosphere of classical learning, bathed in an ambient of academical ethos. A halo of romantic sentiment illumined it.*[17]

Still, in spite of its impressive launching and the ability of its teachers, the Academy had very limited success, for there were never more than 16 pupils in attendance. To try to increase attendance, another building more centrally located was rented and fees were reduced from £8 to £5. Nevertheless, by 1849, the Government was greatly concerned at its lack of progress. On February 15, 1849, a petition was presented in the Assembly that an efficient English school be established. This petition pointed out some of the defects of the Academy: the exclusively classical nature of the courses, the high rate of tuition, and the lack of a suitable site. As a consequence the Assembly requested a report from the Board of Directors of the Academy. This report, submitted to the Assembly in January 1850, has a curious relevance to recent controversies in the Province regarding religious vs. secular schooling.

In his report,[18] the Reverend Newman commented that the cost of the Academy had been great, the good done inconsiderable and, since the people of St. John's, including some of the Directors, had revealed their lack of confidence in this system of education by continuing to send their children elsewhere, he doubted that the Government should continue to support such a school. He maintained that the most obvious, though certainly not the only objection to the Academy, was

---

[17] Howley, *op. cit.*

[18] cf. *Acts of Legislature, 1850, Appendix*, pp. 133-137, PANL.

the absence of all religious instruction. As a consequence, he claimed, discipline in a school of this kind could only be maintained by severity, the fear of punishment or the hope of reward. Even if a course of theology were introduced, this would not solve the problem since religion would still not be treated as the rule of life, but be regarded as simply another branch of study. He therefore suggested that three schools be set up: one for the Anglicans, another for the Catholics, and a third for the Wesleyans. Assuming he would be in charge of the Anglican division, he generously offered to surrender a third of his salary for the support of the teacher of the Wesleyan school — a decision which he was later to regret.

Mr. Nugent was of a different mind. He objected strenuously to the idea of having three schools, deeming it "greatly objectionable economically, politically and philanthropically."[19] Moreover, he had a very poor opinion of the Board of Directors claiming that they were powerless for good, though they could cause an incalculable deal of mischief. Nugent was of a very fiery, independent temperament and we can see why the report of the Board of Directors stressed that one of their problems was their lack of control over the teachers. However, their most serious complaint was the total absence of all religious instruction. In an attempt to find a compromise between the views of the Reverend Newman and Mr. Nugent, the Directors' report suggested that while the school should remain in one building, each teacher should have his own room where he would conduct both religious and secular lessons.

A public meeting was called for March 14, 1850, to pressure the Government to repeal the Act of 1844 "for more efficiency and to be better suited to all classes of the community,"[20] but it broke up in disorder before it could accomplish anything. The commotion centred about the person of Valentine Nugent, so it must be suspected that he had been the cause of much of the disunion in the Academy.

The question was debated at length in the Assembly, and the Act duly amended to place the appointment of the teachers in the hands of the Board of Directors. Henceforth, the Academy was to be divided into three divisions and the sum of £550 was voted for the teachers' salaries: £200 for the master of the Anglican Academy, £200 for the master of the Roman Catholic Academy, and £150 for the Wesleyan master. A rather unusual provision of the Act was that, until a suitable building was available, the teachers should provide classrooms at their own expense for their respective schools. To offset this expense, they were permitted to keep all fees except those required by the Board of Directors. The "Dissenters" accepted this arrangement, but asked that the £2,500 originally appropriated for a school building be divided equally among the three Academies. Thus the Denominational System as it was to exist for the next century and a half came into being.

[19] *Ibid*, p. 139.
[20] *Royal Gazette*, Tuesday, March 19, 1850.

View of the College from the rear.

Chapter 2
THE BEGINNINGS

"...even to the dimensions of a University."
– Bishop John T. Mullock, O.S.F.

Our story primarily concerns the development of the Roman Catholic Academy, but a cursory view of the other two Academies may be of interest. The Church of England Academy was opened in July 1850, with the Reverend Newman as Master and Mr. Charles Coombs as Assistant; Bishop Feild provided premises for the Academy as well as a house for the Master and boarders. The average attendance for that first year was 19 boys, 13 of whom were in the upper school. Reverend Newman was not happy that his income had been much reduced (from £300 to £200), and that out of this amount he had to pay the salary of Mr. Coombs and spend £50 on books and other supplies. To mollify him, the Legislature gave a grant of £95 to offset his expenses. It also granted £30 compensation to James Campbell, a St. John's teacher, "for Legislative endowments having destroyed private schools."[1]

Eventually the Anglican Academy and Bishop Feild's Classical School for Boys amalgamated, but Newman did not continue as Headmaster. After the amalgamation, Bishop Feild reported that in the Church of England Academy there were two Masters, both clergymen, one an MA from Trinity College, Cambridge,[2] and that there were between 30 and 40 students.[3] In 1894, this Academy was renamed "Bishop Feild College."[4]

Not having a Master in place, the Wesleyans had more difficulty in getting started. It was a year later, on October 1, 1851, before they were able to open their Academy at the top of Prescott Street[5] in a house owned by a Mr. Rendell. They had induced a teacher from Scotland, Adam Scott by name, to come to St. John's by paying his passage to Newfoundland, guaranteeing him £200 a year for three years, giving him a house and school rent free, and paying for the necessary school books.[6] Later, the various Protestant denominations amalgamated and this Academy became known as 'The General Protestant Academy." From 1860 to 1875, it occupied the Eton Buildings, the premises previously held by Valentine Nugent.[7] Mr. Scott continued to teach there until 1877.[8]

---

[1] *JHA* 1852, p. 228, PANL.

[2] His name was the Reverend C. Poulet Hanes. cf. Edgar House, *Edward Feild, the Man and His Legacy,* p. 115, Jesperson, St. John's, 1976.

[3] H. W. Tucker, *Life and Episcopate of Edward Feild, Bishop of Newfoundland,* 3rd edition, p. 191.

[4] "Bishop Feild College," *The Book of Newfoundland,* R. R. Wood, Vol. I, p. 308.

[5] *JHA* 1852, pp.175-9.

[6] The Legislature granted £200 towards the expenses entailed. *JHA* 1852, p. 252.

[7] See various indentures held by James J. Greene, Q.C. In 1875, the premises were sold to the St. John's Training School run by the Congregational Church.

[8] *Encyclopedia of Newfoundland and Labrador,* Vol. 5, p. 110.

But to proceed with our main story. Valentine Nugent was the first to set up his school, opening the Catholic Academy in May 1850, at his home, the "Eton Buildings," on Monkstown Road,[9] with Mr. Condon as Junior Master. The school was an immediate success, reporting 47 pupils by the following month.[10] It soon outgrew the space available for it and for some years led a wandering existence. The school, however, was short-lived, for in July 1856, Mr. Nugent was appointed High Sheriff and had perforce to discontinue it.

To explain what happened next, we have to retrace our steps a little. In July of 1850, while these various Academies were opening, the Roman Catholic Bishop, Michael Anthony Fleming, O.S.F., died and his place was taken by Bishop John Thomas Mullock, O.S.F., who had been his coadjutor for the previous three years. Bishop Fleming had resisted all efforts to open a seminary in Newfoundland, believing that he could always obtain a sufficient supply of priests from Ireland. He was also quite apprehensive of the political intrigues that the introduction of local priests might bring.

Bishop Mullock, however, thought otherwise. In a Pastoral Letter published February 19, 1855, he announced that the work on the Cathedral was practically completed and that his next task would be "to establish a Seminary for the education of candidates for the Clergy." However, he had more than a seminary in mind, for, as he told the people in the following year, he intended "to commence the erection of a college which will be an honour and an ornament to St. John's, which will accommodate 40 students with their professors, and 300 day scholars." His plans were even more ambitious than this for, at the same time, he suggested that the college could be enlarged, if necessary, "even to the dimensions of a University."[11] Lest it be thought that he was neglecting the education of the Catholic girls, it should be remembered that, in 1842, Bishop Fleming had introduced the Sisters of Mercy for the education of the more affluent Catholic girls and had built a fine convent and school for them near the north side of the Cathedral. Still earlier, in 1833, he had introduced the Presentation Sisters to take care of the less wealthy girls; while the Orphan Asylum School, operated by the Benevolent Irish Society in their own headquarters, provided for the poorer boys.

Bishop Mullock plays such a large part in our story that, before proceeding further, it might be well to present him more thoroughly. Born in Limerick in 1807, he entered the Franciscan Order at the age of 16 and was sent for training to the Franciscan Monastery in Seville, Spain. Here, besides Latin and Greek, he quickly acquired a fluent knowledge of Spanish and a love for its literature. In 1829, he was sent to St. Isidore's, the Franciscan College in Rome, to complete his studies and to prepare for the priesthood. After his ordination in 1830 — by which time he had also become fluent in Italian and French — he returned to Ireland and restored

---

[9] This was quite a large building, being almost 100 feet wide and 50 feet deep. The residence of James Greene, Q. C., now (2006) occupies this property.

[10] The *Morning Courier*, June 8, 1850.

[11] February 22, 1857, RCASJ 104/1/29.

a Franciscan Monastery in Ennis. Two years later we find him at Adam and Eve's parish in Dublin where he rebuilt the rapidly disintegrating parish church, and where he first met Bishop Fleming. In 1837, he was transferred to Cork. There he rebuilt and adorned the church in Broad Street.

Bishop Mullock possessed rich and wide-ranging intellectual and artistic gifts. He found time, while pastor at Adam and Eve's, to translate some of the works of

Father Enrico Carfagnini, O.S.F.
First President of
St. Bonaventure's College (1856-1863)
and Second Bishop of Harbour Grace

St. Alphonsus Liguori[12] and to introduce him to the English-speaking world. He became a leading figure among the Irish Franciscans and Bishop Howley claimed that he was responsible for the restoration of the Franciscan Order there.[13] Bishop Fleming was well aware of his abilities and had twice recommended him for a bishopric,[14] before eventually obtaining him as his coadjutor in Newfoundland in 1847. As soon as he arrived in Newfoundland, Bishop Mullock threw himself into the work of completing the enterprises which Bishop Fleming had begun.

By 1855, the Cathedral had been consecrated and the fine stone residence for the Bishop and his clergy next to it erected, furnished and occupied. This meant that the

First R.C. Chapel in St. John's located on the site of the present Star of the Sea Hall.
It dates from about 1754. Bishop Michael Anthony Fleming, O.S.F., was consecrated
here in the first episcopal consecration in Newfoundland, October 28th, 1829,
Feast of St. Simon and Jude, Apostles.

---

[12] St. Alphonsus was Founder of the Redemptorist Order. He was noted for his work in moral theology and, in 1871, was declared a Doctor of the Church..

[13] Howley, *Ecclesiastical History II*, p.11, Terra Nova, St. John's, 2005.

[14] SCRC, America Settentionale, Vol 4, f 749v-750v, May 1, 1837; f 113r, June 11, 1837. The bishopric in question was that of Jamaica in the West Indies.

Maurice Fenelon

Thomas Talbot

"Old Palace," a rather ramshackle wooden building on Henry Street, was empty. The Bishop now took advantage of the coincidence of this building becoming available and of the closure of Valentine Nugent's school to announce the opening of his new College. While its permanent home in the Cathedral grounds was being built, it was to be temporarily located in the Old Palace.

Of course, to ensure the success of such a program as Bishop Mullock now envisioned, a competent President and staff were essential, and Bishop Mullock cast his net far and wide to find such a group. Surprisingly, for President his choice fell on the Italian Father Enrico Carfagnini, a fellow Franciscan, a lecturer in philosophy and theology, whom the Bishop had come to know at St. Isidore's in Rome. Father Henry, as he came to be called in Newfoundland, was 36 years of age. He was a native of Scanno in the Abruzzi in Southern Italy. Besides his academic abilities, he was an excellent organizer and was gifted artistically and musically, though his imperfect knowledge of English was a handicap. This last, however, was not as great a problem as one might expect since theology and philosophy were, at the time, taught through the medium of Latin.

As Dean, responsible for the behaviour of the students and general discipline, the Bishop appointed Father William Forristal who was, at the time, parish priest of Placentia.[15] He also was 36 years of age. Father Forristal's first assignment was a recruiting trip to Ireland where he enlisted the services of Maurice Fenelon, a 22-year-old native of Carlow, whose responsibility was to be the teaching of English. Father Forristal agreed with him for a term of three years for a salary of £100 a year, to commence a week after his arrival in St. John's. If he boarded in the College, the cost would be deducted from his salary.

With this skeleton staff, the Bishop opened the College on December 1, 1856, in its temporary quarters; eight boarders and 32 day students were in attendance. The students and staff soon settled into their new abode. Two large rooms were used as classrooms, with Mr. Fenelon teaching English and Mathematics in the west room and Father Forristal teaching Latin and Greek in the east room. The Chapel yard served as a grass-covered playgound.

Some ten years previously, Bishop Fleming had purchased an estate, known as Belvedere, to house a group of Franciscan Brothers who, at the request of the Benevolent Irish Society, had come from Galway in 1847 to assume the manage-

---

[15] Father Forristal later became administrator of the Cathedral and Dean of the Diocese. He died in 1894.

Fr. William Forristal

ment of the Orphan Asylum School. However, the Brothers' stay in Newfoundland was brief, and this building was now empty. Here the boarders and the professors set up temporary living quarters. In his Lenten Pastoral of February 22, 1857, the Bishop announced:

...we have commenced in the old Episcopal Residence a School and Seminary, where your children may be prepared by a solid, a refined, and a Catholic Education for any situation in life. A good English, commercial and scientific educa-tion, together with a knowledge of modern lan-guages, will prepare them for commercial pur-suits, and the study of the ancient languages and mental and natural phi-losophy, for any profession they may wish to adopt.[16] We hope especially in a few years to see some of the sons of Newfoundland ministering at the altar, and breaking the Bread of life to your children. Though the Institution is still in its infancy, it already begins to bear fruit; and though the house where it is at present provisionally located is not adapted for it, still the number of pupils enrolled on its books shows the anxiety of the

Belvedere monastery

[16] It is obvious from this statement that, from the beginning, Bishop Mullock did not intend to restrict the student body to those boys intending to study for the priesthood.

Catholic population to avail themselves of its advantages.... We may then confidently hope that this Institution now commenced, sanctified by the blessing of our Holy Father, peculiarly placed under the patronage of the Immaculate Virgin on whose Feast it was opened, and dedicated to the Seraphic Doctor of the Church, St. Bonaventure, will flourish for many ages, a source of light and sanctification to the people of Newfoundland.

Bishop Mullock was widely educated, a man of great vision, keenly aware of the importance of Newfoundland's geographical location in the new scientific era which was then in its infancy. He had already proposed the construction of a transatlantic telegraphic cable and had been in constant correspondence with Cyrus Field, Samuel Morse (of Morse Code fame) and others attempting this gigantic task. In the Pastoral Letter just mentioned, he outlined his idea of the place which Newfoundland should occupy in the world of the future — a position which it has even yet not fully realized — and the role which St. Bonaventure's graduates should be prepared to play in it:

No longer isolated, Steam and Electricity will render Newfoundland the connecting link between two hemispheres, placed by the Almighty in front of the New, and in close proximity to the Old World, surrounded by an ocean richer than all the mines of America or Australia, the future home of a great and noble people; it is absolutely necessary that the Catholic youth should have an education to fit them for the great destiny before them, and the seminary and school now established will grow with the growth of the people, and preserve for ever the Catholic character of the country.

While the boarders enjoyed their twice daily tramp from Belvedere to the school, Father Henry, not being used to Newfoundland winters, found the journey difficult. One very windy day just two weeks after the school opened, while slithering down the icy slopes of Garrison Hill, he fell and broke his leg. He was laid up for quite some time and was cared for by the celebrated bonesetter, Peter Brennan, after whom Brennan Street is now named.[17]

Meanwhile the Bishop rushed ahead with his building program. His timing was impeccable. In 1852, the Newfoundland Government had decided to build a penitentiary and had imported considerable quantities of Galway granite for this purpose. However, during the planning process, the size of the jail was reduced drastically. As a consequence, a large quantity of these massive granite blocks was superfluous, and Bishop Mullock was able to purchase them for his new building at a modest cost.

---

[17] Peter lived to be a hundred years of age and his tombstone in Belvedere proclaims him "a centenarian and a celibate." With the money left to the Christian Brothers in his will, the Brothers purchased the grounds for the original Holy Cross School.

On April 27, 1857, he laid the cornerstone of his grand new College in an impressive ceremony. The members of the Benevolent Irish Society in full regalia led the procession, followed by a large number of boys and girls and interested citizens, with the clergy and the Bishop also in full regalia bringing up the rear, while the Cathedral bells rang a joyful peal. Just as the ceremony ended, rain drove the assembly into the Cathedral where Bishop Mullock addressed them in a lengthy sermon.

Four months later, in August 1857, the first public examination of the College students was held. The conduct of school exams at that time and for many years afterwards was very different from our present written tests. The students were assembled, in the presence of their parents and invited dignitaries, and were "put through their paces" orally by their teacher. Bishop Mullock attended this first trial and was well pleased with the result.

Pressure of space in the old building forced the work on the new College to be pushed ahead rapidly, with James Purcell as architect and Patrick Kough as builder. As soon as the first floor was finished in March 1858, the classes moved in, although work on the upper floors was still in progress. By the month of October the whole building was ready for occupancy.

October 4, 1858, the Feast of St. Francis of Assisi, the great founder of the Franciscan Order, was chosen for the formal opening. The ceremonies began in the morning with Pontifical Mass celebrated by the Bishop, followed by the blessing of the statue of St. Francis of Assisi which had just been erected in front of the Cathedral. The formal opening of the new College building took place in the evening in the presence of the College students, staff and the local priests. Bishop Mullock gave an address during which he announced that the name of the College was to be St. Bonaventure's after the Franciscan College in Seville where he himself had studied for the priesthood. He then presented the College with an oil painting of its patron, St. Bonaventure, a painting which has hung on the College walls ever since. The Professors and the boarding students, at least eight of whom were studying for the priesthood, then took possession of their living quarters on the upper floors. At the same time many new students were enrolled.

This building is now (2006) very little different in appearance from when it was first built. Considering the Bishop's artistic interests, it is surprising that it presents such a grim facade with so little ornamentation to soften its stark outlines. Perhaps the "penitentiary stones" have something to do with this austerity, but still we would expect something more ornate. It was a rather expensive edifice. In a letter to Bishop Connolly of New Brunswick, Bishop Mullock stated that up to March 1859, he had spent £5,000 on it, for which he had received a grant of £1,500 from the government. With its four storeys and a large attic, it was, and still is, an imposing building. The ground floor consisted mainly of two large classrooms containing "forms"; i.e., desks, each about 10 feet long and accommodating six boys. On the second floor were the College chapel, the staff dining room, recreation room and library. The third floor had the staff bedrooms and a dormitory for the senior boys. The fourth floor and attic also contained dormitories, of which there were four in all.

This painting of St. Bonaventure was presented to the College by Bishop Mullock at its official opening on October 4, 1857, when the Bishop announced that the College was to be called St. Bonaventure's after the College where he himself had studied while in Seville, Spain.

SAINT BONAVENTURE
Bishop and Doctor of the Church
(1218-1274)

Giovanni (John) Fidanza was born in Bagnoregio (Viterbo) in 1218. While a child, he was cured of an illness by St. Francis who is said to have exclaimed "O bona ventura" (O good fortune). The name stayed with him, and he was indeed a "good fortune" for the Church. Wishing to become a Franciscan, he studied philosophy and theology at Paris and, for a long time, was a professor there. Elected Superior General of his Order, he organized and directed it wisely, so much so as to have been called its "second founder and father," for, in fact, Francis had not left very specific constitutions.

To have Bonaventure close to Rome, the Pope appointed him bishop of Albano and cardinal, burdening him with the responsibility of preparing the Second Ecumenical Council of Lyons for the union of the Latin and Greek Churches. His theology, Augustinian in mind and spirit, and strongly Christocentric, made him capable of understanding profoundly the theology of the East.

The Council opened on May 7, 1274, and, on June 28, reached an agreement for the union (unfortunately afterwards broken). But on July 15, Bonaventure died, attended by Pope Gregory X. St. Thomas Aquinas, with whom he had a close friendship, had died a few months previously.

Bonaventure was a man of action and of administration, practical and speculative, endowed with a balanced temperament and human sympathy. He saw a fundamental accord between the arts, science, philosophy, theology and history. Rarely have **knowledge and faith**[1] seen such a harmony in one man, and one, above all, animated by love. He was a great contemplative, a mystic. Because of this he has been honored with the title of "Seraphic Doctor."

---

[1] *Scientia et Fides* – motto adopted by the College and forming part of the school crest.

Chapter 3
THE FIRST COLLEGE COMMUNITY

O Life, how pleasant is thy morning,
Young fancy's rays the hills adorning,
Cold-pausing caution's lessons scorning,
We frisk away
Like school-boys at th'expected warning,
To joy and play.

– Robert Burns, Epistle to James Smith

The increased enrolment meant the need for additional staff, so Bishop Mullock began looking for suitable personnel both at home and abroad. Among the applicants for a teaching position was Thomas Talbot who had been on the staff of the St. John's Academy. He was now in the 40th year of his age. In his letter of application, Talbot modestly stated that he would be prepared to conduct classes in the Latin and Greek classics, French and Spanish languages, geometry and logic, trigonometry and navigation, arithmetic and bookkeeping. In the event, he was engaged to teach various classes in the lower grades.

In the following year, 1859, a much more unusual person joined the staff. Bishop Mullock had written Father John Henry Newman (the future Cardinal) asking for assistance in finding teachers. Father Newman, recently returned to England from Dublin where he had established the Catholic University, mentioned a couple of possibilities and then noted that "There is another gentleman, a convert, who was thinking of setting up a day school at Bayswater under Dr. Manning's[1] direction. I forget his name, but, as I have heard nothing further of the scheme lately, I should not wonder if he might be applied to. I will inquire on this point. You shall hear again from me."[2] This gentleman was William Cowper Maclaurin, M.A. Oxon., who had been the Anglican Dean of Moray and Ross in Scotland. Through his involvement in the Oxford Movement, he had been converted to Catholicism, and hence had lost his position. He had retired to the Southwark Diocese in England where he was living in poverty. When contacted, Maclaurin accepted a position on the College staff as Professor of Classics. Several others were shortly afterwards added to the staff: Señor Comerford joined as Professor of Spanish, a subject very useful in the commercial life of the town because of the fishing trade with Spain; Professor Bennett took charge of music; and Thomas Mullock, the Bishop's brother and Cathedral organist, gave lessons in piano.[3] Monitors from among the "Normal"[4] students assisted the staff in teaching the younger pupils. All this added

---

[1] Dr. Manning was R. C. Archbishop of Westminster, London, England.
[2] June 29, 1858, RCASJ, 104/1/18.
[3] Thus one can see that the College's lively musical tradition began at its very birth.
[4] "Normal" students were those preparing to enter the teaching profession. They received a small stipend from the Government.

up to an impressive, if expensive, staff. The President and lay Professors received $400 a year each, the priest Professors, $240. This was in addition to their room and board, for most of them, clerical and lay, lived in the College.[5]

THE STAFF

The teachers needed a great width of knowledge, for the curriculum was breath-taking. It included Christian Doctrine, Church history, English composition, grammar and spelling (which included derivation of words); English history, geography; Latin, Greek, French and Spanish; algebra, geometry, arithmetic, mensuration, navigation, astronomy and bookkeeping, besides singing and instrumental music. It was fortunate, therefore, that this first College community was a robust and talented one. We have pen pictures of some of the teachers. Mr. Fenelon was "solemn and grave," a strict disciplinarian though capable of an occasional joke. He was a true friend to the boys and they were very attached to him. Of great ability, he had no use for the rod. "Calm, cool, and collected," he placed the responsibility for learning on the boys themselves and they responded well. On fine days, he taught in the ancient Greek peripatetic method, walking with his class along the avenue of poplar trees.

Mr. Maclaurin was elderly, a bit hasty, an old-time school master who believed in the use of the rod even for the older boys. He liked manliness and detested a sneak as was evident on one occasion when some boy removed his "rod" from his locked desk. When extensive inquiries by the staff failed to discover the culprit, Maclaurin told the boys that he was pleased that they were manly enough not to betray a fellow student and that, as far as he was concerned, the matter was finished. Outside school hours, he was not above pulling a trick on the boys. On one occasion he came into the schoolroom where the boys were assembled and remarked that he was surprised that they had not procured some smoked glass to look at the eclipse that morning. The boys immediately rushed hither and yon to obtain and smoke a piece of glass. Then, while they were waiting for the expected view of the eclipse, Maclaurin laughed and announced: "This is the first of April!"

In spite of his broken English, Father Henry seems to have been the ideal choice as President. An article in the *Herald Tribune* of July 2, 1908, written in honour of the Golden Jubilee of the College claims:

> *No more suitable man could have been selected as President at the inception of the College. Dr. Carfagnini was a man of varied learning, enthusiastic, and energetic, and the state of excellence to which the College attained under his presidency and of which the older boys still speak in endearing terms is ample testimony that Bishop Mullock had in Father Henry a man whose inspiring influence was the real foundation of St. Bon's of today.*

---

[5] Not, perhaps, Comerford, Bennett or Tom Mullock.

Father Henry seems to have been a fine organizer and disciplinarian. Besides acting as President, he taught Logic and Philosophy to the students aspiring to the priesthood.

... AND THE STUDENTS

The first students seem to have been worthy of their teachers. They were a lively and intelligent group, as mischievous as schoolboys of any era. "Hazing" of new boys was accepted. It usually consisted of a ducking in the snow when the season had sufficiently advanced for an adequate supply of that material to have accumulated. Invasions of the Bishop's garden or of the soldiers' vegetable gardens at Fort Townshend were common. In typical schoolboy fashion, they would settle any "differences" after school in the "Hollow" behind the (now demolished) fire hall. In the same area, they staged many a battle with the sons of the soldiers of the Fort Townshend garrison when they were not engaged in snow battles among themselves, boarders versus day boys, between whom there was always a keen rivalry.

Quite a few of the students were studying for the priesthood and went on to win high honours in ecclesiastical colleges. Among them was the future Archbishop Michael F. Howley and Michael Morris, eldest son of the Morris family which also included the future Lord Morris. After his ordination, and while serving as parish priest, Father Morris devoted himself to the orphans at Villa Nova, Manuels. Tragically, he fell victim to a typhoid epidemic which ravaged the orphanage. A statue to his memory can still be seen in Bannerman Park in St. John's. Among the students also was an outport student whose first name was Matthew (his family name is unknown). Surprisingly he had the Latin and Greek classics at his finger tips, having studied them under a priest-uncle, and he was of invaluable help to the other, less industrious, students. There too was the future Monsignor Scott. John Scott was a native of Limerick. Contacted by Bishop Mullock during a visit to Ireland in 1857, he had left his home at the age of seventeen to join the Newfoundland diocese. Having completed his philosophical and theological studies at St. Bonaventure's, he was ordained priest in 1863, served in the diocese with great distinction for many years, and died in 1901 beloved by all who knew him.

The boys were given the opportunity to develop their talents in many different ways, spiritually, academically, culturally, and athletically. In cricket, the College team quickly began to excel and, to the chagrin of the local Artillery team, eventually replaced them as the premier club in the town. Father Henry introduced a College band for which he designed a typically Italian uniform: grey in colour with brilliant crimson and gold buttons and braiding, the whole topped by a hat adorned with a nodding plume of crimson. This band consisted of over 30 members. It gave frequent performances and soon became known for its excellence. He also began a student theatrical company which proved so popular that it drew crowded houses, as did a lecture series, organized by him and given by the Bishop and other leading men of the town.

The regimen of the pupils, particularly of the boarding students, was by present-day standards an onerous one. Their day began with morning prayers at 6:30, followed by study until Mass at 7:30 in the Cathedral, usually with Bishop

Mullock as celebrant, after which they had a well-deserved breakfast. At 9:30, they were joined by the day students for classes which continued until 3:00 p.m. with an hour's break for lunch. After school there was dinner at which the prefect presided and one of the students read aloud from some pious book. Then there was time for games, cricket predominating, but also hurley,[6] football and handball, until the bell summoned them for two hours of study, followed by tea, indoor recreation and bed. The meals were what could be expected in a boarding school as the following ditty, popular among the boarders during their Belvedere days, illustrates:

> *Old horse, old horse, what brings you here,*
> *From Sable Island to Belvedere?*[7]

The dormitories were allotted according to seniority, the clerical students occupying their own dormitory, the Normal students another, the other senior students a third, and the juniors the fourth, located at the top of the building. Each boarder was expected to bring his own bedding including his mattress. The iron bedsteads were the wonder of the outport lads accustomed as they were to wooden beds with wooden slats. A prefect, chosen from the senior students, was in charge of each dormitory and his position was not to be envied. Among his duties was getting the boys up for morning prayers and study at both of which he presided. He was also responsible for leading night prayers. The theological students, being the 'élite' of the school, had little to do with the other pupils, their dormitory and their classroom being on the second floor — the other classrooms were on the ground floor.

Saturday was a half-day. At noon, the junior classes assembled in the reception room where each boy was expected to recite a short poem from memory or else sing a song. Saturday and Sunday afternoons, were devoted either to games or to long walks. As one might expect, the boys detested having to parade through the main streets of the town during these walks but loved the long country hikes.

Bishop Mullock preached in the Cathedral every Sunday and every day in Lent, and attendance at his sermons was *de rigeur*. He visited the College at least once a week and never missed the semi-annual public examinations and prize-giving for which he had gold and silver medals cast and awarded to deserving students.

Before the Christmas vacation, and again before the closing of school in August, rigorous examinations were conducted. These were most solemn occasions. A newspaper account[8] of the first such examination in December 1860 describes how the examination hall was crowded with the families of the students

---

[6] Hurley, an Irish tradition, and which required large playing fields, did not long survive except on a casual basis.

[7] This was a variation of an old English naval ditty: "Old horse, old horse, what brings you here? You've carried me gear for many a year! And now, worn out with sore abuse, They salt you down for sailor's use." (cf. *Artemis*, Julian Stockman, Scribner, 2002, p.15.)

[8] *The Record*, Dec. 29, 1860.

and many other persons including several members of the Government. The students (about 70 in number) were ranged on a raised platform at one end of the hall. The proceedings began with musical items by the students. The instruments played were the seraphine (a sort of primitive harmonium), the violin, and the octave (a flute or piccolo). Bishop Mullock entered, accompanied by Father Henry and some prominent gentlemen from the city, and took his place at a table in front of the stage. Then the junior students were examined by Mr. Fenelon in geography, English grammar, the use of the globes, elementary astronomy, arithmetic, writing, both plain and ornamental, and finally book-keeping. Mr. Maclauren then conducted the older boys in Latin, Greek, French, algebra and geometry. He was followed by Mr. Comerford who examined the boys in Spanish. When these tests were completed, the students gave a series of recitations from English poets and orators. To conclude the proceedings, one of the students gave an address and presented the Bishop with a silver cross, still to be seen in the Basilica museum. Incongruously, on the cross was engraved: "From the pupills (*sic*) of St. Bonaventure's College"—presumably the spelling of the students left something to be desired![9] This was the first such public examination to be held in the "Bishop's Library" after its erection. In his report to the Government in 1860, Bishop Mullock wrote that "it will be partially a Library for the use of the Public as well as of the College. I have a collection already of over 2500 volumes as the nucleus of a Public Library and many of these books are rare and valuable."

Bishop Mullock had always intended that the College include a major seminary in which students could complete their preparation for the priesthood for the diocese, and he encouraged several candidates to come out from Ireland and elsewhere for that purpose. It was for this reason that he assembled such a large library. Nor was he straying from the truth when he claimed that many of these books were "rare and valuable." Recent research, in fact, has shown that it is a collection which any university in Canada would be proud to possess. Such items, for example, as a 1524 edition of the *Gospel of Mark* by Erasmus, a 1599 edition of *The Prince* by Machiavelli, a first edition (1615) of the second part of *Don Quixote* are just samples of the riches which the library still possesses. The wonder is how he could have assembled such a valuable collection which, in turn, by its variety of subjects and languages reveals the breadth of his own learning. The fact that that several of these books were on the Index of Forbidden Books may be an indication of his own attitude towards scholarship.[10]

---

[9] Amusingly, when St. Bon's reopened in 1999, the first billboard announcing this event stated that it was "an independant (sic) Roman Catholic School," thus maintaining the tradition of "creative" spelling which had marked the College's original opening.

[10] The Index of Forbidden Books listed those books which were considered a danger to the Faith and which, consequently, Catholics were forbidden to read unless permitted to do so for some scholarly purpose.

Unfortunately for the Bishop's purpose, just at this time the parents developed a preference for sending their offspring to Rome or Ireland for their seminary training so that, in fact, only two local students, John Kinsella and William Born, and several foreign students, including the future Msgr. John Scott, Father Thomas Hennebury (both from Ireland) and Msgr. Anthony Fyme (from Holland) actually completed their entire theology course at the College. However, other future priests also received part of their education here in these early days. They included Dean Nicholas Roche, Monsignor William Veitch, Monsignor Vincent Reardon, Fathers Joseph Donnelly, William Doutney, William Fitzpatrick (future President of the College) John St. John, and Richard Walsh[11]. Over the years, the Bishop's intention of encouraging vocations to the priesthood was fulfilled far beyond expectations.

In his report to the government mentioned above, Bishop Mullock wrote that "the great benefit of the Institution will not be apparent for several years when the generation now obtaining a higher education will become active members of Society." Nevertheless, the College quickly became the focus and pride of the Catholic community throughout the Island. As early as 1864, Michael J. Kelly, the Superintendent of Catholic Schools could report that: "... some of our best teachers have come from that Institution. In fact, it is one of the main elements that we have to depend upon to improve our Schools...."

---

[11] A complete list of priest graduates of the College is given in Appendix 1.

Chapter 4
DIFFICULTIES ARISE

In my time there was no regular band, no theatricals.,
no regular cricket or football clubs....
There was nothing of the spirit of sport that is now so much in evidence.

– Lord Morris[1]

This idyllic situation, however, continued for only a few years. To be consistently successful, an institution of this kind with no coordinated curriculum, with a staff of individualistic scholars, each with his own methods and without any formal training in the art of teaching, requires the continued presence of a strong personality at its head; one with a clear understanding of the goals of the institution and with the ability to inspire the staff and students while imposing suitable discipline. It is to this kind of leadership, for instance, that the great public schools of England owed their success. Unfortunately, after its initial stages, St. Bonaventure's was not so fortunate. In 1863, after serving the College well since its birth, Father Henry became involved in a serious confrontation with the Bishop. Various causes have been assigned for this conflict, among them, that he objected to Bishop Mullock's admitting non-Catholics to the College, that he preferred to send clerical students to the Urban College in Rome rather than to St. Isidore's. However, Bishop Mullock, in a letter to a confrère in Ireland,[2] was emphatic that it was a matter of money, that Father Henry wanted to control the finances of the

Fr. Michael Walsh,
2nd President

College, including the annual government grant, a concession which Bishop Mullock was not prepared to grant. Whatever the reason, Father Henry left the College and Newfoundland in a huff to the great anger of the Bishop.[3] His loss to the College was incalculable. None of his immediate successors possessed his dynamism and organizing ability, and the brilliancy of the College's beginnings gradually started to tarnish.

To succeed Father Henry, Bishop Mullock chose one of his own diocesan priests, Father Michael Walsh,[4] parish priest of St. Patrick's Parish in St. John's. Father Walsh, a native of Cappahayden in Ireland, had come to Newfoundland in 1837 as an assistant to his uncle Archdeacon James Walsh, Parish Priest of St. Kyran's in Placentia Bay. In 1857, he had been appointed first Parish Priest of

---

[1] "Recollections of Old St. Bonaventure's," *The Adelphian,* 1907, Vol. IV, #1, p. 54.
[2] Mullock to Cavanagh, Provincial O.S.F., St. John's, July 19, 1865, Mullock Papers, CBASJ.
[3] He gave expression to his outrage in his diary of that year.
[4] Brother of Father John Walsh, PP of Renews (d.1912).

**Fr. T. McGrath,
3rd President**

St. Patrick's in St. John's. Father Walsh was a kind, amiable man, a scholar and a theologian, but he was not in good health. Nevertheless, he remained in charge of the College for five years before resigning in 1868 and becoming Parish Priest of Placentia. He died in Harbour Main in 1871.

Replacing Father Forrestal as Dean during Father Walsh's term of office was **Father Richard Howley,*** D.D. Father Howley was the younger brother of Archbishop Howley. A brilliant student who, having obtained his doctorate in theology at the College of Propaganda Fide in Rome, was appointed professor at All Hallows College, Dublin, where he had spent two years as a pupil. In 1865, he returned to Newfoundland and was appointed professor at St. Bon's, teaching philosophy and moral theology He seems, however, to have been, like many geniuses, rather eccentric and difficult to deal with. Two years later, in 1867, he resigned from the College. His place was taken by Father Thomas McGrath[5] who had been administrator of the Cathedral. In 1868, Father McGrath succeeded Father Walsh as President. This appointment, however, was not a success. Father McGrath was a brusque, outspoken person who created fear in the boys to whom, for obvious reasons, he became known as "Whiskers." He lasted only one year and was, in turn, replaced by Father J. R. Lovejoy (1869-72), another unhappy appointment. Lord Morris, in his recollections of St. Bon's at that period,[6] noted that:

> *Father Lovejoy was a very corpulent man, far from healthy, and the nature of his ailments so affected him that it was a regular and usual thing, during the hearing of our class, for him to fall into a deep slumber at the commencement, and remain so until the hour was up.*[7]

On paper, Father Lovejoy's staff seemed quite formidable. It consisted of Father Dan Lynch,[8] Mr. Thomas Talbot, Mr. (later Father) Fitzpatrick, Mr. O'Regan and Mr. Bennett. But Father Lynch's teaching (of philosophy) was irregular and Mr. Fitzpatrick was frequently ill (he had tuberculosis). Talbot and O'Regan were the mainstay of the staff but, a few months into Father Lovejoy's term of office, both resigned; O'Regan through ill-health (he died on his way back to Ireland); Talbot to enter public life as a member of the Assembly after giving the College twelve years of stalwart service. With all these problems, it was not

---

[5] Father McGrath (1835-77), a native of Kilkenny, was ordained in 1862. Because of ill-health, he returned to Ireland in 1877 and died in Tipperary that same year.

[6] Edward Morris, "Recollections of Old St. Bonaventure's", *The Adelphian*, 1907, Vol. IV, #1, p. 54.

[7] From this description, it would appear that Father Lovejoy suffered from some form of nacrolepsy.

[8] Father Lynch was killed in a gas explosion in Montreal in November 1875.

Fr. J. R. Lovejoy,
4th President

surprising that the College was experiencing difficulties.

Meanwhile, to the consternation of all concerned, on March 29, 1869, Bishop Mullock, the mainstay of the College, died unexpectedly of a massive heart attack at the early age 62. It was Easter Monday and the Bishop had paid his respects to the Presentation and Mercy Sisters. After visiting the Benevolent Irish Society, he climbed up the steep Garrison Hill. No sooner had he reached his residence than he apparently suffered the attack. Father Richard Howley was summoned and administered the last rites. Almost immediately afterwards, the Bishop breathed his last. True to his Franciscan traditions, at the time of his death, he possessed only £20.[9]

There was quite a tug-of war over who should succeed him. The Franciscans exercised all their considerable influence in Rome to continue St. John's as a "Franciscan See"; the local clergy thought that the time had come to have a bishop appointed from among their own ranks. In the event, neither was satisfied. Rome appointed Father Thomas Joseph Power, a native of New Ross, Co. Wexford, who, at the time of his appointment, was rector of Clonliffe College, the major seminary for the Archdiocese of Dublin. He seems to have been the personal choice of Cardinal Cullen by whom he was consecrated bishop in the Irish College in Rome on June 12, 1870. It was perhaps ominous that less than a month earlier, on May 22, 1870, in the same city, Father Henry Carfagnini had been consecrated Bishop of Harbour Grace[10] by the same Cardinal Cullen. Bishop Carfagnini was to be a thorn in Bishop Power's side for most of his episcopacy.

The first non-Franciscan to become Bishop of St. John's, Bishop Power was noted for his intellect[11] and for his preaching. He was an expert in the liturgy of the Church and, according to Bishop Howley, "he raised to a height of particular grandeur the music and ritual of the Cathedral."[12] He was a kindly, gentle person, pious and zealous, with great interest in the welfare of his diocese, but given to rash promises while a great procrastinator, hardly suited to deal with the unrest which the Newfoundland Church was experiencing at the time. Constantly aware of the turmoil in the neighbouring diocese of Harbour Grace where, as a correspondent was to express it later, "there was war to the knive"[13] between Bishop

---

[9] Holland to McDonnell, November 17, 1875, *SP* #16, CBASJ.

[10] In the *interregnum*, Harbour Main and Holyrood were taken from the St. John's diocese and added to that of Harbour Grace. Later in the same year, the west coast of the Island was also separated and made a prefecture with Monsignor Thomas Sears as Prefect Apostolic.

[11] He was a graduate of London University.

[12] cf. article on Bishop Power by J. G. Higgins in the *Centenary Souvenir Book* (1855-1955) of the Archdiocese of St. John's

[13] McDonnell to Hoare, September 9, 1875, *SP* #9, CBASJ.

Fr. F. A. Slattery, O.S.F.,
5th President

Fr. William Fitzpatrick,
6th President

Fr. William Fitzgerald,
7th President

Carfagnini and his people, especially the Irish, he was afraid to give the least cause of complaint to his congregation. The College needed to be "taken by the scruff of the neck" but this he seemed unable or unwilling to do, and the College drifted along.

On Father Lovejoy's retirement as President of the College in 1872, **Father P. A. Slattery, O.S.F.**,* (1872-76) succeeded him. A native of Waterford, Father Slattery had come to Harbour Grace after his ordination in Rome in 1859. He was more durable than Father Lovejoy but no more successful. He was deaf and hence lost his grip on the school, though one thing he did do well was to regularise its finances. It was of this period that Lord Morris could sadly report:[14]

> *It was not the fault of the teachers, it was largely due to the system of continually changing the staff if the period from '70 to '74 was not the Augustan era of the College. I went to the school full of the traditions of the College '60 to '70 — the years that had turned out many brilliant students with which the history of the College must be forever associated. ... I found it hard to believe that these traditions were not mere fictions, rather than substantial realities. ... In my time there was no regular band, no theatricals, no regular cricket or football clubs ... There was nothing of the spirit of sport that is now so much in evidence.*

To try to remedy the situation, a layman, Professor P. J. O'Neill was appointed Headmaster, Father Slattery remaining as President.. This led to a brief revival. Professor O'Neill was an M.A. from Trinity College, Dublin, a gold medalist. He was a "classical scholar, keen mathematician and an enthusiast for English Literature. He was a kindly, sympathetic teacher and captured the con-

---

[14] Morris, *op. cit.*

fidence and esteem of his pupils. Assisted by Mr. F. J. Doyle, who taught commercial subjects, he soon evolved order out of chaos."[15]

At the end of 1876, however, Father Slattery resigned. He and Bishop Power had been at odds for some time,[16] so possibly the Bishop was not sorry to see him go. He was succeeded by Father William Fitzpatrick, assisted by the newly-ordained **Father William Fitzgerald**.*[17] Father Fitzpatrick was a native of St. John's and had joined the staff of the College in the late 1860's while still a clerical student. He taught Spanish and French and, in 1874, had been appointed Dean. He was of a very delicate state of health, suffering from TB,[18] and was to die only five years later while still President. Most of the teaching was still being done by Professor O'Neill and Mr. Doyle.

Some idea of the critical situation in which the College found itself at the beginning of the school year in September 1876 can be gained from the following figures. There were only 37 students in attendance, consisting of 12 day-boys (their numbers increased shortly afterwards), six boarders and 19 pupil-teachers.[19] There was a grant of £700 from the government, plus £30 for each student-teacher, to which was added the fees of the day-boys. Yet the College was £300 in debt.[20]

Now another element entered the picture, one which, though at first it further compounded the difficulties of the College, was ultimately to be its salvation. After repeated entreaties over many years, the diocese[21] had at last obtained the services of the teaching Order of Christian Brothers to take over the struggling Orphan Asylum School (shortly to be renamed St. Patrick's Hall Schools), which the Benevolent Irish Society had been attempting to keep alive since its foundation in 1826. The arrival of the Christian Brothers in January of 1876 implied far more than the arrival of a few more teachers. It meant the introduction, for the first time in Newfoundland, of a group of teachers who taught as a unit, were all trained in the same methods, used the same graded text books (most of which had been written by members of their own Congregation to ensure their suitability) and

---

[15] W. J. Carroll, "the Mid-Seventies," *The Adelphian* Vol. 4, #1, June 1907, p. 65. The *Newfoundlander* of January 28, 1875, in noticing his appointment, quotes from the *Dublin Nation* of June 1, 1875, as follows: "We are very happy to learn that P. J. O'Neill Esq. A. D., &c., has been recently appointed Professor in the Catholic College of St. John's, Newfoundland. Mr. O'Neill was, during intermediate and university career, remarkable not only for his great abilities and close attention to his respective studies, but also – and this is better – for his honour, honesty, and purity of character."

[16] An observer notes that "Father Slattery used to give it 'right and left' to the Bishop." Holland to McDonnell, January 12, 1877, *SP* #42. CBASJ.

[17] Father Fitzgerald was a native of Dungarvan in Ireland. He had come to Newfoundland as a Deacon and had been ordained by Bishop Power on January 6, 1877 (cf. Holland to McDonnell supra.)

[18] P. K. Devine, in his reminiscences, noted that Fr. Fitzpatrick was confined to his room most of the time (1878-81) that he, Devine, attended the College. cf. *The Adelphian* 1931, p. 50f.

[19] These 19 student-teachers were from the various educational districts and their support was largely paid by the government. The boarders and day-boys paid their own fees.

[20] cf. Holland to McDonnell, September 6, 1876, *SP* #34, CBASJ

[21] The reason Bishop Power was more successful in this respect than his predecessors may have been that he had been President of Clonliffe College in Dublin and was a personal friend of influential Brothers.

**Fr. William Ahern,
8th President**

employed the same code of discipline. In effect, it was the first modern school in Newfoundland. And although there were usually well over a hundred boys in a class, the results were dramatic, resembling the impact of the introduction of the automobile into the horse and buggy age. So much so, that parents began to take their boys away from the College to enter them in the Brothers' school.

This created a dilemma for the Christian Brothers. On the one hand, their apostolate was to the poorer children and they did not want to refuse any of these where there was room to accept them. On the other hand, they could hardly demand a means test from applicants, nor could they afford to offend those whose offerings would be mainly responsible for their support.[22] An interesting instance of this dilemma occurred one day when the Bishop spoke to them, disapproving of their accepting such pupils; but, a few days later, "by special request," he had a 'respectable' boy entered into their school.[23]

In spite of his illness and in spite of the problems that the advent of the Christian Brothers was causing him, Father Fitzpatrick cordially invited the Brothers to share the College residence while they were waiting for their monastery to be built on a nearby property.[24] Five Brothers moved into residence on October 28, 1877, and were assigned bedrooms on the third floor and a large room on the second which served as community room and kitchen. They remained in residence until August 21, 1880, when they moved into their magnificent monastery at Mount St. Francis located just opposite the College.

The College Board at this time consisted of Bishop Power, Father Fitzpatrick, J. I. Little, Q.C., the Honourable Thomas Talbot, W. P. Walsh, Daniel J. Greene, and Maurice Fenelon. Their most pressing concern was the debt caused by the low enrolment and the high salaries of the teachers.[25] When, in April 1878, Professor O'Neill applied for an increase in salary, the Board notified him that, instead of increasing his salary, they would have to reduce it from £200 sterling to £200 local currency. He was not willing to accept this so, in August 1878, he resigned and returned to England where he began the study of law. The Board was also obliged to raise the tuition for boarders and pupil teachers[26] from £30 currency to £35. The

---

[22] The Brothers refused all government support and relied on an annual collection for their survival.

[23] cf. Holland to McDonnell, May 3 & 5, 1876, *SP* #25, 26, CBASJ.

[24] Since their arrival in St. John's, the Brothers had been living in a house on St. John's Lane.

[25] In 1877, the debt had been £600; by 1881, it was to reach £1,436. (cf. Minutes of College Board, March 7, 1882, CBASJ).

[26] The Board seems to have had an erratic policy towards the pupil-teachers. They were considered rather "low-brow," at times they were admitted to the College as boarders while at others they had to find lodging in the town.

government grant for pupil teachers was £29 a year, so future pupil teachers would have to raise the additional £6 themselves, not an easy thing to do since most of them came from the outlying settlements.

Professor O'Neill's replacement, Mr. John F. Morris, another member of the Morris family, was also a highly successful teacher, but his tenure was brief since, in November 1879, the College Board, for reasons unknown, notified all the lay teachers that their services would no longer be required after February 14, 1880.

In May 1880, Bishop Power travelled to London to search for a suitable replacement for John Morris. He returned with Charles E. Hodson, M.A. (Camb.) who had been teaching higher mathematics at Kensington University College. Mr. Hodson began teaching at the College in the end of August but it was a brief experiment for he resigned in the following January. On the fourth of the same month, Father Fitzpatrick died and was buried in his parents' plot in Belvedere cemetery, greatly mourned by all who knew him. Father Fitzgerald was appointed to succeed him, and Father Daniel O'Brien was appointed to the staff.

Though young and inexperienced, Father Fitzgerald soon proved a dynamic leader. He was a capable musician, and, besides Greek, Latin and science, he also taught drama and singing. He instituted both the Holy Name Society, of which the College students were the first members, and the 'Children's Mass' in the Cathedral at which he was the usual preacher.

To try to attract greater support for the school, the Board decided, in March 1882, to invite Bishop McDonald, Bishop of Harbour Grace, and Monsignor Thomas Sears, the Prefect Apostolic of the West Coast, to become members of the Board. The next meeting of the Board in April was attended by both these prelates. Having determined that, in spite of the indebtedness, the staff of the College would have to be increased, a teacher, Mr. J. Ryan, was engaged to care for the pupil teachers at a salary of £200 currency a year. In January 1884, Martin Furlong was hired to assist him at a salary of £40 a year and Mr. Ryan's salary was increased to $1,200.[27] Mr. Furlong resigned at the end of the school year to study law.

Father Fitzgerald now began a vigorous, but abortive, building effort. The first result of this was the installation of hot water heating. Next, he built a ten-foot wide corridor at the rear of the building where the students could exercise in inclement weather, and renovated other parts of the building. He planned to take off the upper storey of the College and build an addition back from the study hall. These plans had even gone out to tender when the opposition of Bishop McDonald[28] of Harbour Grace frustrated them.[29] Meanwhile, he launched a determined drive to obtain more students but without much success, for the academic results at the College

---

[27] Note that, as this time, the currency in use was gradually changing from English pounds to local dollars with a pound being roughly equal to five dollars.

[28] Bishop McDonald was so incensed at not being consulted about these additions that he resigned from the Board.

[29] cf. *SP* #23-28. CBASJ.

could not compare with those in the St. Patrick's Hall Schools. It did not help matters when, in the spring of 1884, the dreaded diphtheria disease appeared among the students and they had to be dispersed for some time. Eventually, even Father Fitzgerald found the challenge too great. In the summer of 1888 while on vacation with his brothers in the United States, he wrote Bishop Power to say that he would not be returning to Newfoundland.

His successor was **Father William Ahern**,* destined to be the last priest President of the College for over a hundred years. Father Ahern, a native of Waterford,[30] studied at All Hallows Missionary College, Dublin, and was ordained by Bishop Power in 1883 for the diocese of St. John's. He joined the staff of the College in 1885 and became President in 1888.

With Father Fitzgerald's departure, the Bishop and the College Board had become thoroughly discouraged. Morale among the staff and students was at its nadir. For some years, the other two Newfoundland prelates had been advocating that the College be handed over to the management of the Christian Brothers, but Bishop Power hesitated to take such a drastic step knowing the admission of failure it would entail and the reaction that would inevitably occur on the part of some of his priests.

By April 1889, however, the choice was clear: either to close the College or to ask the Brothers to take it over. He put the matter to the Board which unanimously agreed to ask for the Brothers. Consequently, the Bishop forwarded this request to Dublin to Brother Anthony Maxwell, the Superior General of the Brothers, with what results we shall see in the following pages. Thus began the passage from one era in the chequered history of the College to another very different one.

---

[30] There is some confusion regarding the place of his birth which was either in Waterford, Ireland, or Brooklyn, N.Y., more likely the latter as he went there after leaving Newfoundland.

Chapter 5
TURMOIL IN SUMMER

This city is now passing through a great trial. One can easily realize the times of plague, when the little white coffins, two and three in the day, pass the door. You may see in the dusk of the evening a funeral with two persons following towards Belvidere[1]. It is sad also to see the word "Diphtheria" in large letters on yellow posters stuck on every house affected. The magistrates have ordered this to warn people not to enter. It is a dreadful disease — whole families have been wiped out, not a child left to the distracted parents. No child under 14 yrs. is allowed to Mass or any such place, and much misery is caused by the dread of contagion.[2]

The next act in our educational drama was played out against the terrifying background of a raging diphtheria epidemic which began in the early spring of 1889 and lasted into the fall; an epidemic which played its own part in the collapse of the College and was to cast its sinister shadow over its continued existence. At first the epidemic attacked mainly the young. Deaths were frequent. In April, the Brothers in St. Patrick's Hall Schools reported: "The numbers in our junior schools are low. For the past three months diphtheria has been raging. Mr. James Howley buried a fine boy eleven years of age last week."[3] By May: "Diphtheria spreading this week. Schools so thin we can't send returns. ... Three men employed opening graves at Belvidere."[4] A few days later, "They (the doctors) are sending a request this evening signed by all the medical men to have schools and churches closed for some time as Diphtheria is spreading so fast.... There is great consternation."[5] By the 28th, "This evening's account is, for the week, sixty-nine new cases of Diphtheria and nine deaths. ... All houses in which disease appears are to be quarantined, and children under 14 not allowed to Churches."[6] Shortly afterwards Brother Fleming wrote that the disease seemed to be on the decline:[7] "Only 42 cases last week against 57 the previous week and 69 before that. Seven deaths last week against 11 the week before." Sadly, it flared up again for, on the 24th, Brother Slattery described two scenes he had just witnessed:[8]

---

[1] "Belvidere" was the accepted spelling at that time.

[2] Slattery to Holland, *SP* #129, June 9, 1889, p. 5.

[3] Flood to Holland, *SP* #114, April 14, 1889. James Howley was the noted geologist and author of *The Beothucks or Red Indians* (1915)

[4] Fleming to Holland, *SP* #123, May 8, 1889, p. 3.

[5] Idem.

[6] Fleming to Maxwell, *SP* #128, May 28, 1889, p. 1.

[7] Fleming to Maxwell, *SP* #131, June 12, 1889, p. 1.

[8] Slattery to Holland, *SP* #132, June 24, 1889, p. 3.

Diphtheria is still raging. Yesterday a funeral passed—two little coffins side by side. Out of five children, they were the third and fourth the poor parents lost. Today another sad sight. The funeral consisted of a man and two boys—the father and two only survivors of six children. It is most mysterious in its ravages and seems to be little understood by doctors. The people are panic stricken and fly all contact with the infected.

It was in this atmosphere of fear and confusion that the transfer of the management of the College was announced. One might perhaps have expected that, faced with such a social disaster as the epidemic represented, the people would have not cared one way or the other who ran the College. But, in fact, reactions were as passionate as they were diverse:[9]

The topic of the hour in the clerical, conventual and secular circles in St. John's is St. Bonaventure's College and the Christian Brothers. To mention the several and diverse opinions of each circle is not my intention. The first circle feels humiliated but, on the whole, resigned; the second is much divided, some for and some against the change, the third is unanimously in favour of it. In fact the public are delighted at the change and have on every occasion expressed their joy and satisfaction.

By all reports the approval of the change by the Catholic people was virtually unanimous. The College Board also was totally in agreement,[10] while the Staff could hardly wait for the Brothers to take over. "Father Ahern is like a bird in a cage anxious to be free from it, he thinks every day too long. Father Ryan equally anxious."[11] The priests of the diocese understandably felt somewhat humiliated that "the Bishop and Board expect the Brothers to succeed where they have failed,"[12] but this soon passed away in the realization that the change was all for the good.

There was one small group of priests, however, who remained strongly opposed. In general, these were the "native" priests who had done some or all of their training at St. Bonaventure's. Their leader was Father Michael Morris whom we have mentioned earlier as a member of the first College class in 1856. Father Morris was a complex personality. A man of extraordinary dedication, he had taken on himself the operation of a boys' orphanage at Villa Nova in Manuels and had taken up to 200 boys under his care. He was convinced that the College should remain under the control of the priests. The previous summer, on Father Fitzgerald's departure, he had even urged the Bishop to allow him to take over the College while still remaining in charge of the orphanage. In fact he had asked to be

[9] Flood to Holland, *SP* #121, April 30, 1889.
[10] See Slattery to Holland, *SP* #119, April 17, 1889, p. 1.
[11] Fleming to Holland, *SP* #127, May 27, 1889, p. 1.
[12] Slattery to Holland, *SP* #122, April 30, 1889, p. 1.

OLD ST. BONAVENTURE'S, VALE!
(Editor "Evening Telegram.")

St. John's, June 27, 1889

Mr. Editor –In the *Colonist* of yesterday APPEARED A PARAGRAPH DECLARING THAT OLD St. Bonaventure's was about changing hands. A more exact heading would have been: *"Destruction of Higher Education:" a fitting ending to twenty years bungling.*[1] It was unkind of the *Colonist* reporter to omit chronicling that the "joyful event," like all acts of supreme treachery, was celebrated by a grand *dejeuner*, quite equal to the spread at the *Atlantic*-at which the usual toasts were drunk. The *Archididasculus*[2] in replying said: "It was the happiest day of his life, as it saw the realization of the dearest wish of his heart. For nearly two decades of years he had laboured earnestly to destroy all higher education in Newfoundland; and although it was an unconscionably long time to take, he appealed to them if the results were not brilliant. Like slow poison, his methods were sure and safe. He had trusted to the scripture precept about the blind leading the blind, and he had taken care that in all these long years no one but incapables, bunglers, and blind pilots would have charge of the "Old Brig." And if today she was stranded on the rocks he claimed the full credit of it; and in proof of his words, he challenged any one to point out or name *ten or even five clever young men in our Catholic community to-day* who could say that they had been educated during these eighteen years at Old St. Bonaventure's. Was that not a splendid record?

It was true that he had burned his fingers pretty badly in trying to get sops and jobs for those incapable professors he had imported to carry out his views. More than once he had been sorely crossed and hampered by the nonsensical patriotism of some irreconcilable natives, but he had pretty well muzzled them, and to-day he could claim that he had won all along the line; and he thanked Heaven that in his time at least there would never again be the spectacle of *a native sitting in a professor's chair, or teaching in the old college on the hill.* It was true that last year despite all the force and grace of his "Vindex" letters, documentary proofs were forthcoming that showed that the old college, founded by his predecessor in office, and built by the people's money, was designed as a seminary where young Newfoundlanders would be trained in philosophy and theology; but so much the worse for the facts and *crank* that produced them. He didn't take stock in that kind of grammar. He had himself talked a lot of nonsense about *elevating natives* when he first came into office; but he found it didn't do, and he could say from experience that the imported article was far more satisfactory. He found that natives were far too clever when they got fair play; they were too ambitious. Witness how they succeed in church and state when away from Newfoundland, and he believed that if they got a taste of the sweets of higher education, and that education with a flavor of patriotism and native feeling and thought, good-by to his reign and the good old easy-going times. The Secretary, resplendent in a white shirt, here proposed that all hands sing the *Dies Irae* before parting; but the chairman insisted that a more fitting hymn to close the solemn farce would be "Sound the Loud Timbril," which was accordingly entoned with all solemnity, and the gathering broke up.

ONE OF THE OLD BOYS.

The above letter was answered shortly afterwards by the following:

NEW ST. BONAVENTURE'S, AVE!
(*To the Editor of the Colonist.*)

Sir:- I have little desire to enter the arena against a writer in Friday's "Telegram", signing himself "One of the Old Boys." It is a futile task to discuss any question with a writer who quotes words never uttered, and ascribes motives never entertained. But as a Catholic, I desire to enter my indignant protest against the most malicious and venomous attack ever made, in this island, on any ecclesiastic. The letter is a splendid specimen of what its writer calls "nonsensical patriotism," as it contains a most childish, nay, disgusting "lot of nonsense about elevating the natives"; and if it be a specimen of the "higher education" he received at Old St. Bonaventure's, there is little doubt "the imported article is far more satisfactory." This writer speaks of some natives as being "pretty well muzzled." It is a great pity the operation failed in his case, as it would save Catholics the grave scandal given by his production.

The writer signs himself "One of the Old Boys," but evidently makes a mistake. That letter was never written by *one* of the old boys—it was produced manifestly by the "Old Boy" himself.

---

[1] Bishop Power had succeeded to the Diocese in 1870.
[2] Head teacher

Only the father of lies could dictate such a vile attack on the highest representative of ecclesiastical authority in the island

Being one of the "Old Boys," he had an opportunity of being trained in "philosophy and theology," in those golden days of old he speaks of with much regret. If he is a typical student of those times, few Catholics will regret that "there are not *five such* clever young men" in our Catholic community today. *One* such "Old Boy" is enough. Then, if his letter be the fruit of his "philosophy and theology" we should be thankful for the discontinuance of the course.

He says the college was built by the people's money. As one of that denomination, I am very much pleased to think that there is at length some prospect of the *people* getting even more interest on the investment than they have received since the foundations were laid. We are coming into our rightful inheritance. The granite walls of old St. Bonaventure's are too solid to be stolen away and they will long stand a monument of the people's generosity and for the people's use. But when the "Old Boy" asserts that it was built as a seminary for the training of young Newfoundlanders in "philosophy and theology" – in other words for ecclesiastical students alone - I beg leave to contradict him. It was for others too: for the lawyer, the doctor, the engineer, the man of business, and for all Catholics requiring something more than an elementary education. The seminary was no more intended for theology than for law, medicine or engineering. Having finished there his preliminary mathematical and classical studies, the student was supposed to continue at some other seat of learning, the particular and technical subjects appertaining to his particular vocation. The law student took up his legal studies in a lawyer's office, the student of medicine repaired to London, Dublin or Edinburgh to finish in the advanced studies proper to his profession; while the ecclesiastical student turned his face to Laval, All Hallows, or the Propaganda; and there, for years, at the feet of the most renowned professors in the world, enlarged and ennobled his mind by studying the profound truths of philosophy and theology. It is as reasonable to complain that law, medicine or engineering is not taught as to bemoan the absence of a theological chair. All these studies are purely technical and must be pursued in those centers especially established for their cultivation. Much as I should desire it, I am sorry I have no son showing any inclination for the priesthood, but there are a couple of boys, in whom I am deeply interested, who will have to fight their way in other fields of the world's warfare.

I protest against the policy implied in this scandalous letter, that the interests of these and many others are to be sacrificed for the sake of the few young men whom God may call within the sanctuary. By all means let aspirants to the priesthood be well trained in philosophy and theology; but let them pursue the study in one of those great centers of learning, where it can be followed with advantage and success. In "One of the Old Boys" may be seen the sad results of loose theology and third rate philosophy. His "poison" is not "slow." It strikes at the vitals of Catholicity, unity and authority.

If this writer wishes to know what the people think, let him go amongst them and learn. He will soon find that there are not "five Catholics" in all St. John's – "young" or old – "'men" or women – "clever" or otherwise, who take his view of the proposed change. The "native protest" was still-born. Amongst the people he will find ardent hopes and certain confidence that the future prospects of the college will be worthy successors of the balmist days of the past; and that under the tried and trained experience of the Christian Brothers it will fully realize the sanguine expectations of its most ardent admirers. His letter was headed, "Old St. Bonaventure's, Vale!" I join sincerely in the valediction, but would wish to add, "New St. Bonaventure's, Ave!" Farewell the Old – All Hail! the New!

Having done with the "Old Boy", I have a word to say about his agent, without whose assistance his venom could not be disseminated. The vilest Orange print of Toronto, or Belfast, would not dare to publish such an atrocious attack on any ecclesiastic. We are 20,000 Catholics of St. John's. Are we so fallen, and so despicable, that this unprincipled newspaper may insult the highest dignitary of our Church before our eyes? Will Catholics patronize or tolerate in their homes, a newspaper whose columns reek with foul abuse of the Reverend Bishop, who represents the Infallible Church of Christ." Reverse the position: in a Protestant population of 20,000, would any Catholic paper dare insult their highest church dignitary? If it did – well, "Twenty thousand Cornishmen would know the reason why"! Were there no "Telegram" anxious to publish, there would be no "Old Boy " found to write such an infamous production.

I am, Sir,
AN OLD CITIZEN

allowed to form a teaching Order for this purpose.[13] Both requests the Bishop had refused. Now he began a determined campaign to force Bishop Power to reverse his position, causing the Bishop much embarrassment as Father Morris was a member of a prominent St. John's family. He persistently lobbied both the Bishop himself and many influential Catholics. On June 27, 1889 there appeared in the *Evening Telegram* an anonymous letter bitingly attacking the Bishop for his decision and accusing him of attempting to dismantle higher education in Newfoundland so as to destroy a native clergy.[14] Although he strongly denied it, it was generally accepted that Father Morris had written this letter. Consequently, it was thought that he had gone too far. All his supporters deserted him and rallied around the Bishop and the Brothers. Disappointed and disheartened, he retired to his orphanage where disaster soon struck.

Some of the boys contracted typhoid fever, apparently through drinking contaminated water. For a while, Father Morris tried to care for them himself with the assistance of his staff. But the disease spread like wildfire throughout the institution, and, by the time the medical authorities were contacted, 60 boys were down with it and several had died. Then Father Morris and some members of the staff, all of whom were working day and night, also contracted the disease. Two of the staff died and Fr. Morris was removed to his family home where, on August 1, 1889, he also passed away. Brother Slattery paid this tribute to him:[15]

> *All St. John's — indeed all Newfoundland, stands mute at his sudden and tragic end ... He is dead, but he won't be forgotten. He had his faults, but his good qualities were many and great. He was one of the most temperate men I ever met, while his clothes were almost shabby. Under other circumstances he would have accomplished wonders.*

His body lay in state for three days in the Cathedral. He was buried in Belvedere with the Governor and the entire Assembly in the procession. The city stores were closed and flags flown at half-mast. Later a monument was erected to his honour in Bannerman Park where it still stands.

But before this tragedy, poor Bishop Power, with the town in the midst of an epidemic and the Church in turmoil over the proposed transfer of the College, was faced with another bombshell. On April 30, 1889, in answering the Bishop's request for the Brothers to take over the College, Brother Holland, writing to Brother Fleming on behalf of the Superior General of the Brothers, had indicated that the Superior General was not at all in favour of doing so. In a later letter

---

[13] Fleming to Holland, *SP* #126, May 13, 1889, p. 1.

[14] For a copy of this letter, see insert. It is probable, however, that this letter was not written by Father Morris at all, but by Father Richard Howley who was on very bad terms with the Bishop, at least Br. Slattery came to think so.

[15] For an account of this tragedy see "The Tragedy of Villa Nova" by Michael McCarthy, *The Monitor*, August, 1978, RCASJ.

(May 13, 1889), the Superior himself explained why. There were two main reasons: one, that he was extremely hard pressed to fulfil his present commitments; and secondly, that in any case, he thought the Brothers should "stick to their last." They were founded to teach poor boys and they should leave to others "the management of higher and more important establishments."[16] He also expressed the very sensible fear that the Brothers might not be able to live up to the expectations of the Bishop and the people of St. John's.

The Brothers were thunderstruck at this apparent refusal. In panic, they wrote individually to the General and his Assistant, Brother Holland, protesting that their position in St. John's would be untenable if the offer were refused. Brother Fleming wrote strongly:[17]

> ...you will place the Brothers here in a very awkward position and indeed the Bishop also. He has gone pretty far in the matter, and I can clearly see that your objecting to take it will be the beginning of an amount of unpleasantness for which you are not prepared. You lose your hold on the people who have been so kind and who are all without exception anxious that it should be taken by the Brothers. You will likely have the boys ordered out of the school, and I won't be at all surprised besides incurring the great displeasure of the Bishop and Priests.

And Brother Slattery, writing on the same day, put in a special plea on behalf of the people of St. John's.

> ... in all the wide world is there a spot more deserving of gratitude from the Brothers than this good city of St. John's. Rich and poor alike would be serviced by our having the College. The first, by having a proper place for their children, the second by having more room in St. Patrick's Hall."[18]

He also pleaded on behalf of the Bishop "He acted most generously in the matter of the College. ... He will feel intensely if his offer is refused."

Under such pressure the Superior relented and reluctantly agreed to the take over. There were still practical problems to be surmounted. There was a debt of $12,000 on the College, but the Brothers believed that there would be no difficulty in paying this off. More important was the question of ownership. Originally the Bishop had agreed to hand over the College, "lock, stock and barrel," but there were legal problems with this in canon law. Bishop Power's advisors objected and the Brothers, realizing that, even if they had complete legal ownership of the College, "(n)o one believes but that a future Bishop, if determined on the point, could take

---

[16] Maxwell to Fleming, *SP* #125, May 13, 1889.

[17] Fleming to Holland, *SP* #123, May 8, 1889, p. 1.

[18] Slattery to Holland, *SP* #124, May 8, 1889, p. 1.

the College from the Brothers, even if secured by documents of cast steel. The Brothers' strongest title deeds will be not on parchment but in the hearts and affections of the people."[19] So eventually it was agreed that only the endowment should be handed over, and that the Brothers, should they ever leave, would be indemnified for whatever monies they had invested in the College.[20]

When all was agreed, Brother Maxwell worked rapidly. Brother Fleming, accompanied by Brother Kennedy was ordered to Ireland to make final arrangements. Meanwhile, since the priests had left the College, Brother O'Hurley was asked to sleep there until the new staff arrived. So, amidst such difficult birth pangs, the second era in the continuing saga of the College's tumultuous history began.

---

[19] Slattery to Holland, *SP* #132, June 24, 1889.
[20] This provision was never carried out, nor did the Brothers request it.

**The First Brothers' Community at St. Bon's.
Br. J. L. Slattery, Br. P. J. Culhane,
Br. T. A. Prendergast, Br. J. J. Crehan**

Chapter 6
THE NEW BROOM[1]

*To regulate such an establishment, to bring the different elements of
its necessary machinery into harmonious working, to raise an Institution
like this from its present "abject condition" to one worthy of the Colony
and of our Brotherhood,*

— Brother J. L. Slattery

On August 5, 1889, Brother Maxwell notified Brother Slattery of his appointment as President of St. Bonaventure's College and told him that two Brothers were on the way from Ireland to join his staff. These Brothers were James Joseph Crehan and Thomas Andrew Prendergast. At the end of October they were joined by a lay-Brother, John Conrad Byrne.

Brother James Joseph Crehan* was such a unique character that he deserves a brief memoir of his own. A native of a small Irish-speaking village near Dungarvan, Co. Waterford, James Crehan had never spoken a word of English until he was seven years of age when his family suffered the all-too-familiar fate of Irish peasants of the time — eviction, and were forced to seek refuge in the town of Clonmel. There, James attended the Christian Brothers' school, and he and his brother Edward quickly distinguished themselves for their intellectual brilliance. Edward joined the Holy Ghost Fathers, became President of the famous Rockwell College in Cashel and later Provincial Superior of his Religious Congregation. James, after joining the Brothers in 1874 and receiving the name in religion "Brother Joseph," spent some years teaching in Ireland before being assigned to Newfoundland at the age of 27. He was an all-round genius and, although he remained only seven years at the College, he had a most profound effect on that institution and its students. Deeply interested in all branches of learning, he was, according to his companion, Brother Prendergast, probably the first person in North America to take an X-ray picture. The picture in question was that of the Brother Prendergast's hand,[2] the year being 1896. In a tribute to Brother Crehan at the time of his death, Professor J. L. Ahern of Waterford wrote:[3]

*I often showed him some difficult mathematical problems. He simply
took out his pencil and a scrap of paper and solved them right away. This
happened on many occasions. The extent of his knowledge of English*

---

[1] For a fuller description of these eventful years (1889-1895) read my *Fair or Foul the Weather,* Creative Book Publishing, St. John's, 1999.

[2] Brother Prendergast wrote years later: "A picture of one of my hands showing all the bones, joints, etc., of the fingers and back of the hand, as distinctly as can be obtained to-day, was to be seen fifty years ago in one of the show-cases of the old College building," *Obituary of Brother J. J. Crehan, CBER,* 1945, p. 433. Roentgen had announced his discovery of the X-ray in December, 1895.

[3] *Ibid.,* p. 447.

Literature, Latin and French astonished me. He could speak for hours on the different ideals of the classical and romantic poets, and he often recited passages from Scott, Wordsworth and Tennyson. I often submitted to him some obscure lines from the Odes of Horace, and he had not the slightest difficulty in translating them.

He was also well versed in theology, Church history and other branches of religious learning. But, with all that, he was deeply religious. "He was simple, humble, kind, fond of the poor and the orphan, and could be seen years and years ago on the side of the street in his native Clonmel, teaching poor, neglected children some of the essentials of our Holy Faith."[4] In appearance he was short, decidedly plump, and in later years wore his hair long. This, with his sober black clothes gave him a remarkable likeness to a familiar figure in a cereal advertisement and he acquired the nickname "Quaker Oats." It would be difficult to find a person better suited to the demanding work he was now to take on with the senior pupils of St. Bonaventure's.

Brother Thomas Andrew Prendergast,* a younger man of 20 years, was born near Carrick and also attended the Brothers' school in Clonmel. By another coincidence, his elder brother became a well-known priest-theologian. Brother Andrew was of "medium height, light sand-coloured hair, somewhat ruddy complexion, soft-spoken voice, small penetrating eyes which sparkled as an accompaniment to his own witty sallies"[5]. He was "physically active and radiating intelligence, whose kindly face was lighted by a smiling "good morning" as he entered (the classroom)."[6] He became noted as the most successful teacher for public examinations in Newfoundland.

Of Brother Byrne little is known except that he was born in Carlow, had entered the Congregation as a school-Brother, had failed in that responsibility and had become a lay-Brother. He was 44 years of age when assigned to St. Bonaventure's. Possessed of a quiet, unostentatious piety and a firm will, he was responsible for the domestic arrangements of the College for the next 22 years, and had the distinction of being the first Christian Brother to die in Newfoundland, an event which occurred in May 1911 when he was 66 years of age. He was first buried in the grounds of Mount St. Francis, but later his body was exhumed and placed in the Brothers' plot in Belvedere.

**Br. J. L. Slattery,
9th President**

---

[4] *Ibid.,* p.435.

[5] Brother Thomas Perry, *Ibid.* p. 466. The present writer lived with Brother Prendergast for three years from 1936 to 1939 and at that time, although decidedly eccentric, Brother Andrew still possessed the merry twinkle and witty sallies of former years.

[6] Brother P. Dominic McCarthy, "Obituary of Brother T. A. Prendergast", *CBER,* 1954, p. 459.

THE COLLEGE OF ST. BONAVEN- ture, under the patronage of the Most Rev. Dr. Power, will be opened by the Christian Brothers as soon as the Board of Health grants permission.

Meanwhile it is desirable that early application for admission should be made, in order that classes may be formed immediately after opening.

The education given will be complete and thorough, embracing all the subjects necessary for Business. the Professions, and for aspirants to the priesthood.

At this College boys may without leaving the country. advance from the elementary stage to the Matriculation and Arts, and Science Examinations of the London University.

Fees, for Day Boys, $12, $15 and $18 per annum, according to class. For Boarders—Board Washing and Tuition, $160 per annum.

The only extra charges are: for Instrumental Music Books and Stationery, and Medical attendance.

Prospectus giving programme of studies and full details, is now ready, and may be had on application to

aug21,fp tf   **J. L. SLATTERY.**

Re-Opening of Saint Bonaventure's.

The classes in St. Bonaventure's College (under the charge of the Christian Brothers) will embrace a very much larger sphere of usefulness area than before. By reference to advertisement in this paper, it will be seen that it will not be necessary for aspirants to the priesthood to leave the country to prepare for Holy Orders, or to matriculate in the London University. This will not only be a great saving in time for boys, but will save a large amount of expense to parents and guardians of scholars. Owing to the fact that diphtheria has all but disappeared it is expected that the the College will re-open about the first week in September.

Announcement of re-opening, 1889

PROSPECTUS.

St. Bonaventure's College, St. John's, Newfoundland, under the Patronage of the Most Rev. Dr. Power.

St. Bonaventure's College is conducted by the Christian Brothers, who aim at giving the pupils a complete and thorough education—elementary, commercial and classical. At this College boys may, without leaving the country, advance from the elementary stage to the subjects prescribed for the matriculation and the arts and science examinations of the London University.

The chief object of the education system of the Christian Brothers being the religious instruction of their pupils, the moral and religious training of the students is most carefully attended to.

No effort is spared to secure the exact and efficient training of all the pupils in the studies pertaining to commercial life.

The studies are divided into three courses:

1. The elementary course is intended for young boys, who will be kept apart from the rest of the students, in dormitory, class and refectory. A resident matron will give them all the care their tender years may require.

2. The commercial course is adapted to boys preparing for business or more advanced studies.

3. The advance course comprises those studies necessary for students preparing for university examinations, for the professions or for the priesthood.

The collection of apparatus necessary for the study of natural science, has been greatly enlarged, and no expense will be spared to make it all that the requirements of the students may demand.

The scholastic year is divided into three terms:
1. Christmas to Easter.
2. Easter to Midsummer.
3. Midsummer to Christmas.

FEES FOR DAY BOYS:

Elementary Course $4 per term. $12 per annum.
Commercial Course 5 per term. 15 per annum.
Advanced Course . 6 per term. 18 per annum.

FOR BOARDERS:

Tuition, Board and Washing..$160 per annum.

All fees payable in advance at the beginning of each term. Instrumental Music and Medical attendance are extras.

Students, unless personally known to the Brothers, are required, before entering, to present a letter of recommendation from a clergyman and a certificate of health from a physician.

Each boarder shall provide himself with at least two suits of clothes and an overcoat, four day shirts, three night shirts, two sets of flannels, six collars, four pair of socks, three pair of boots, a pair of house shoes, two pair of pillow cases, two pair of sheets, two pair of gloves, six handkerchiefs, hair-brush, tooth-brush, combs, etc.

Three months' notice is required before the withdrawal of a pupil.

PROGRAMME OF STUDIES.

1. Elementary Course:—3rd and 4th reading books, grammar, geography, writing, arithmetic, drawing, singing, etc.

2. Commercial Course:—5th and 6th reading books, English grammar and composition, French, geography, history, writing, arithmetic, bookkeeping, Euclid, Algebra, mensuration, shorthand, typewriting, drawing, singing, elocution, etc.

3. Advanced Course:—The subjects of the commercial course, Greek and Latin classes, modern languages, natural philosophy, chemistry, trigonometry, navigation, etc.

Pupils of the second and third divisions will be required to take up only such subjects as may be considered suitable for them.

Communications to be addressed to—

J. L. SLATTERY.

PROSPECTUS - 1889

Brother John Luke Slattery* was, at the time of his appointment, a big, burly man of 42 years of age at the height of his powers. Born in 1847, he attended the Christian Brothers' school in Nenagh and joined the Congregation at the age of 17. After his training and 11 years spent teaching in Dublin, he was transferred to Cork, and, in his four years there, he endeared himself to both Brothers and boys by his "good nature, happy disposition and thorough efficiency in the schools. He was kind, yet firm, agreeable and at times even jovial, never repellent, ever great-hearted and magnanimous."[7]

He came to St. John's in 1881 to take over the senior class at St. Patrick's Hall Schools. This he taught with such extraordinary success that one prominent St. John's lady, comparing St. Patrick's Hall Schools to St. Bonaventure's College, was moved to ask:[8] "How can it be possible that you can do as much as three priests, two lay professors and a professor of drawing, and having more boys than they do?" In agreeing to become President of the College he was well aware of the challenges which he faced for he had been a close friend and confidant of Father Fitzgerald who had often spoken to him of his many difficulties at the College. In writing the Superior General accepting the position he described these challenges:[9]

> *To regulate such an establishment, to bring the different elements of its necessary machinery into harmonious working, to raise an Institution like this from its present "abject condition" to one worthy of the Colony and of our Brotherhood, all these form a Programme far beyond my ability to accomplish. I clearly see the enormous difficulties before me.*

But accept it he did. Brother Maxwell had chosen wisely.

On August 14, 1889, Brothers Crehan and Prendergast arrived in St. John's via the *S.S. Peruvian* and settled briefly into Mount St. Francis Monastery to recuperate from the voyage. Then, on August 29th, Brothers Slattery and Crehan moved to the College to be joined two days later by Brother Prendergast. The sight that met their eyes would have been enough to dismay the stoutest hearts. The building was deserted. The previous staff had, naturally, taken away all their belongings, including their beds. This applied also to the boarders who, as we have noted, had always been required to provide their own bed and bedding. The boarders' apartments were in the same condition as when they had been abandoned helter-skelter at the end of the previous school year. Even the dirty water was still in the wash basins.[10]

> *We entered here without a penny and had to furnish throughout as the priests took all their things away. We had not a book, nor a bed, for ourselves or the boys. Not a room was furnished except by the spiders.*

---

[7] "Br. J. Luke Slattery," *CBER*, 1910, p. 197ff.

[8] Fleming to Maxwell, *SP* #70, April 20, 1884.

[9] Slattery to Maxwell, *SP* #133, August 5, 1889.

[10] Slattery to Maxwell, *SP* #168, November 22, 1890.

Besides this, the building had been neglected in the disarray of recent times, so their first task was to get rid of the debris of years, and to clean and paint the various rooms, "tearing down and building up and making dingy places look bright."[11]

They rolled up their sleeves and set to work, and on September 9, 1889, the College was formally reopened by Bishop Power in the presence of many dignitaries, including Archdeacon Forrestal, who had been one of the two first teachers in the College when it opened in 1856, and Thomas Talbot, now High Sheriff, another of the early teachers. There were 55 day-boys in attendance, a demonstration of the confidence the people had in the Brothers. Two weeks later, on September 23rd, the boarders were admitted; the large dormitory accommodating 24 and the small one, eight, both on the fourth floor. On October 5th, the Normals arrived, bringing the total number of students to almost 90.

Shortly after the opening it was discovered that the cook had been acting dishonestly for years past. She was dismissed, and Mrs. Leece "an honest woman and a fair cook," took her place. Mrs. Furlong was engaged as matron, with Kate Power to assist her "and the College will never have better servants."[12]

The situation of the Normals was, to our present way of thinking, rather peculiar. While the ordinary boarders paid about $40 a year, the Normals were supported by the Government at a lower rate. Some of them paid the difference themselves and hence enjoyed all the privileges of the boarders, but the others slept in the attic (the fifth floor), ate at a separate table, polished their own boots and made their own beds! This traditional system endured for the first five or six years of the Brothers' regime when the distinction gradually disappeared though the Normals continued to pay a lower 'pension'. The College Annalist relates an amusing incident in connection with the polishing of boots, another indication that schoolboy antics last from generation to generation.[13]

For the first few months a boy (hired) cleaned the boots, &c. but as the boarders were utilizing him for bringing in contraband goods, he had to be dismissed and was replaced by Rachel Lynch who remained at her post in the College until the spring of 1902.

In a related problem, Brother Slattery reports:[14] "Tobacco gave us a little trouble but I think we have completely eradicated old habits. But it requires continuous vigilance. The new comers give most trouble."

Together with the financial difficulties, and the frequent turnover of staff, the Normals had always presented a serious continuing problem for the College. Sometimes they had been boarded in the College, at others they had been

---

[11] Fleming to Holland, *SP* #112, August 20, 1889, p. 1.

[12] College Annals, 1889, p. 53, CBAJS. There are two books of Annals that deal with the same period. This is the shorter of the two accounts.

[13] *Idem.*

[14] Slattery to Maxwell, *SP* #168, Nov. 22, 1890, p. 1.

expected to live in the town.[15] Bishop Power and some of his priests were opposed to permitting the Normals to board. They considered them "low," "vulgar," "ill-conducted," and it would appear that Brother Fleming was of the same view. Brother Slattery, however, did not agree. He claimed that it was the system that was at fault and that "with judicious arrangements, and the supervision and training of the Brothers, the habits and manners of the Normals would be as free from reproach as those of any other students."[16] In a previous letter he had explained the source of the trouble:[17]

> The "system" was wretched — each student supplied his own room — from bedstead to basin. The well-to-do folk made a flourish while the poor Normal should make his "appurtenances" correspond with the slenderness of his purse. Each was supposed to polish his own boots. Before entering — but for different reasons — neither class had often done this unenticing piece of work. The result was only what might be expected. Other matters, broken mugs and jugs, want of supervision in the dormitory and refectory, gave it a bad name & no wonder. Boys sick, at home, found all their bedding absent on their return. It was stolen and never recovered. Last winter a most respectable boy while out playing had his bedding stolen. He lay on the boards that night, got sick, went home and never returned. The untidy appearance of all things around was unjustly attributed to the Normals, but it was the System — or rather the want of any — that lay at the root. The soiled water left in the basins when the boys were going on last summer vacation, was there in the basins on their return, seven weeks later. Decent people turned against the whole place and its ways.

As it turned out, Brother Slattery was right, and before very long the Normals were a credit to the institution. Another decision of his had an ironic twist. It will be remembered that, for some time, boys had been deserting St. Bon's in favour of St. Patrick's Hall Schools much to the dismay of the priests. But when Brother Slattery decided to take in younger boys, both as day-students and as boarders, the shoe was on the other foot. Boys began to leave St. Pat's for St. Bon's. Brother Fleming was disturbed; he had lost both his principal teacher and his best students. "What will poor Mount St. Francis do," he wrote pathetically to Brother Holland, " if every man who can pay a pound is taken away? I fear our numbers will fall short.... Our staff in St. Patrick's Hall will be very weak now—as soon as you can, come to our aid."[18] But that was not Brother Slattery's concern, he had enough on his own plate.

[15] cf. Slattery to Holland, *SP* #129, June 9, 1889.

[16] Slattery to Holland, *SP* #132, June 24, 1889, p.1.

[17] Slattery to Holland, *SP* #129, p. 2.

[18] Fleming to Holland, *SP* #135, August 20, 1889.

So, for the first three months, the future of the College looked very promising; everyone (except possibly Brother Fleming) was very pleased. Then disaster struck!

On the last day of November 1889, just as the College was settling down nicely, the dread disease of diphtheria, which had been raging throughout the town,[19] broke out among the boarders. Immediately, school had to be cancelled, the dayboys sent home, and the familiar yellow posters placed on the doors. All admittance had to be refused, except to priests and doctors. Soon six boarders were ill. A week later, Brother Slattery and Brother Prendergast, two servants and another boy were struck down. Fortunately, Brother Crehan escaped the infection and was able to tend to the sick, assisting Doctor Edward Shea, the College physician, who was unremitting in his care for them. "From early morning till midnight he was at our call."[20]

Sadly, on December 15th, one of the boys died from the disease. He was George Gibbons, son of a "planter" at St. Mary's; he had entered the College only three weeks previously. Since Brother Slattery was such a warm-hearted person, the effect of this calamity on him was shattering. Four months later, in a letter to Ireland, he unburdened himself: "Even now my heart sinks when the sad remembrance of our fearful experience comes before me... I am not ashamed to acknowledge that I often wept like a child when things seemed going from bad to worse."[21]

Two days earlier, in an attempt to avoid further spread of the disease, the seven boarders who were still healthy had been taken by Brothers Crehan and Byrne to a summer home, Friendly Hall, at the top of Kenna's Hill. This building was bare and had to be completely outfitted for their use at considerable expense. By December 22nd, the sick were convalescent enough to be moved to Friendly Hall while the College was thoroughly disinfected. To accommodate them, the healthy boys were moved from Friendly Hall to a cottage near the College called Silver Oak Lodge.

By the end of the month of December, staff and students were well enough to reassemble in the College. But, as if to mock their efforts, a new boarder from St. Pierre, named, very appropriately, Joseph Le Fèvre, came down with the disease just a week after he was admitted. Then Brother Byrne caught the disease from him. Both had to be sent to hospital, the school once more disinfected, and its reopening postponed.

All this took place in the worst winter in living memory and in the midst of a flu epidemic which struck all the staff except the indomitable Brother Crehan.[22] To

---

[19] The statistics for the previous June will give some indication of why it was so feared. For the week of June 10, 1889, there were 42 new cases and 7 deaths. During the following week, there were 49 new cases and 5 deaths, from June 18 to 24, there were 45 new cases and 13 deaths, and the following week, 36 new cases and 4 deaths; for a total of 172 new cases and 29 deaths. Source: The *Colonist,* June 28, 1889.

[20] Slattery to Holland, *SP* #154, March 4, 1890, p. 1.

[21] Slattery to Holland, *SP* #155, April 1, 1890.

[22] Slattery to Maxwell, *SP* #153, February 17, 1890, p. 2.

crown their misery, when the school did re-open on January 20, 1890, with the temperature at -13° F (-25° C), the furnace burst. Yet, in spite of everything, by the middle of February all was in working order again.

Remarkably, in the midst of all this turmoil and in spite of his own bouts of illness, Brother Slattery had seized the opportunity of the vacant classrooms to alter radically the physical set-up of the school. He divided the large classroom into two, turned the parlor and old kitchen into another classroom, converted the boys' study to a gym, changed the boys' entrance from the rear of the building to the front, and finally, removed the handball court at the end of the building. Thus he was able to open the windows of the large classroom which the presence of the ball court had necessitated being blocked up. He even laid plans for the improvement of the bumpy field in front of the College.

Except for still another brief outburst of diphtheria in April, which caused the loss of a week's classes, the rest of the school year was a peaceful one for Brother Slattery and his staff. When school ended, he began to look forward to a restful summer, but to his dismay, in June, he was summoned to Ireland to take part in a General Chapter[23] of the Brothers. Reluctantly he obeyed.

---

[23] Every ten years, the Superiors were required to meet with representatives of the Brothers to examine the state of the Congregation. This meeting was known as a General Chapter.

Chapter 7

RE-ENFORCEMENTS ARRIVE

Our boys are good and edifying in their conduct and behaviour.
Above all, the 43 who board with us, I must praise as the best boys I
ever met.

— Br. J. L. Slattery

When, at the conclusion of the meeting in Ireland, Brother Slattery returned to St. John's, refreshed in mind and spirit by this long sea voyage, he found that two additional members had been added to the staff. One, **Brother Michael Baptist Flood**,* had been on the staff of St. Patrick's Hall since his arrival in St. John's from Ireland in 1881. He was in delicate health and found the heavy classes at St. Pat's very difficult. He had been recalled to Ireland, but Br. Slattery had suggested that, instead, he be given a trial at the College where the classes were smaller and his musical talents could be better utilized. This transfer was agreed to.

The other new member was **Brother Patrick Joseph Culhane**.* Born in Glinn in Co. Limerick in 1868, Patrick Culhane had first tried his vocation to the priesthood but had transferred to the Christian Brothers just the year before. He had barely completed his novitiate year when he was sent to join the College staff, a very inexperienced 22-year-old but, as it proved, an excellent choice.

Brother Slattery was delighted with these reinforcements. The number of students increased as well. By the end of November 1890, there were 97 students on the roll. Br. Slattery was surprised to discover how pious the boys were, especially the boarders who proved very different from the "low" lot he had been told they would be. Seven or eight of them were studying for the priesthood. He noted that "Our boys are good and edifying in their conduct and behaviour. Above all, the 43 who board with us, I must praise as the best boys I ever met."[1]

Just before Christmas, the Government School Inspector, Mr. James J. Wickham, examined the College, and his report was highly laudatory.[2] Several points in his report are of special interest: there were six students in the top class who were all following the London University Matriculation Curriculum; in spite of a large overdraft, almost $1000 had been spent on scientific equipment during the year; there had also been a large outlay on the grounds to level the field in front of the College and to incorporate the Bishop's Garden into the school property.[3] Finally, the inspector noted that Brother Flood had introduced the tonic sol-fa system of singing, the first educational institution in the country to do so.

During this year, while attending to his normal school duties, Brother Slattery took on three major initiatives. His first came about as a result of his pleasant sur-

---

[1] Slattery to Maxwell, *SP* #203, December 24, 1891, p. 1.

[2] A complete copy of the report can be found in Appendix 2.

[3] Bishop Power had donated his garden, situated where the Forum and its parking lot are now located, to the College.

prise at the quality of the students, particularly the once despised boarders, and confirmed by an incident at Easter time. The Brothers were about to make their annual eight-day retreat in preparation for Easter when two of the boys asked to join them. Br. Slattery explains what happened:[4]

> We consented – but only for three days. One by one others joined on till we had twenty three!! Many of these had ideas for the priesthood and others for ourselves. Well, I was never more edified. Many of them scarcely left the Chapel, till out of mercy, they were sent to walk round the grounds. As for Rosaries, Stations, &c, it was one exercise from morning till night. One great blessing we have is that all our grown boys are either for the priesthood or religion and are most edifying. The younger ones easily follow.

Brother Crehan was of a similar opinion for he wrote to the Superior General that "I have never met finer boys than many of our pupils."[5] Several of them, he noted, had quite made up their minds to join the Brothers. Realizing that, for years to come, there would be major difficulty in obtaining sufficient reinforcements from Ireland, Brother Slattery sought permission from his Superiors to establish his own Brother-formation program at the College. He argued that, as student teachers, the recruits would be financed by the Government and that they could receive their teacher training at St. Patrick's Schools and the newly established Holy Cross Schools in the West End of the city. After much persuasion, he was permitted to set up an experimental preparatory program at the College under the care of Brother Joseph Crehan. Four fine boys applied for admission and were accepted. A section of the building was set aside for their accommodation.

The second initiative was of a different nature. The Government was concerned about the quality of education in the country and issued a public request for suggestions to improve the school system. There was, at the time, a strong movement urging the adoption of a unified secular public school system instead of the existing denomination system. Brother Slattery realized the danger this movement presented to the Catholic schools and presented his own proposals for the improvement of the existing system. Among his suggestions were the following, many of which readers will recognize as part of the basis of our present educational system:

a) Teaching was to become a profession rather than a job. Teachers were to be adequately paid according to their qualifications and, on retirement after thirty years service, a suitable pension. Scholarships were to be provided to encourage young people to take up the profession.

(b) A Central Board was to be set up to certify teachers, oversee examinations, oversee the opening of new schools and supervise the distribution of government

---

[4] Slattery to Maxwell, *SP* #181, April 6, 1891, p. 1.
[5] Crehan to Maxwell, *SP* #164, October, 15, 1890, p. 2.

grants. Inspection was to be done by district rather than by denomination. In areas where no one denomination could support a school, there were to be common schools with a mixed Board.

Brother Slattery's proposals were accepted as being the best submitted and the Government prepared a Bill based on them. After a stormy passage through the Legislature and many alterations, this Bill became the law of the land. So the Council of Higher Education (the CHE) which did so much to improve educational standards in Newfoundland and Labrador as well as the establishment of teaching on a professional basis owed their introduction to his initiative.

For his third initiative, with what seemed to many people in the town sublime audacity, Br. Slattery decided to enter four of his top students for the London University Matriculation examination. This was an extremely difficult test, and no student from Newfoundland had passed it for the previous five years. Moreover, his boys were only sixteen years of age while the normal entrant would be in his/her twenties. In the event, none of the students passed the exam, but Brother Slattery was happy that they had gone "so near the mark" and that they had done better than the students from the other Colleges. He was sure that in the following year they would succeed for, as was customary, all were going on again.[6]

The school year ended on a very up-beat note as the first public examinations and prize day under the new regime were held in St. Patrick's Hall on St. Bonaventure's Day, July 14, 1891. The Bishop, the Board of Governors, about 20 priests and many leading citizens were present and the event was an unqualified success. Afterwards, Bishop Power wrote the Superior General to say that "the management of the College deserves the highest encomiums... the moral standard of the Institution affords the greatest hope for the future well-being of the Roman Catholics in this City."[7]

The following year, the growing reputation of the College caused the number of students to swell to 115, among whom were 43 boarders of whom 16 were student teachers. Some of the Brothers had visited St. Pierre during the summer to improve their French. They had been very hospitably received by the Brothers there, and now one of the latter, Frère Louis, came to reside at the College to learn English and to teach French. Unfortunately, he brought with him three St. Pierre boys who gave considerable trouble, but he himself made such an impression that when he had to leave in February, the Brothers were very sorry to see him go. Thus began an association between St. Bon's and St. Pierre that lasted for almost a century.

On June 24, 1892, the year was apparently crowned by the consecration of Father Michael F. Howley as Bishop and Vicar Apostolic of St. George's where he had served as Prefect Apostolic since 1885. Since Bishop Howley had been one of the original pupils of the College when it opened in December 1856, and was the first native Newfoundlander to be elevated to the bishopric, there were naturally

[6] Slattery to Whitty, *SP* #198, October 14, 1891.
[7] Power to Maxwell, *SP* #190A, August 5, 1891.

St. John's after 1892 fire, looking west from Devon Row;
trees in Cavendish Square (on right) escaped fire.

B.I.S. building after the 1892 fire.

52

great celebrations in the College. The students presented him with an Address and an entertainment; the staff with a formal dinner.

It will be noticed that I used the word "apparently" when speaking of this historic event, because just two weeks later, St. John's was visited by one of the worst of its periodic disasters. For weeks the weather had been very warm with not a drop of rain. A hot wind blew steadily seawards. A few minutes after four on the evening of July 8, 1892, a fire broke out in a stable, caused by a careless stablehand smoking a pipe. In a few minutes, the flying sparks ignited the roofs of several houses nearby (the houses were all made of wood and the roofs tarred). From there, sparks, carried by the wind, alighted on other housetops. Soon, the fire spread to right and left. St. Patrick's Hall with its Brothers' schools was threatened. The Brothers from both communities (St. Bon's and Mount St. Francis), accompanied by the St. Bon's boarders rushed to the scene. The fire brigade was helpless, for there had been a demonstration of fire-fighting techniques the week before and the nearby reservoir had been emptied and not replenished. So the Brothers manned the roof of the St. Patrick's Hall while the boarders, forming a line, passed buckets of water from hand to hand up to them. For three hours, they fought the flames, dousing burning spots as they appeared. When the corner of tower of the Hall caught fire, Brother Slattery climbed over the railings around the roof and on to the top of the dormer windows. Here, 60 or 70 feet about the ground, standing on the small arching support not more than a foot wide, he flung buckets of water up at the blazing corner. Just as this threat was conquered, the alarm went up that that joists of the main roof were ablaze. With considerable difficulty, the Brothers hastened down the stairs; the coat and vest of one of them caught fire, but he was not injured. Scarcely had they escaped into the open, black as pitch, drenched and exhausted, when the whole ceiling fell with a crash, flames bursting out through the broken glass of every window. An instant later and their retreat would have been shut off. But, in spite of their heroic efforts, St. Patrick's Hall was destroyed, with only its walls left standing. Fortunately the Cathedral and the surrounding buildings were spared, but two-thirds of the city,[8] including the beautiful Anglican Cathedral and other Protestant churches, was destroyed. Twelve thousand people were rendered homeless.

Shocked by the terrible disaster they had witnessed, two of the boarders became unhinged. One soon recovered, but the other caused some anxiety until Brother Flood accompanied him to his home some 30 miles away where the familiar sights calmed him.

To help provide for those rendered homeless, the boarders were sent home some weeks earlier than usual, and the College was filled with the dispossessed,[9] many of whom had been staunch supporters of the school. Among them was

---

[8] A similar fire in 1846 had caused much the same damage.

[9] The Government sent up copious supplies to feed them. It did the same for Mount St. Francis and the Convents.

**Fr. M. J. Ryan, Ph.D.
winner of the 1st Jubilee
scholarship, and 1st
St. Bon's graduate to
matriculate at London
University**

Thomas Talbot[10], one of the first teachers at the College and now a member of its Board of Governors as well as being Sheriff of the City. Mr. Talbot had no relatives in Newfoundland and remained in the College until his death in 1901 at the age of 90.[11]

All this accumulated tension had its affect on Brother Slattery's health. It was reported by one of the other Brothers that he "spends half the night at times rambling about his room asleep or dreaming... he feels at times a violent palpitation."[12]

But this see-saw of emotional highs and lows was not yet complete. In August, the results of the London University Matriculation Examination were announced. All four candidates from St. Bon's had passed, three in the first division and one in the second. Francis Connolly, one of the first three, had been awarded the Jubilee Scholarship worth the magnificent sum of £100 ($480) a year for two years.[13]. Among the others was Edward P. Roche of Placentia, the future Archbishop of St. John's. Emphasizing the magnitude of their achievement was the fact that the three candidates from the Wesleyan College, aged 24 and 25, had not passed.[14] This victory did more than add to the reputation of the College; it changed the whole attitude of the people towards the Matriculation Exams. Soon we find the other Colleges entering more and younger candidates and providing St. Bon's with serious academic competition. Thus the standard of education in Newfoundland received a welcome boost.

---

[10] Others were Mr. D. J. Greene, Mr. & Mrs. O'Mara, Mrs. Cummins, Mr. Foran and family, Misses Halley, Vinicombe, Joy and others. (College scrap-book, July 1892).

[11] Talbot was a wealthy man and the Brothers were rather expecting to be mentioned in his will. As it happened, he left everything to the Church, and Bishop Howley used the legacy to erect Talbot Hall at Littledale.

[12] Fleming to Whitty, *SP* #228, September 25, 1892.

[13] I have been unable to find the origins of this scholarship except that it was established by the House of Assembly, moved by George Henry Emerson, Q.C., 76th section of the Education Act. It was called the Newfoundland Jubilee Scholarship to be used "in the London University." None had been granted in the previously five years. Earlier winners had been: Rev. Doctor M. J. Ryan, C. N. Conroy, M. W. Furlong, Miss Dove. (cf. *Evening Telegram*, September 1892).

[14] Two of the boys, Edward Roche and Andrew Jordan, entered All Hallows Seminary in Ireland; Frank Connolly and William Howley went to England to study law. Unfortunately, this was before the advent of *The Adelphian* and no photographs are available.

Chapter 8
AN ERA ENDS

...And many a friend upon the quay...
Heard through the mist the distant roar
Of billows telling to the shore
In language all could understand:
"A MAN is leaving Newfoundland."

– Dan Carroll

John Sullivan
Highest marks in London
U. Exams 1893

Br. P. V. Strapp

𝔍n spite of the great fire, the school year of 1892-93 got off to a good start, with the student roll rising to 120, including 52 boarders and Normals, and with the appearance of the property considerably enhanced by means of a new gate and fencing. The interest of the Brothers in vocations to the priesthood was beginning to bear fruit. Several of the graduates had begun their priestly studies in Ireland, Edward Curran at Holy Cross Seminary and John Ashley at Mount Mellary. They joined Andrew Jordan and Edward Roche who were both at All Hallows. In the yearly examinations at this last institution, Edward Roche placed first and Andrew Jordan second in class, attesting to the excellence of their preparation as well as their own ability. In December of the previous year, two ex-pupils had gone to Rome to study for the priesthood: James Joy from Holyrood, who entered Propaganda College, and William Murphy from Catalina, who joined the Irish College. In August 1893, James White,[1] who had been prefect at the College, entered Carlow College in Ireland, having already completed a year's philosophy at St. Bon's. In the following July, another candidate for the priesthood, Alfred Maher, was to enter All Hallows where he placed 5th of the 30 who took the entrance exam. Joseph Kielly, one of the young candidates for the Christian Brothers, received the habit[2] and thus formally entered the Congregation, the first to do so in North America.

During the year 1893-94, the Brothers' community received two notable local additions. On New Year's Day, a young lad of 16 years of age, John Sullivan by

---

[1] White was the son of Mr. Philip White of Her Majesty's Customs.

[2] The Brothers traditionally wore a long black 'habit' with a broad cincture at the waist, and a Roman collar. A candidate received this habit when he entered the novitiate, i.e., the canonical year of spiritual training.

name, entered the Brotherhood as Brother Benedict.[3] A brilliant lad, blessed with a photographic memory, he was one of the two St. Bonaventure's candidates for the London Matriculation Examination. When school resumed in September 1893, it was found that he had not only passed in First Division but had received the highest marks ever obtained on the Island. Copperthwaite from Wesleyan College passed in the second division.

In October 1893, another young man, 26 years of age, entered the Christian Brothers' Congregation. Patrick Strapp was from Harbour Main where he had been teaching for several years. His name in religion became Brother Vincent. He was to be synonymous with the College until his death in 1952.

At the Distribution of Prizes on July 13, 1894, which again took place in the Bishop's Library, nearly 300 spectators were present. Besides many clergy, there were Justice Sir James Winter, Hon. Thomas Talbot, Hon. Edward P. Morris, George Emerson, Daniel J. Greene, W. P. Walsh, Colonel Fawcett. One can see what a prestigious event it had already become. The Distribution was followed next day by a "Sports Day," thus establishing a tradition which continues to the present day.

A glance at the 1894 prize list reveals the growing number of classes in the school. At the top was Matriculation[4], preceded by two years of Matriculation Preparation, next Third Class, and two years of Fourth Class. In Fifth Class, the subjects were: English and Grammar, geography, Christian Doctrine, geometry, writing, ciphering. Finally, there were two years of Sixth Class (the lowest): subjects being Christian Doctrine, arithmetic, reading, spelling, and writing. In July 1894, 46 Normals and teachers took the Grade examinations in accordance with the new regulations. These exams took place in the Bishop's Library, with the Inspector, Mr. Wickham, in attendance. The better qualified graduates were immediately recruited for various schools throughout the Island.[5]

Brother Slattery did not forget the physical needs of the College. In 1894, the College proudly entered the modern age with the introduction of electric light, and in September 1894, the school was fitted with a fire escape. All this, of course, entailed additional expense and, since his Superiors were pressing him to reduce the debt on the College, he was naturally delighted when, in December 1893, Mr. Charles Kickham willed $4,000 to the College, the interest from which was to assist students for the priesthood.

But the College would not be true to itself if a year were to go by without tragedy. In October, Brother Slattery became seriously ill, apparently a recurrence

---

[3] He was the son of James Sullivan, the gardener at Villa Nova, Topsail. After his training was completed and having spent several years teaching in Ireland, Brother Benedict was transferred to the Brothers' school in Kimberley, South Africa, in 1905. Here he spent the remainder of his teaching life. He died while on holiday in Bristol, England, on April 6, 1943.

[4] The designation of the classes keeps changing and it is difficult to follow all their peregrinations.

[5] Byrne (Holyrood) and Burke, (Brigus) obtained First Grade; Matthew Power (Torbay), Tom Goff (Salmonier), and P. Burke (Conception Harbour) Second Grade.

of diphtheria. He was sent to the Fever Hospital, then located at the top of Signal Hill, where he came near death. Fortunately, he recovered and by October 23rd was well enough to return to the College, much to the relief of Brother Flood who had been in charge during his absence and whose temperament was unsuited to such responsibilities. Brother Slattery's description of the hospital, a former barracks erected by the French during one of their temporary occupations of St. John's, is probably the only link we have with this historic building, long since destroyed.[6]

For another person, however, the outcome of his illness was not so fortunate. In early December 1893, Bishop Power caught a heavy cold and, in spite of every attention, died a few days later. He had been a great friend and supporter of the Brothers, and, as evidence of their relationship, the Brothers were the "chief mourners" at his funeral, walking immediately behind the coffin in front of the clergy. The appointment of his successor was awaited with "fear and trembling," for several of those mentioned as possible successors were of a different stamp.

While the new system of public examinations was proving very helpful, those responsible for education realized the need to stimulate interest in learning throughout the Island. Consequently, in the spring of 1893, Brother Slattery met with the heads of the Anglican and Wesleyan Colleges, Mr. Blackall and Mr. Holloway, and together they persuaded the Government to allocate $4000 a year for prizes and scholarships for the higher classes. The public exams and the scholarships and prizes now open for competition rapidly changed the educational scene in Newfoundland. The schools, the colleges in particular, now realized that they were in direct competition with one another and that their results would be open to public scrutiny. As well, a considerable number of scholarships was at stake. Feelings ran high. On June 11, 1894, the London Matriculations exams began with eight competitors, five from Wesleyan College, two from St. Bon's and one from the Anglican College. The main hope for St. Bon's was sixteen-year-old Harry Strapp. The scholarship was worth $960, a very attractive allurement. The examinations were held in the Colonial Building and the schedule was grueling: Monday, 2-6 p.m., Latin; Tuesday, 10 a.m.–1 p.m. French; 2-5 p.m., arithmetic and algebra; Wednesday: 10 a.m.–1 p.m., Euclid (geometry); 2-5 p.m. magnetism and electricity; Thursday, 10 a.m.–1 p.m., English grammar; 2-5 history; Friday, 10 a.m.-1 p.m., mechanics. The completed papers were sent to England for correction.

Two weeks later, on June 25th, the new CHE high school exams began. Across the Island there were 950 entrants in two grades: senior for those under 17 years of age, and junior for those under 15. The College had 75 entrants. These exams were prepared and corrected by the University Correspondence College, Cambridge, England. The exams themselves were held in the students' own schools but were rigidly supervised by external examiners. For example, Brother Slattery and Mr. Blackall of the Church of England College exchanged places. When writing to Ireland while supervising the exams, Brother Slattery noted: "For the past week I

---

[6] See *Fair or Foul the Weather,* p. 54.

have had entire charge of the Protestant boys and girls and of all their exams. I must say I have found them very honorable and honest. Not the remotest attempt at foul play or the like." He amusingly described himself as writing with "Protestant ink."[7]

During the summer of 1894, the Annual Sports were held and were a great success with about 4,000 people present, among them Governor and Lady O'Brien, as well as the Commodore and all the officers of the warships that were visiting St. John's. Never one to miss an opportunity, Brother Slattery arranged with Commodore Curzon-Howe[8] for a "Grand Military Tournament, Assault at Arms, &c," at the College in aid of his coming Bazaar.

The public was now taking full advantage of the beauty of the College grounds, and every fine evening during the summer, hundreds could be found strolling around or sitting on the embankments watching cricket matches, while the younger element engaged in various forms of athletic activity. Sporting events between the Colleges had been in existence for some years. The *Evening Telegram* described a cricket match between St. Bon's and the Wesleyan College on July 3, 1893, and noted that Mews and Copperthwaite excelled for Wesleyan and White for St. Bon's.

After repeated urging from his Superiors, Brother Slattery had set himself to reduce the debt on the College, a debt which the Brothers had assumed when they had taken over the management of the school, and which had been steadily increasing because of the heavy financial demands of recent years. He decided to hold a monster Bazaar and enlisted the aid of the Catholic ladies. At their first meeting, almost 300 ladies attended. Thus came into existence the St. Bon's Ladies Auxiliary, which has played such a valuable part in the life of the school. An illustration of Brother Slattery's extraordinary influence in the city was that, when the Ladies Auxiliary were to hold an excursion in aid of the Bazaar, the principal merchants of the town agreed, at his request, to close their establishments all day Friday instead of the usual half-day Thursday so that their employees could attend.

Various people staged benefits in aid of the Bazaar, including C. H. Danielle of Octagon fame,[9] who put on a Ball and Supper at the Royal Pavilion at Quidi Vidi. The Grand Military Tournament, at twenty cents a head, netted $400. On July 22nd, a band from the visiting French Warship *Naiade* gave a profitable concert in the College grounds. Through Monsignor Kelly, the Rector of the Irish College in Rome, Brother Slattery obtained from His Holiness, Pope Leo XIII, a beautiful cameo set in gold as a prize. From the Superior General, Brother Maxwell, he received a fine watch and from Sir Ambrose Shea, now Governor of the Bahamas, he obtained $50. The students of St. Bonaventure's themselves donated a roll-top office desk. So all seemed to augur well for the success of the Bazaar.

---

[7] Slattery to Whitty, *SP* #291, June 30, 1994.

[8] Grandson of Admiral Howe, British hero of the American Revolutionary War.

[9] Danielle came to Newfoundland in 1885 as a dancing instructor and restaurateur. He established the Octagon Castle on Topsail Road which became a popular resort for the elite of St. John's. The Royal Pavilion was one of his previous projects.

Just as Brother Slattery was beginning to assume that all would be well with the Bazaar, matters took a sudden turn for the worse when two events threatened its success. Alex Howley and Henry Strapp both passed the London Matriculation examination, though Strapp did not get the Jubilee Scholarship which was won by Ralph House of Bishop Feild College. Then, the results of the CHE exams were published. They were a triumph for the Catholic schools and particularly for the College. Out of the four scholarships offered in Senior Grade, St. Bonaventure's obtained three;[10] of the six available in Junior Grade, the school won five; of the 56 special prizes offered for specific subjects, the school received 30. The other results were equally excellent. The College's supporters were ecstatic; those of the Protestant schools were dejected and, human nature being what it is, the latter quickly lost their enthusiasm for the success of the College Bazaar. Secondly, just at this critical moment, the Government called an election, and all attention focused upon it. Nevertheless, in spite of these and other obstacles, the College netted approximately $6000 or £1200 from the affair, enough to reduce the debt dramatically and to mollify the Superior General.

In December, another and much greater tragedy! After a long period of mismanagement, both local banks closed causing panic among the stockholders and people generally, and depriving many of their life-savings. In a letter to Ireland, Brother Slattery explained what happened:[11] "The fishermen went in debt to the planter, the planter to the merchant, the merchant to the Banks, the Banks to the Government, the Government to money lenders abroad. One brick fell from the building and the mighty edifice of the God Credit fell immediately." Brother Slattery himself had an important part to play in preventing this disaster from becoming even worse. Through a letter to the press which was read out in the House of Assembly, he was able to persuade the Government not to adopt a measure to bail out the banks, a decision which would have spelled financial disaster for the Island.

The College had money invested in these banks and suffered financially from their failure, offsetting somewhat the benefit of the Bazaar but not enough to prove crippling, especially since, during the summer, Commodore Curzon-Howe arranged a second display in the College grounds which netted $320.

In the midst of this confusion, however, there was rejoicing when the announcement was made that the new bishop of St. John's was to be Bishop Michael Howley. When he arrived in St. John's at the end of February 1894, the College, staff and boys, welcomed him with enthusiasm, particularly when, after saying Mass at the College, he spoke to the boys and addressed them as "fellow students."

Having reached the end of his term as Superior, Brother Slattery wrote to the Superior General in early 1895 tendering his resignation and stating his conviction

---

[10] First place was won by Henry Strapp, second was William Kitchin later to become the beloved Monsignor Kitchen who served for so many years at the Cathedral.

[11] Slattery to Maxwell, *SP* #312, January 4, 1895.

First college sports, 1894.

Grand military tournament, St. Bon's campus, summer, 1894.

that the College had a "useful and brilliant career before it."[12] Rather than accept his resignation, however, Brother Maxwell suggested that he take a vacation in Ireland when they could discuss the affairs of the College at length. This offer at first "sent a thrill of pleasure"[13] to Brother Slattery's heart, but, on reflection, he realized how it would look to the Catholic people if, in the midst of post-bank-crash deprivation, he were to take such an expensive holiday. Reluctantly, he wrote the Superior General declining the invitation. In the same letter, he noted that a new postulant, **Patrick McCarthy**,* had arrived and that Brother Benedict Sullivan would take his Intermediate Arts exam in the following week[14] and his B.A. next year. He wrote that Brother Vincent Strapp was a great acquisition, an excellent teacher and very pious. Unfortunately, to offset this acquisition, Br. Baptist Flood, who had been unhappy at the College for some time, was transferred to Mount St. Francis (St. Patrick's Hall Schools).

This year, 1894, Brother Slattery began the practice of publishing an Annual Report (the forerunner of *The Adelphian*). The Report noted that in the three years since St. Bonaventure's students had begun to enter the London Matriculation Examination, more students had matriculated from the College than from the entire Island since these examinations were first established. The Report also noted that there were 176 on the roll, of whom 33 were under ten years of age, 41 under 14, and 58 above that age. One hundred twelve boys were day students, and 61, including 23 pupil teachers, were boarders. The loss of Brother Flood had been a serious blow to the musical program of the College, so, at Eastertime, Brother Slattery was delighted to obtain the services of Professor Flynn, a well-known music teacher. Professor Flynn had been organist at the R. C. Cathedral in Harbour Grace for the past 20 years and had recently moved to St. John's.

The examination results in 1895, the second year of their inauguration, were equally good for the College. John Fenelon won first place in the senior grade, James Benning, second in the junior. The College won three of the five scholarships and 23 of the 56 prizes. Among the other junior grade winners were Vincent Burke, George Kearney, Thomas O'Reilly, Michael Connolly, James Howley.

The College Sports that summer included, besides the usual running, jumping and throwing events, the tug-of-war and the obstacle race. More unusual was the bicycle race. Some time previously a cycling course had been built around the campus and this was now utilized for a cycle race. The race had an unexpected ending. There were two entrants and as they raced neck to neck around the track, a dog ran out between them causing both competitors to fall and bringing the race to a premature conclusion. Professor Power's band provided the musical accompaniment to the various drills.

---

[12] Slattery to Maxwell, *SP* #315, January 22, 1895. In a later letter, Brother Slattery suggested Brother Crehan as a suitable successor. (*SP* #322, March 26, 1895).

[13] Slattery to Maxwell, *SP* #336, July 13, 1895.

[14] Brother Benedict succeeded in this exam, the highest ever attempted in the Island up to that time.

Scholarship Winners, 1896.
George Kearney, Ronald Kennedy, William Kitchin,
Michael Connolly, John Fenelon.

Bishop Howley, 1894-1904.
Archbishop Howley 1904-1914.

An interesting and unexpected use of the College facilities during the summer was for a priests' retreat. The new Bishop was convinced of the need of such a retreat and arranged with Brother Slattery for the use of the dormitories which were turned into "cells" or little rooms. Two Bishops (the other was Bishop McDonald of Harbour Grace) and 30 priests attended and, according to Brother Slattery, everything went off "first class." In the autumn, two more students entered seminaries, Robert Kent to All Hallows and James MacNamara to Mount Mellary.

Brother Slattery's final year (1895-96) began quietly enough, with numbers only fair as might have been expected, given the existing financial situation of the Island though, during the year, they slowly increased. In November, the College was visited by Bishop Neil McNeil, the new Bishop of the West Coast, who expressed himself as being very impressed by the efficiency and excellence of both the College and St. Patrick's Hall Schools.[15] But the pressure was beginning to tell on the staff. Brother Crehan began to suffer from rheumatism and indigestion, Brother Prendergast from the nervousness which was to plague him for the rest of his life, Brother Slattery's heart was acting up again.

In January 1896, Brother Slattery received the expected letter from Brother Maxwell: "As your term of office has expired and you have expressed the wish to be relieved from the burthen, I am about to accede to your request. You will then, as soon as convenient, make up your accounts and arrange outstanding debts in connection with the College. And then when you have all done, kindly let me know, say by telegramme. I will then give further directions."[16] On March 24th, a second telegram arrived, recalling Brother Slattery to Ireland to become a member of the Brothers' community at Waterpark College, Waterford.

When the news of his departure spread around the town, there was a general outpouring of regret. Various "Addresses" and other expressions of respect were presented to him. A local newspaper, depicting the great influence which Brother Slattery had had on his students, noted poignantly:[17]

> *The boys of St. Bonaventure's, about 30 in all, left for their respective homes by rail to-day. Rev. Bro. Slattery was at the station to wish them good-bye, perhaps for the last time. As the conductor shouted 'all aboard,' three hearty cheers were given by the lads for their respected Principal, and every boy seemed to feel the parting keenly. Such close connection has always existed between them that every lad who has received instruction from that gentleman is deeply grieved at the sudden departure of one who took such a fatherly interest in their work and gave them every assistance in his power.*

[15] Slattery to Whitty, *SP #340*, November 13, 1895. Bishop McNeil was later to become Archbishop of Vancouver, and still later, Archbishop of Toronto.

[16] Maxwell to Slattery, *SP #351*, January 8, 1896.

[17] *Evening Herald*, March 28, 1896.

Three days later, March 31, 1896, Brother Slattery was on his way to Ireland. The well-known local poet and artist, Dan Carroll, memorialized his leaving in verse:

Like tear-dimmed eyes when friends depart,
Our city lights looked out to sea,
Our city, whose deep, grateful heart
Low-sobbed a sad good-bye to thee:
And many a friend upon the quay,
That midnight when you sailed away,
Who watched thy ship the Narrows passed
Till gleamed one beacon from her mast,
Heard through the mist the distant roar
Of billows telling to the shore
In language all could understand:
"A MAN is leaving Newfoundland."

St. Bon's Crest 1906.
This crest was actually the crest of the De La Salle Brothers of France which the Christian Brothers had adopted as their own with the insertion of the year 1802, the year the Christian Brothers were founded by Blessed Edmund Ignatius Rice.

Chapter 9
CHANGING OF THE GUARD

All I request is that impossibilities are not to be expected from me.
                                                    – Brother G. B. Lavelle

The St. Bonaventure's community had not long to wait to find out who Brother Slattery's successor would be. In April 1896, the news arrived that his successor was to be Brother Joseph Crehan. Unfortunately, this appointment was not a success. Some time previously, Brother Crehan had criticized Brother Slattery to his superiors for not giving sufficient help in the classroom, but he was soon to find out why. Though of massive intelligence, Brother Crehan was not suited to the daily demands and frustrations of administration and quickly realized that he was not able to cope with the practical responsibilities involved.[1] He notified his superiors accordingly and, after only a month in office, was summoned back to Ireland. He left on June 30th, and Brother Fleming from the Mount St. Francis community was placed in temporary charge until a new appointment could be made.

Br. J. J. Crehan
10th President

Br. G. B. Lavelle
11th President

The new President arrived on Sunday, September 13th. He was **Brother Garrett Bernard Lavelle**,* a native of Westport in western Ireland and just forty years of age. Of keen intellect, he was also an excellent teacher and, while in Ennis, had scored such marked success that pupils flocked to the school from the surrounding areas. At the time of his appointment he had been the senior teacher at Waterpark College for four years and had obtained even greater success there. He was of a very different temperament than Brother Slattery as soon became evident. Where the latter was warm and diplomatic, Brother Lavelle was stern and imperious, and, as events were to prove, could be petulant.

He could not have been happy to be transferred to such a distant and unfamiliar place as Newfoundland just as the new school year was to begin. Soon he was even more unhappy as he grasped the magnitude of the task with which he was confronted. Only two days after his arrival, he wrote to Brother Maxwell: "It is out of the question to think that I could reach on the work which up to the present had

---

[1] As Br. Slattery had noted of him earlier, "…any worry or annoyance has a most injurious effect on his health." (*SP* #250, Slattery to Whitty, July 19, 1893, p. 2.).

to be done by two Brothers, that is, Brothers L. Slattery and J. Crehan. I don't care in what capacity I am here. All I request is that impossibilities are not to be expected from me."[2] His spirits were not improved when Brother Fleming was moved back to Mount St. Francis where Brother Flood had gone some time earlier, and when it seemed that Brother Strapp was also about to be transferred. Even worse, when the results of the previous year's examinations were published, though William Kitchin had passed in First Division, young Brother Anthony Murphy in Second Division in the London Matriculation Examination, and John Fenelon, son of one of St. Bonaventure's founding teachers (Maurice), led by long odds in the Associate Grade; otherwise, St. Bonaventure's had done relatively poorly. It must have poured gall on Brother Lavelle's wounds when he discovered that St. Patrick's Hall Schools had achieved much better results overall.

Whether the Superiors were unaware of the extent of the difficulty or whether they did not have the manpower to assist we do not know. But they did not respond to his plea for help, so he was forced to struggle on. He did make some adjustments to ease his burden. He asked Brother Culhane to teach the Latin and Greek and he requested that the Novitiate be closed since, in spite of the dividends it was beginning to pay in terms of manpower, it added greatly to his burdens. He was determined, moreover, to keep Brother Strapp who was already proving an efficient teacher of the smaller boys. In these matters, the Superiors did respond. The novitiate was closed, young Brother Anthony Murphy was transferred to St. Patrick's Hall instead of Brother Strapp, and the lone sixteen-year-old postulant, Patrick McCarthy, a native of Northern Bay, was summoned to Ireland to continue his training there. The Superiors also moved Brothers Fleming and Flood back to the College, the former to take care of the accounts, and the latter to supervise the music. Brother Lavelle was proving difficult to please and did not welcome either transfer. Nor did it help that the ensuing winter was most severe and that he began to suffer from rheumatism.

Nevertheless, the numbers of pupils in the College continued to increase. By February 1897, there were 22 boarders and 125 day-boys; the changing balance in favour of day-boys was noticeable.

In June, an historic event occurred in St. John's: the laying of the corner stone for Cabot Tower.[3] On this occasion Bishop Howley, one of the main initiators of the work, gave a notable address. It was at this time also that the Bishop inaugurated the Catholic Cadet Corps, one section in the East End and one in the West End of the town. During the years of its existence, St. Bonaventure's students took an active part in this Corps which, together with the corresponding Church Lads Brigade (Anglican) and the Methodist Guards Brigade, was to play a leading part in Newfoundland's contribution to the war effort in the First World War.

---

[2] Lavelle to Maxwell, *SP* #361, September 15, 1896, p. 1.
[3] Cabot Tower was erected to honour the 60th anniversary of Queen Victoria.

CATHOLIC CADET CORPS.

A MEETING was held at St. Bonaventure's College this morning for the formation of a Catholic Boys' Brigade for the city. The chair was taken by J. J. Callanan, Esq., and there was also present: His Lordship the Bishop, Hon. E. P. Morris, Jas. P. Fox and T. J. Eden, Esqs., and others. The principal discussion took place over the name, respecting which nothing definite was decided, but it is more than probable that the name will be the **St. John's Catholic Cadet Corps.** A committee was formed consisting of the Bishop, Hon. E. P. Morris, Hon. John Harris, Supt. Sullivan, J. J. Callanan, Jas. P. Fox, T. J. Edens, L. J. Gearin and C. Hutton, Esqs. Jas. P. Fox was appointed Secretary, and . J. Edens, Treasurer, and a sub-Committee was appointed to draft rules, look after a drill hall and other matters, and report at another meeting to be held on Monday next. The corps will be under the command of Mr. Jos. Shea, and will include both East and West End members.

THE FIRST MEETING FOR THE
FORMATION OF THE
CATHOLIC CADET CORPS

This announcement appeared in the
Evening Telegram, August 26, 1896.

Catholic Cadet Corps, St. Bon's, c. 1898.

In spite of his unhappiness, Brother Lavelle was not idle. During the following summer, while preparing for the 1897-98 school year, he refurbished the library with padded seats all around and installed glass book cases and electric light. He had all the classrooms painted, two of them refloored with hardwood, one provided with glass cases, and the Hall also floored and painted.

However, he was made much happier when he found that two new Brothers were being assigned to his community, Brother Joseph Norris from Ireland[4] and Brother John Columba Fennessy[5] from Holy Cross School where he had been teaching successfully since its opening in 1890. The staff was now a formidable one. It consisted of Brother Lavelle, Brother Prendergast, Brother Culhane, Brother Strapp, Brother Norris, Brother Fennessy, with Brother Byrne as lay-Brother. Brother Flood had, in the meantime, been recalled to Ireland and had sailed on June 20, 1897; Brother Sullivan, also summoned there to continue his training, had left on August 13, 1897.

The results of the public exams for June 1897 raised Br. Lavelle's spirits still more. St. Bonaventure's had done remarkably well, far better than he had expected. Of the 79 students presented for examination in all the grades, all but four passed. In Associate Grade, James Cowan obtained third place (one of three scholarships) in the Island. In Senior Grade, Eric McKay received first place, R. Kennedy, third place, and Vincent Cleary, fifth place, (three of five scholarships). In Junior Grade, Sidney Herbert came first; Cyril Cahill, third; James Howley, fifth; and Thomas Carter, eighth; (four of ten scholarships). Best of all, when the results of the London Matriculation Examinations were announced on October 19, John Fenelon had passed in First Division and had won the Diamond Jubilee Scholarship worth $600. It was a stunning performance. In spite of all Brother Lavelle's misgivings, something must have been going well at the College.

In the annual Report which Brother Lavelle, following his predecessor's example, had published, he mentioned that nine ex-pupils were engaged in seminary studies: three in Rome, five in Ireland and one in Montreal. Of those in Rome, Alex Howley had obtained his Bachelor's degree in philosophy; John Ashley and James Joy, their Bachelor of Theology. Father Edward P. Roche, the "first fruits" of the Brothers' management of the College, had returned to Newfoundland to begin his pastoral career here.

Perhaps a note is in order here on the impact of the new system of examinations on the intellectual life of the Island. In the London Matriculation Examinations of 1896, Newfoundland passed ten candidates, while the rest of the colonies passed only eight among them. It was becoming apparent also that the

---

[4] Brother Norris came to Newfoundland from the Brothers' school in Derry. He returned to Ireland four years later in 1901. It appears that he did not persevere in the Congregation.

[5] Brother Fennessy was to have a long and distinguished career at St. Bonaventure's, particularly in teaching the younger boys, training the altar boys, directing plays and operettas, and in coaching games, especially cricket at which game he was so successful that the other Colleges eventually lost interest. He died at the College on March 31, 1939. His "Life" is found in *The Christian Brothers Educational Record*, 1940, pp. 172-182.

other Colleges were quickly adapting to the new system and were well able to hold their own with St. Bonaventure's. However, in spite of the apparent success of the examinations, sober heads were beginning to question their value. Brother Lavelle himself deplored the apparently unhealthy competitive spirit which they seemed to engender with the possible neglect of weaker students.[6] Others questioned their value for children not destined for higher studies. One result of this was that the Brothers at St. Patrick's Hall Schools began to re-examine their attitude towards these exams,[7] while the Bishop took the difficult step of forbidding the Presentation Sisters to enter their students for them.[8] Eventually the Brothers at St. Patrick's Hall Schools and Holy Cross Schools decided to forgo the exams. While this may have been a reasonable decision at the time, in the long run it resulted in the virtual exclusion of poorer children from higher studies for many years.

The school year, 1897-98, passed relatively without incident; Brother Lavelle now much more contented with his position. In his published Report of the school year, he stated that the College had won considerably more academic honours than any of the other institutions. Among these winning awards, we again meet the name of Sydney Herbert who, having secured first place in Junior Grade the previous year, now did the same in Senior Grade. He had swept all before him and was to achieve still greater honours in succeeding years. A debating society had been introduced but had still to achieve its full potential; a typewriter had been purchased for the commercial program; Professor Flynn continued, with great success, the program of tonic sol-fah introduced by Brother Flood some years previously. Brother Lavelle listed the most pressing needs of the College: a large hall for assemblies and concerts, a gymnasium "provided with all modern equipment," a chemistry laboratory where the College's fine collection of scientific apparatus could be effectively utilized. Perhaps tongue in cheek, he listed other desirable additions: a good ball court (handball), a billiard room, and a large swimming bath about 50 feet by 30 feet.[9]

The College Sports, which took place on June 30, 1898 were beginning to take on the form which became traditional. Besides the usual athletic events, there was a musical drill, a maze, a gymnastic display under Professor Ross. Professor Power provided the musical accompaniment to the drills.

[6] Nevertheless, he invariably published comparisons between the records of St. Bonaventure's students and those of the other Colleges, and was extremely unhappy when the College teams were beaten. (SP #438, November 10, 1898, p. 1.)
[7] Kennedy to Hennessy, SP #406, October 22, 1897: "No matter how hard we work, we can't keep up the Catholic percentage to the proud standard of former years. If we could get out of them, a great deal of unpleasantness would be avoided." (He was speaking of St. Patrick's Hall and Holy Cross Schools.) Fleming to Hennessy, SP #410, December 2, 1897: "I never could see any profit we could derive from them. Our boys are not so well prepared for business as they had been previously to the examinations, and I am fully convinced they are not so well instructed in religious matters, and no way are they so well prepared for the battle of life."
[8] Kennedy to Whitty, SP #401, August 9, 1897.
[9] The handball court(s) and the billiard room were eventually realized but the swimming pool was rejected in favour of a more practical ice-skating rink.

The 1898-99 school year began with an inspiring ceremony in the College chapel when Father James White, just ordained in Ireland, said his first Mass there. The numbers on the Roll now jumped to 217, the largest increase being in the junior section. In October, Sir John Bramston and the Earl of Westmeath, accompanied by Bishop Howley, paid a gracious visit. On June 26th, the C.H.E. exams began with 20 students in Junior Grade (now called "Preliminary"), 20 in Senior Grade (now called "Intermediate") and only one in Associate Grade.

The results of the public exams were again excellent. Sydney Herbert continued his winning ways, achieving first place in Associate Grade (he was too young to enter for the London Matriculation), and obtaining first or second place in every subject for which he entered. In his Report, Brother Lavelle claimed that the success in the public examinations had been remarkable, that "the number of scholarships won by our pupils this year exceeds the entire number won by all the boys throughout the entire country!"[10]

Though not directly connected with the College, a most unusual event occurred during May which is worth recording. It will be remembered that some years earlier, Brother Crehan had introduced an x-ray machine to Newfoundland. In early May 1899, a Miss Nugent suffered a bullet wound to the head. Probably at the suggestion of Dr. Shea, Brother Lavelle, accompanied by Professor Holloway, brought the x-ray apparatus to the General Hospital to attempt to discover the exact position of the bullet. It proved difficult to obtain an exact impression because the patient was unable to remain immobile for the 45 minutes required for a good exposure. The longest time she was able to do so was ten minutes, and only a very weak negative was therefore obtained. It was reported that this was probably the first time x-rays had been employed in a hospital in Newfoundland.[11]

Much the same pattern was followed in the succeeding year, 1899-1900. The Roll reached 226. Two more ex-pupils, John Ashley and Edward Curran, were ordained to the priesthood. In September, the Governor Sir H. McCallum visited the College. In October, a College Football League was established, competing for a silver cup donated by the City Football League. Much to Brother Lavelle's chagrin, although the College started well, winning its first two matches, it lost all the rest, and the Cup in this first year of its competition passed to the Methodist College. The keener competition brought with it, as usual, its fair share of bickering, one College being accused of inserted a "ringer" for a crucial match, while a penalty shot awarded in another game was hotly disputed by the losing side.

In November, a new heating system was completed by Mr. W. J. Ryan at a cost of $2,200; Brother Lavelle complained that he had to pay a duty of 30% on all the materials imported for it. In April, the long-desired billiard table was imported at a cost of £50. In June a lattice railing was placed around the Campus. The Altar Boy Society flourished with 76 members, of whom 50 would be present at a typical Sunday Vespers. Its officers were: Treasurer, William O'Flaherty; Secretary, James

---

[10] *St. Bonaventure's College, Annual Report, 1899,* p. 4, CBASJ.
[11] cf. *Daily News,* May 18, 1899. We are not informed as to what eventually happened to Miss Nugent.

Howley; Prefects: James Donnelly, Francis Carter, John Meehan, John Mitchell, John Rawlins, Augustine White and Edward Wilson.

Once more, Brother Lavelle was pleased with the results of the public exams and did not hesitate to compare them with those of the other schools. In Associate, the College passed four students, a result equaled but once in previous years. In Intermediate, all the College pupils passed in either the Honours or the First Division, with Anthony Power achieving first place in the Island. In Preliminary, John Penney had the unique distinction of obtaining full marks in Latin as well as leading his grade.

In his annual Report, Brother Lavelle made one perplexing comment. He said: "The difficulty of procuring funds is the great obstacle to having our College thoroughly equipped with all requisite improvement. We should wish to impress on our friends the difficulties of our position in this matter, in order that something practical may be done to effect the removal of these hindrances which hamper the institution on its road to progress." To what difficulties was he referring? Was he criticizing the Government or the Bishop? There is no way of knowing.

There was, however, obviously some problem, for, in January 1901, Brother Lavelle was suddenly summoned back to Ireland by telegram. From correspondence in the Congregation's archives, it would appear that this was at his own request. Apparently, he was questioning his religious vocation. It would appear, also, that these uncertainties continued throughout his life although he remained faithful to his dedication to the end. He left on January 13th by the *Assyrian.* There is no doubt that, scholastically, he had had a fine record of success. Yet, even in his closing address to the boys, he could not refrain from referring to the "difficulties" he had encountered: "That my efforts have not been more successful was sometimes due to the absence of these means which it was not in my power to command."[12]

---

[12] *St. Bonaventure's College, Annual Report, 1900 and 1901,* p. 33, CBASJ.

The Merchant of Venice.

Chapter 10
FILLED TO OVERFLOWING

*Two Brothers teach over 80 boys in quarters lent by the Bishop.
The room is composed of an old coach house and
a room which was formerly used as a meeting room.
Science is taught in the garrett.*

– Brother Downey[1]

Brother Lavelle's replacement arrived quickly. **Br. James Joseph Downey*** landed in St. John's on the 15th of the following month (February 1901). Moreover, he brought with him Brother Michael Jerome Lannon to join the staff of the College. In September still another addition arrived, Brother Edward Stanislaus Daly. Perhaps by now, the Superiors had begun to realize the enormous weight of the burden they had placed on Brother Downey's predecessor.

Br. J. J. Downey
12th President

Brother Downey, 46 years of age, was a native of Dublin, Ireland. Before coming to Newfoundland, he had been Superior of two of the Brothers' schools in Ireland, in Youghal and in Derry, where he had been noted for the success of his pupils in the Intermediate examinations. His kindly disposition and good humour provided a welcome relief for the pupils of St. Bonaventure's after the rigors of the previous regime.

His companion, Brother Michael Jerome Lannon, a native of Waterford, Ireland, was just 23 years of age at the time of his arrival in St. John's. Very different from Brother Downey, he was thin and wiry with a shock of wavy brown hair, a bundle of nervous energy. Though short in stature, he possessed a demanding personality that strove for precision both in what he did and in what he expected from others. He was gifted in music, literature and dramatics, particularly in public speaking and debating, all qualities of great value to the school.

Brother Daly, though just 21 years of age, had been teaching in Ireland for the past five years. He was tall, thin, athletic and very musical. Though young, he was one of those teachers who have a deep personal influence on their pupils. One of the latter, Senator Jack Higgins, Q.C., afterwards confessed that he was broken-hearted when, six years later, Brother Daly left the school. One can see that, whatever their past omissions, the Superiors were now being very supportive of the school. Brother Daly soon learned to skate, and one of his duties became the making of a rink on the campus during the winter months.

---

[1] Downey to Moylan, *SP* #450, January 19, 1903, p. 3.

Taking advantage of these additions to the staff, Brother Downey re-organized the classes, beginning in September 1901. He and Brother Prendergast took responsibility for the Associate class, Brother Culhane for the Intermediate, Brother Lannon for the Advanced Preliminary, and Brother Daly for the Junior Preliminary. Brother Fennessy took the forth and fifth classes, and Brother Strapp, the first, second, and third.

In the following month, Good Friday, April 5th, another great friend of the College also died. He was Monsignor John Scott. Born in 1840 in Limerick, Ireland, where he made the acquaintance of Bishop Mullock, John Scott came to Newfoundland at the age of 17 to study for the priesthood. He was one of the few clerical students who pursued all his ecclesiastical studies at St. Bonaventure's and was ordained in the Cathedral of St. John the Baptist on August 30, 1863. He was, for many years, administrator of the Cathedral and was greatly loved by all who knew him.

In May, Brother Whitty, Assistant to the Superior General, arrived to inspect the Brothers' institutions in St. John's and was apparently pleased by what he discovered. He found 248 boys on the College register, the largest enrolment ever. The only disturbing feature was that Brother Prendergast was beginning to show signs of that mental instability which was to plague him for the rest of his long life and prevent him from using to the full his many talents.

During the summer, Brother Downey engaged Phil Hanley, painter, and James Nangle, carpenter, to give the school a general facelift. Among other improvements, heating and electric lighting were installed, the campus resodded and seats placed at various strategic places around it. Better still, on November 26, 1901, the final payment of $1,523.46 on the College debt was paid; Brother Downey thereby achieved one of the main goals he had set for himself on arriving.

By now, the College routine was so well established that it proceeded more or less on an even keel from year to year, with varying emphases depending on the views of those in charge. Academic successes followed one another with the usual ups and downs, as did athletic accomplishments. The *College Prospectus* of 1901 notes that "St. Bonaventure's hockey star does not seem to have risen yet. Every game was lost though stubbornly contested...Once again the College has been very successful at cricket...The football season brought a fair amount of success. The cup was lost by one point." In 1902, Anthony Power won the Jubilee Scholarship of $600; he matriculated at London University together with Richard McGrath.[2] One of the scholarship winners in the Intermediate Grade was Francis Carter, who, sadly, drowned while swimming in early July. During the spring of 1902, two ex-pupils of the school were ordained: Rev. William Kitchin and Rev. Alec Howley (nephew of Bishop Howley), both of whom had had brilliant academic successes while in the seminary.

---

[2] Not the future Bishop McGrath.

An unusual event was a banquet given by the College in December 1902 to celebrate the conferring of an honorary LL.D. by Ottawa University on the Honorable Edward P. Morris who had been a pupil of the College some thirty years previously. Mr. Morris was Minister for Justice and Attorney General, and was soon to become Prime Minister. The degree was conferred by Bishop Howley who gave the customary oration in Latin.[3]

The increasing enrolment was now bringing it own difficulties. In a letter to the Superior General, Br. Downey described the acute accommodation problem:[4]

> ....*Principal School (26'x18') - 36 seats for rather small boys.– 40 present daily varying in age from 16 to 20....*
> *Junior School (26'x18') - Seats for 40, Sixty present ...*
> *Preliminary Grade (Principal Class) – (26'x18') – room formed out of parlour and kitchen, over the furnace. One half room a foot higher than the other. Seats 32; 34 present....*
> *Preliminary Grade (Junior Division) and Fourth & Fifth Standard – Two Brothers teach over 80 boys in quarters lent by the Bishop. The room is composed of an old coach house and a room which was formerly used as a meeting room....*[5]
> *Science is taught in the garret....*

The need for more and better accommodation was obvious. It was fortunate that at this time Bishop Howley, who was keenly interested in building projects, had just finished the high altar in the Cathedral[6] and was looking for some similar work to do. He had already approached Brother Downey about extending the College.[7]

In October 1902, Brother Downey wrote to the Superior General:[8]

> *The Bishop on yesterday introduced the question of the extension of the College. His idea seems to be that he would give us money at a very low interest with no obligations attached as to the payment of Principal.*

---

[3] The Latin text can be found in the College handbook for 1903, p. 33.

[4] Downey to Moylan, *SP* #450, January 19, 1903, p. 3.

[5] This is where the food bank is now located under the Bishop's Library.

[6] He had moved the main altar back about seven feet to create a more spacious Sanctuary. See *Your Guide to the Basilica of St. John the Baptist*, 1984, p. 39.

[7] At an assembly of all the students of the Brothers' schools on St. Bonaventure's campus on September 11th, he announced his "intention of soon taking steps to erect a new wing to the College which would make provision for the teaching of science and Technical and Manual work as carried on at present by the Brothers in Ireland" (Log Book, p. 13, CBASJ). At the same time, he was urging the Benevolent Irish Society to add an extension to St. Patrick's Hall. This latter extension became known as the O'Donel Wing.

[8] Downey to Moylan, *SP* #448, October 17, 1902.

In fact, he said that, though the whole thing should be drawn up on a business basis, yet he might be able to remit the Principal. His idea is to add something like the Library at the other side of the building. He has an "Aula Maxima" on the brain and I have a playhall on mine...I think they could be easily combined...then in the upper storey we could have schools. He told me to think the matter out well as to what we would require and that he would probably see his way very soon to do something.

In the same letter, he noted that "our classes are very full. We have ten in our Associate Class, 25 in Intermediate and about 50 in Preliminary."

In spite of the overcrowding, examination successes continued. Augustus White secured first place among the candidates in the London Matriculation Examinations and won the Jubilee Scholarship. George Malcolm also passed in First Division. In Associate Grade, seven St. Bonaventure's students passed, forming more than a third of the entire boys' pass list of the Island. Eleven students passed in Intermediate; two, Matthew Joy and Arthur Flynn, in Honours Division. In Preliminary, 36 boys passed, four winning scholarships, John McGrath,[9] led the Grade.

It attests to the growing interest in Inter-Collegiate sports that, on January 20, 1903, Bishop Howley came to the College and gave the boys a holiday "to practice hockey." Perhaps as a result of this additional practice, on February 4th, the College defeated the Methodists by a score of 8 to 1, the first hockey victory the College had ever had in the four years of the competition! The game was played at noon in The Prince's Rink. The members of the victorious team were: Tom English (Capt.), Andrew Nolan, Jack Rawlins, George Malcolm, Gus White, John Penny and Francis O'Neill. Sadly, they were beaten in the final match by the Feildians by a score of 4 to 0.

At times, the boys were inspired to heroics. On May 19, 1903, because of a small-pox scare, all the Brothers and boarders were inoculated by Doctor Mitchell. Two days later, the cricket season opened with a match between St. Bonaventure's and Bishop Feild. St. Bonaventure's best bowler, Gus White, was ill, but finding that the batsmen were doing poorly, he got up from his sick bed, came to St. George's Field and took his turn at bat; then, when the Feildians came to bat, he bowled so well against them that St. Bonaventure's emerged victorious. In the next game against the Methodists on May 30th, several of the St. Bonaventure's players were so ill that they should have been in bed but, nevertheless, played well enough to win a closely fought match.

However, in spite of the apparent "even tenor of its ways," all must not have been well at the College, for in June, Brother Whitty returned for another visit and, in the following month, **Br. Downey*** was recalled to Ireland.

---

[9] John McGrath was only 12 years of age and making his first attempt at the scholarship. Having obtained it, he left school to become a stenographer at the House of Assembly.

Chapter 11
IMPORTANT DEVELOPMENTS

There is no school in the colony in which a bright boy
can be profitably kept after fifteen years of age.
– Letter to The Herald, *August 15, 1904*

Once more, however, the Superiors came to the rescue for when **Brother Patrick Berchmans Ryan*** arrived in August to join the College staff, he brought with him the news that Brother Joseph Culhane had been appointed President.[1] Br. Culhane proved to be an excellent choice, for, besides his physical energy and his knowledge of the local scene, he was noted for his discretion. In later years, he became known to the Brothers as "Joseph Most Prudent," a title taken from the litany of St. Joseph.[2]

Br. P. J. Culhane
13th President

Brother Ryan, a native of Tipperary, was 28 years of age when assigned to the College. Quiet and retiring, he was deeply spiritual. An excellent mathematician, he had taught in various schools in Ireland and England, and was on the staff of Cork College when summoned to exchange places with Brother Downey. He was a very patient man, and he had ample opportunity to practice this virtue during the following winter about which Brother Culhane reported to his superiors: "…we have passed through the severest winter that I have spent in Newfoundland. Apart from the great cold, etc., owing to the elevated position of the College we had great difficulty in getting sufficient water. For days we had but the merest dribble coming in by the regular supply and every drop had to be carefully preserved."[3]

Spiritually, that first school year, 1903-04, of Br. Culhane's administration proved to be a satisfying one. In September, Deacons McCarthy and Fyme were ordained priests and celebrated Mass in the College. Shortly afterwards, ex-pupils James Greene, James Walker and John Kavanagh sailed for Rome to study for the priesthood at Propaganda. A perusal of the College Year Book for 1903 provides a summary of how well the College ex-pupils were doing in their various fields. At Louvain, James Coady was completing his theological studies and would soon be ordained. At All Hallows in Dublin, William O'Flaherty had completed his

---

[1] Tradition among the Brothers has it that, on hearing the news, Br. Prendergast, who had been expecting to be nominated, was so disappointed that he suffered his final breakdown.

[2] In one way, however, his choice was unfortunate – at least for the purposes of this volume, for with his appointment, the College Annals ceased to be written and were not resumed until 1911. However, from 1902 to 1906, he kept a log book which, though mainly concerned with athletic affairs, partially filled the gap.

[3] *SP* # 456, Culhane to Whitty, April 24, 1904, CBASJ.

philosophical studies, having captured the prize for elocution, and had begun studying theology. In the same institution, Stanislaus St. Croix had won prizes in several subjects, while George Malcolm and John Rawlins were doing well in their first year. Thomas Gough had won several prizes at Mount Mellary and was now in Carlow College continuing his ecclesiastical studies. Michael Power and Joseph Pippy had received their B. Theol. Degrees at Propaganda College, Rome, and had distinguished themselves in their studies. The procession of priestly vocation continued into the following year for, in August 1904, Edward Wilson, Peter Kelly, and Edward O'Brien left for All Hallows Seminary, Dublin; while in September, another ex-pupil, Father James Coady, recently ordained at Louvain, returned to Newfoundland.

Secular successes, too, were gratifying. Bertram James had obtained his B.Sc. degree from McGill University; Charles Howlett had entered his second year at the Royal College of Dental Surgeons of Ontario, having distinguished himself in his first year; Engineer Richard Howley, R.N., had been promoted to H.M.S. *Victorious*; several ex-pupils were doing well in various banking positions. The impact of the College on the standards of achievement in Newfoundland was obvious.

Overshadowing these achievements, however, were three major events which occurred during 1904 and which had significant impact on the life of the College. First was the elevation of the diocese of St. John's to the dignity of an archdiocese, with jurisdiction over the other two Newfoundland dioceses. Bishop Howley was appointed its first Archbishop. His installation took place in February 1904, and was greeted with universal rejoicing, particularly by the St. Bon's staff and students, for the new Archbishop, besides being the first Newfoundlander to be raised to this dignity, was a distinguished ex-pupil of the College.

THE ADELPHIAN

Secondly occurred what seemed a relatively unimportant event at the time, the appearance at Easter, 1904, of the first edition of the school magazine, entitled *The Adelphian*,[4]. Rather ambitiously intended to appear four times a year, *The Adelphian* contained scholarly articles from ex-pupils, fledging attempts at the same by present pupils, original poems, reports on sports and other College activities, obituaries of recently deceased pupils and ex-pupils and results of recent examinations. Gradually, *The Adelphian* settled down to one edition a year but became enlarged from some fifty pages to over 100 pages. The Jubilee issue of 1907, for example, contained some 150 pages. With rare exceptions, *The Adelphian* appeared every succeeding year of the College's existence until its demise in 1962.[5] The editor for many years was Brother Strapp whose intimate knowledge of the history of the College led to the preservation of many of its records. *The Adelphian*

---

[4] *Adelphian* is Greek for "Brothers."

[5] Since then, while still entitled *The Adelphian,* it has taken on the form of a school year book rather than the historic record it was originally intended to be.

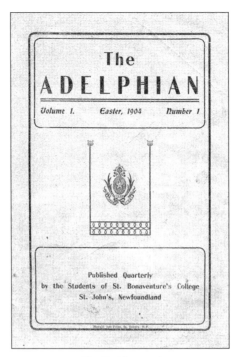

The first issue of
The Adelphian, Easter, 1904.

First editors of *The Adelphian*.
(Sitting) J. J. Penny, E. J. Wilson, J. J. Fitzgerald.
(Standing) A. M. Power, S. M. Herbert, A. S. White.

provided an invaluable and, possibly, unique record of the history of the College and of the Province as well.

THE RHODES SCHOLARSHIP

Of all the events which took place in St. John's in 1904, however, the one that caused the most excitement was the inauguration of the Rhodes Scholarship. It was worth £900. There was to be one such Scholarship for the Island, and the lucky winner would have all his expenses paid to obtain his degree from Oxford University. Besides, there was the prestige which the scholarship would bestow on both the winner and his school. To obtain this award, not only must the candidate obtain distinction in the London Matriculation Examinations but must also be outstanding in character, athletics, and social concern.

A Selecting Committee of eminent local citizens was appointed, reflecting the denominational aspect of the country. For the first year, they were: The Governor (chairman with casting vote), Chief Justice Horwood, Mayor Shea, Honourable J. S. Pitts, and the three Superintendents of Education: Canon Pilot, Doctor Curtis and V. P. Burke. There were very different and warmly held views as to the regulations under which the Rhodes should be awarded; principally, whether it should be confined to boys who had done all their studies in the colony (there was no question of girls!), or should it be open to Newfoundlanders educated elsewhere. Doctor Parkin, manager of the Rhodes bequest, came to the Island from England to decide these questions and, after much debate, a list of regulations was drawn up and agreed upon, the most important rule being that the scholarship should be confined to boys educated in the Island.

This last point was bitterly contested and led to greatly bruised feelings. A group of 12 respected citizens, only one of whom was a native Newfoundlander, wrote to the Rhodes Committee protesting this provision and revealing their attitude towards the Island's schools: "There is no school in the colony," they wrote, "in which a bright boy can be profitably kept after 15 years of age. There are three schools in the colony denominated Colleges, but which are in reality merely High Schools in their senior departments, and these unable to give other than an indifferent preliminary training in classics."[6] However, in spite of these protests, this provision was maintained.

Academically, that spring must have had a very demanding time for the students. On June 13th, the London Matriculation Exams began. There were 13 entrants: seven from Methodist College - (Hatcher, Baird, Knight, Moran, Noonan, McIntyre, Scott); four from St. Bon's - (John Penny, Edward Wilson, Matthew Joy and Peter Kelly); and two from Bishop Feild – (Bonner and Adrian). The exams were held at the Colonial Building and lasted for four days. On June 20th, the C.H.E. exams for Primary, Preliminary and Intermediate began. St. Bon's entered 40 students in Preliminary and 27 in Intermediate. On June 25th, the C. H. E. Associate exams started with a common center at Methodist College; St. Bon's

---

[6] See *The Herald*, August 15, 1904.

RHODES SCHOLARSHIP

Mr. Sidney Herbert is Elected the First Rhodes Scholar for Newfoundland.

The committee on whom devolved the duty of selecting the first Rhodes Scholar met this morning, and selected Mr. Sydney Herbert of St. Bonaventure's College. The Committee of Selection were His Honour the Administrator, Canon Pilot, Rev. Dr. Curtis. Hon. J. S. Pitts. Mayor Shea and Mr. V. Burke. The candidates from whom the scholar was elected were Messrs. Power, Herbert and White, all of St. Bonaventures, all of whom qualified for the Scholar ship by gaining an exemption from the Responsion Examination of the Oxford University.

Sydney Herbert was born at Pilley's Island on November 18th, 1883 and entered St. Bonaventure's College Sept. 4th, 1896. In June, 1897, he led the Junior Grade, C.H.E., taking prizes in several subjects. In June. 1898, he led the Senior Grade. C.H.E., gaining prizes in Latin, French, German, Arithmetic. Geometry and Drawing. He took the Associate Exam. in June. 1899, and again was leader of his grade and took first place in French, Latin and English, and second place in Mathematics and Science.

He thus led each of the three grades in successive years, a record which has been done by only one other boy in Newfoundland—J.J. Fenelon. Master Herbert was but 15_ years of age when he led Associate. He left St. Bon's in July, 1899, and entered the employ of the Electric Light Company and remained with that company till last Xmas, when he entered St. Bon's as a boarder to study for the exams recently held for the Rhodes' Scholarship. To this brilliant young Newfoundlander, and to the staff of St. Bonaventure's College, *The Telegram* extends congratulations, and feels confident that the name and honour of Newfoundland will be upheld by Mr. Herbert at Oxford.

- The Telegram, September 8th

First Newfoundland Rhodes Scholarship.
A. S. White, S. M. Herbert, A. M. Power.

entering ten students. These exams continued until July 2nd. On the evening of June 28th, the C.H.E. exams in Practical Music were held, with St. Bon's as the center. It is interesting that only girls took these music exams, nine in Intermediate and five in Preliminary. In the midst of these tests, the various Colleges held their Sports Days and other athletic events. The students must not have had much free time.

The Rhodes Scholarship Exams started on July 12th, and lasted until the 23rd. There were three candidates from St. Bon's: Sydney Herbert, Anthony Power, and Augustus White; two from Bishop Feild College, N. Morine and C. Hunt; and one from Methodist, H. Bond. Two other Bishop Feild students, Winter and Dunfield, also took the exam to obtain their higher certificate but not to apply for the scholarship. All the Newfoundland students chose Latin, Greek, French, Mathematics and English History as their subjects, which meant that, in all, they had to write fifteen papers.

The suspense as to the successful candidates did not last long. On August 13th, a cable was received from the Secretary of the Examining Board in England stating that, while Bond, Herbert, Morine, Power and White had obtained certificates, only Herbert, Power and White had achieved exemption from Responsions (i.e., they did not have to take the usual University qualifying exam).[7] Since this exemption was a necessary condition to obtain the Rhodes Scholarship, it was clear that the successful candidate must be from St. Bonaventure's. Congratulations poured in from all quarters, many pointing out how unfounded the protests of the "Group of 12" had been.

Meanwhile, as the Selecting Committee prepared to make their selection, the three candidates returned to St. John's from where they had dispersed for a hard-earned vacation; Power[8] from Bay Bulls, White[9] from Barren Island, P. B., Herbert[10] from Baie Verte. All three set to work to draw up their *Curriculum vitae,* while the College authorities prepared certificates as to their character and general worthiness. On September 5th, a dinner was given in the Episcopal Library for the three young men, with the Archbishop and city priests present as well as the College Board. Two days later the Selecting Committee[11] met to consider the credentials of the applicants. On the following day, September 8th, the candidates appeared before the Committee, and then the Committee made its selection. The fortunate winner was Sydney Herbert who, on September 15th, sailed for England to take his place in Oxford University as Newfoundland's first Rhodes Scholar. He was to be followed by a long line of outstanding students from the College.[12]

---

[7] Students who obtained a high pass in Greek, Latin and mathematics did not have to take the normal Oxford entrance exams, i.e., the "Responsions". Those who just passed these three exams obtained "certificates", i.e., they were permitted to sit for the Oxford entrance exam.

[8] Anthony Power was the son of former Councillor M. Power of St. John's.

[9] Gus White was the son of Philip D. White and brother of the Reverend J. C. White.

[10] Sydney Herbert was the son of H. M. Herbert who held a responsible position at the Baie Verte mines. Sydney had left school in 1899 to work with the Reid-Newfoundland Electric Light Co., but had resigned in 1903 and re-entered St. Bon's as a boarder to work for this scholarship.

[11] The Governor did not attend, possibly to avoid political embarrassment. One of the candidates was the nephew of the Premier and another the son of the Leader of the Opposition.

[12] The complete list of Rhodes Scholars from the College can be found in Appendix 3.

Chapter 12
DOUBLED IN SIZE

...the ever expanding demands of modern Education absolutely
require this enlargement if we hope that the College will continue
to hold that honored placed in the very van of the literary phalanx,
which it has thitherto so honorably attained.
— The Archbishop and Bishops of Newfoundland

The need for additional accommodation continued to command the attention of the College authorities, and, on May 23, 1904, the Board of Directors met in the Episcopal Library, with Archbishop Howley presiding, to address this need. After lengthy discussion, an addition to the College building was agreed upon at an estimated cost of $25,000. Detailed plans were prepared. At a further meeting on July 14th, the plans were modified and the estimate rose to $40,000. There is surprisingly little written material available about the construction of the new building. The plans were changed several times but eventually the design of the present building, now (2006) named Mullock Hall, was agreed upon. To enlist the assistance of the Catholics of the country in this ambitious project, the three Bishops issued a joint Circular Letter, explaining the need for the extension to the College and urging the people to support it. Plans for the new building having been concluded, tenders were let at the beginning of May, 1905. The contract was signed on the 27th of the month. The expected cost had now risen to about $60,000. The designer and architect was Mr. Jonas Barter, the successful contractors were M. and E. Kennedy, with W. J. Ryan as contractor for heating and plumbing, and the McGrath Brothers responsible for painting and glazing.

Brother Culhane was proving an energetic organizer. With two important events in the offing, the laying of the cornerstone of the new building and the Golden Jubilee of the foundation of the College in 1857[1], he began to prepare for them by the formation of an Old Boys' Association and a Ladies Auxiliary. On March 25, 1907, he called a meeting of ex-pupils in the Episcopal Library. They responded enthusiastically and it was agreed both to form an Old Boys' Association and to celebrate the Jubilee of the College during the year. Brother Culhane asked any of those present who had interesting reminiscences of the old College days to write them down and send them in for publication in the special jubilee issue of *The Adelphian*.

At a subsequent meeting on April 23rd, the Constitution of the new Society was decided upon and its first officers elected. These were: President, Sir E. P. Morris; 1st Vice President, M. W. Furlong; 2nd Vice President, F. J. Morris, K.C.; Treasurer, W. J. Carroll; Secretary, J. J. McGrath, B.L. They were a distinguished group. Sir E. P. Morris was Minister of Justice and Attorney General, Martin W.

---

[1] As we have noted, classes actually began in the old Palace on December 1, 1856.

Furlong and James J. McGrath were distinguished lawyers, Frank J. Morris was the speaker of the House of Assembly and W. J. Carroll was sub-sheriff of Newfoundland. Members were expected to pay $1 a year. Some indication of the importance that the College had achieved was that the election was given first page prominence in the subsequent issue of *The Newfoundland Quarterly*.[2]

At an enthusiastic meeting of the Old Boys' Association on May 6, 1907, a "Council of Twenty" was elected from the Old Boys, two for each five-year class period. They were as follows: 1855-60: Captain English and F. J. Doyle; 1860-65: M. K. Green and J. J. Murphy; 1865-70: D. A. Flynn and M. J. Kelly; 1870-75: Honourable J. Harris and M. A. Devine; 1875-80: Reverend Doctor Murphy and J. Winter; 1880-85: J. P. Crotty and T. Thorburn; 1885-90: W. R. Howley and W. Collins; 1890-95: V. P. Burke and W. H. Tobin: 1895-1900: John Fenelon and Doctor Howlett; 1900-05: D. A. Flynn Jr. and Fred Bradshaw.

Three days later, on May 9th, a meeting of the officers with the Council decided that the Golden Jubilee of the College should be celebrated on the Fourth of July in conjunction with the laying of the cornerstone of the new wing and the annual Sports Day. The turning of the sod took place on May 23, 1907.

In June, the promised, greatly expanded edition of *The Adelphian* appeared. It contained a history of the College as well as reminiscences of College life by many distinguished ex-pupils from its earliest days up to 1900 and is the fundamental source of our knowledge of the early history of the College.

The Fourth of July arrived. In the morning, at 10 o'clock, the cornerstone of the new building was laid in the presence of Archbishop Howley and Bishops McNeil (St. George's) and March (Harbour Grace), Governor and Lady MacGregor, and many other distinguished guests. At 2:30, the annual sports began in the presence of the same dignitaries and occupied the afternoon. At night, the College was illuminated[3] and a reunion of ex-pupils and friends was held in the Episcopal Library with the C.C.C. band in attendance and various musical items proffered. Mr. P. Hanley gave a display of fireworks. Over 400 guests were in attendance, the library being tastefully decorated for the occasion.

On July 30th, more practical affairs occupied the meeting of the Old Boys, namely, how to pay for the new addition. After much discussion, it was decided to ask those who could afford it to guarantee sums from $5 upwards for the next ten years. Collectors were appointed. At a further meeting on February 24th of the following year, 1908, provisional results were announced. The past pupils had guaranteed $600 a year for ten years, and citizens generally had guaranteed $500 for the same period. Mr. J. J. Tobin contributed $100; Mr. W. P. Walsh gave $100 and a guarantee of $50 a year for ten years; Mr. J. J. Murphy guaranteed $100 for the same period; Sir E. P. Morris, Hon J. Harris, and Mr. M. W. Furlong $50 each for

---

[2] Vol. VII, No. 1, July 1907.

[3] Each window was decorated with a transparency from the skilled hand of the well-known artist, Dan Carroll.

ten years; Mr. T. J. Edens contributed $200. In all, an amount of approximately $1200 a year for ten years had been guaranteed.

The Adelphian of Christmas 1908 lists the donations given up to that time. It is noteworthy how widespread the donations were. For instance, the late Sir R. G. Reid had bequeathed $2500 to the cause, the Governor gave $25, The parish of Torbay, $110; Witless Bay, $120; Renews, $120; St. Mary's, $54; Harbour Grace, $50; Carbonear, $40; the Diocese of St. George's, $350. The Ladies Auxiliary had handed over a cheque for $2000.

The Ladies Auxiliary had been formed in October 1907. Its purpose was to "pay the yearly interest on the money necessary to enlarge the College, and, later, to help to pay off the principal."[4] A meeting was held in the T. A. Hall on October 30, 1907, with about seventy ladies in attendance. Its first officers were: President, Lady Isabel S. Morris; 1st Vice-President, Mrs. Agnes Mitchell; 2nd Vice-President, Mrs. Martin Furlong; Treasurer, Mrs. Garrett Byrne; Assistant Treasurer, Mrs. P. J. Shea; Secretary, Mrs. May Carroll; Assistant Secretary, Mrs. W. Tobin. Members were expected to pay fifty cents a year. The men's association was limited to ex-pupils of the College, but the ladies were more ambitious and extended their invitation to "every woman in the island and many abroad."[5] This Ladies Auxiliary was very successful and by the end of 1916 had contributed $16,000 for the cost of the new wing. On February 1, 1917, since a bequest of Mr. Cummins had provided sufficient funds to pay the remaining debt on the building, it was decided that the Association was no longer necessary, and so the Association was formally disbanded, after having played a magnificent part in the progress of the College.

The new building was occupied on the opening of the new school year in September 1909. Still in daily use, it reflects the rather grandiose concepts of the Archbishop more than the practical ideas of the Brother President. Much of the main portion is taken up by a regal staircase which restricts the space available for classrooms and boarding accommodations, while the adjoining wing consists principally of a large hall, called the "Aula Maxima," on the ground level, and a magnificent two-level chapel occupying the third and fourth floors. In contrast to modern classrooms' heights, the main floor is seventeen feet high, the others fourteen feet. As Archbishop Howley commented in the *Adelphian* of 1909: "The contrast between the two building (the old and the new) is indeed striking. The new building stands proudly upright in all the dignity and grace of modern proportions,[6] with lofty windows, aesthetic finishings....The old College, on the other hand, seems to retire modestly into the background overawed by its more aggressive successor."

---

[4] *The Adelphian,* Vol. VII, No. 1, July 1907.
[5] Letter announcing the formation of the society (undated), CBASJ.
[6] This building, subsequently named "Mullock Hall" later lost some of its dignity when the portico over the main entrance had to be removed because of structural difficulties.

Turning of the first sod for Mullock Hall by Bishop Howley, May 23, 1907.
On the Bishop's left is Brother Culhane. On his right is Brother Slattery.

Building of Mullock Hall, 1907.

Donations for its furnishing were many. Dean McGrath, P.P. of Bell Island, donated the main altar for the chapel. A recently discovered letter[7] written to him by Brother Culhane describes its arrival. It is dated March 24, 1909:

Dear Father McGrath,

Mr. Tobin made all arrangements for having the seven cases conveyed to the College on last Saturday. Three of the cases were of huge size and it took several men to handle each. Today Mr. Kennedy's men opened the cases and took the different sections of the altar to the chapel. The main body of the altar was in but two parts and it was quite a task for the workmen to get these two parts upstairs.....

At present the different sections lie here and there on the chapel floor, but 'tis not hard to form an estimate as to the appearance which the altar will present when erected. It will be simply grand.... His Grace (Archbishop Howley) saw it this evening and is highly pleased. He at once set to work laying out the platform &c, and soon the work of erection will begin. It is hard to know which part of the altar pleases most. The Last Supper Group is beautifully executed. The expression in each face of the Calvary group is very striking. But it would take pages to give even a faint idea of the whole – and that, too, even before the parts are put together. I know you will be delighted with it.

We have ordered pews from Mr. Callahan.

I am, yours very gratefully,
P. J. Culhane

Besides Dean McGrath's gift of the altar, other donations were received from the pupils and ex-pupils. The Fifth Standard donated the candles for the altar boys; the Preliminary and Intermediate boys, the four branch candelabra for the altar; the senior students donated a veil for the tabernacle; Pat Kennedy of Preliminary Class donated the chimes; the monstrance for Benediction of the Blessed Sacrament was the gift of the Old Boys; Mrs. J. J. Tobin presented a statue of St. Gerard Majella; Mrs. T. J. Edens presented statues of St. Brigid and St. Aloysius in memory of her daughter Mary. The boarders provided a sanctuary lamp which burned before the Blessed Sacrament altar for many years. The chapel was blessed on St. Bonaventure's Day, July 14, 1909, Archbishop Howley saying the first Mass and Dean McGrath celebrating another immediately afterwards.

In the midst of all these events, scholarship was not forgotten. At the annual Prize day on October 30, 1908, Brother Culhane was able to list the following accomplishments of the students of the College. Two boys had passed the Rhodes

---

[7] Courtesy of Doctor MacDonald.

2-7 Club.

Catholic Cadet Corps - c.1913.
Father Mike Kennedy is fourth from left in the back row.

Examination: J. McGrath and T. Halley (J. McGrath was too young to compete for the scholarship this year). Two boys had passed in the London Matriculations Exam — Tom Lamb (First Division) and John Carter (Second Division). The College had won the Jubilee Scholarship for the second year in a row (J. G. Higgins and Tom Lamb;) had taken first and second place in Associate Grade for the third consecutive year; had taken first, fourth and fifth places among boys in Intermediate (Leonard Edens, Leo Sharpe and F. Keating); had taken first and second place in Preliminary (John Barron and E. Crawford); had taken eight of the 11 scholarships won by the boys in the C.H.E.; had taken the greatest number of prizes — 12; had passed the greatest number of boys — 71; had educated half of the boys whose names appeared in the Honours Division of the C. H. E.

All of this must have been a great encouragement both to the Archbishop and to Br. Culhane. *The Newfoundlander* of 1907 (exact date not given) paid the latter a fine compliment. "The College has had many successful presidents," it reported, "but it is questionable if the present principal, Rev. Bro. Culhane, has ever had a superior in his line. The school has advanced by leaps and bounds in his time and any boy can get as good an education right here in our midst, as he can in any city in the world, that is, of course, within certain limitations."[8] Br. Culhane was a keen supporter of games, and the same paper also noted that the College had won the Football Championship for the past three years, the Cricket Championship for the past two years, the Hockey Championship for the past year, and, at present, held all the inter-Collegiate Trophies for Athletics.

One result of the new more spacious accommodations was that the practice of three-day retreats was begun for the older students. The first such retreat took place on March 6-8, 1910, and was conducted by Monsignor E. P. Roche. This practice continued for many years and was a fruitful source of vocations to the priesthood and the religious life.

During the year 1909, three new clerical ex-pupils were ordained: Doctor James Greene, John Kavanagh and Edward O'Brien. In the following year, there were four such ordinations: Reverend Edward Wilson, James Walker, Peter Kelly and John Rawlins. Scholastic triumphs continued with Jack Higgins winning the Rhodes Scholarship in 1909, and John Fox in 1911.

THE TWO POINT SEVEN CLUB

All, however, was not study and prayer. In 1909, the senior boarding students decided to organize a secret society, to be known as the Two Point Seven Club. They wore an emblem in their buttonholes with the College flag of blue and gold on which was the figure 2.7. The purpose of the Club was innocent enough, simply to wind up the school year by having a Banquet at Woods Restaurant on Sports night, July 2nd (hence the name of the Club, also so called because it had fourteen members).

---

[8] Striking a blow, no doubt, at the "Group of Twelve" who had protested the Rhodes Scholarship regulations. (cf. Chapter 10).

Br. W. P. Smithwick

Lord Morris

When Sports Day arrived, leave was granted to the Boarders to be out until 8 p.m., but when the roll was called, all the Seniors, including the Prefect and sub-Prefect, were missing. All the others had retired to bed. Eventually the Brothers did the same with the exception of the Principal who remained a lone sentinel. Ten, eleven o'clock passed and the Principal began to be seriously concerned. Meanwhile a gala repast was being celebrated by the 2.7 Club at Woods Restaurant, with many toasts, songs and speeches. Eventually the evening came to a close and the culprits wound their way up Garrison Hill. All doors were barred but a window in the study was found unclasped and quickly opened. The group crept upstairs in apparent safety, but just as they were about to open the dormitory door, a light was switched on, and, to their great surprise and dismay, there stood the Principal in all his wrath. Next morning came the accounting, but after an apology, all was forgiven and the group left the College in good standing.[9]

In 1909, on April 26th, another historic event in the life of the College occurred when, at a meeting of the ex-pupils, it was decided to form a football team for the Newfoundland Football League, the colours of the team to be the College colours, "blue and old gold."[10]

So began an Association which was to be a power in Newfoundland sports for many years.

The year 1911 was an inspiring one in the life of the College. In the previous year, His Holiness, Pope Pius X, had lowered the age at which it was permissible to receive Holy Communion. Consequently, on May 17, 1911, seventy small boys received their First Holy Communion in the College Chapel.[11]

A week later, on the 24th, Brother J. C. Byrne died at the age of 66. He was a domestic[12] Brother and had come to the College just a few months after the Christian Brothers had taken over its management in 1889. He was first buried in the grounds of Mount St. Francis, adjacent to the College, but later his remains were transferred to the Brothers' plot in Belvedere Cemetery. His place at St. Bon's

---

[9] This incident was recounted by Joseph M. Greene, M.H.A., in the 1931 issue of *The Adelphian*. He gives the names of the 2.7 Club as being: Mogue Power, Tom Devereaux, Hugh Hayes, Reg. Burke, Tom Nangle, Jim Flynn, Mike Dinn, Cyril Kenneally, John Ryan, Paddy Coady, Tom Walsh, Tom Dubordieu, Steve Norris and Joe Greene.

[10] Newspaper clipping of 26.4.09 in S.B.C. Scrap Book 1907-1917, CBASJ.

[11] Their names can be found in *The Adelphian* of June 1911.

[12] That is, he attended to the physical needs of the school rather than teaching class.

was taken by Brother W. P. Smithwick who arrived from Ireland on September 2, 1911.

On June 23, 1911, the Papal Delegate, Most Rev. P. F. Stagni, arrived on an official visit. He was received in the College on the following day and, a day later, ordained the new bishop of St. George's, Bishop Michael F. Power, who had attended the College from 1890 to 1898. Bishop Power said his first Mass as a bishop in the Chapel on the 26th. On July 2nd, the Delegate was entertained at a formal luncheon in the Aula Maxima.

The College maintained its success in scholastic and athletic affairs. In 1912, John Barron won the Jubilee Scholarship; he and four others passed the London Matriculation. Kevin Keegan matriculated at Trinity College, Dublin, and J. B. O'Reilly was accepted by McGill University. In Intermediate, St. Bon's received four of the six scholarships offered. In 1914, Nicholas Duchemin and W. C. McGrath won the two scholarships available in Associate. In cricket, the College team won the shield for the third year in a row.

Other interesting events occurred during these years and should not go unrecorded. On May 23, 1904, there was a meeting of the Board of Directors to congratulate prominent ex-pupil Edward Morris on being created a Knight by the King of England. Later, in 1918, Sir Edward was elevated to the peerage and become Lord Morris, the one and only native Newfoundlander ever to sit in the British Parliament.

In September of the same year, Archbishop Howley wrote to the *Evening Telegram*, explaining the relation between Allandale Road and Bonaventure Avenue. Having been accused of wanting to change the name Allandale Road to Bonaventure Avenue, he explained:

> *Some twenty-three years ago (1871-2), the road leading by the Episcopal Palace and in front of St. Bonaventure's College was closed and a road was opened further westward towards Fort Townshend, which passed on to meet the Circular Road, near the old Ball Alley. This was an entirely new road, and was named at the time "Bonaventure Avenue.". Allan Dale Road[13] is a country road, branching off this Bonaventure Avenue, at its junction with the Circular Road. It runs almost at right angles to Bonaventure Avenue, passing by the northern side of Belevedere Cemetery, to Allan Dale and Long Pond.*

Although the education the College provided was mainly classical, still it did not prevent the students from being quick to avail of modern scientific and technical developments. An interesting example of this was provided by Thomas J. Walsh, an ex-pupil working in West Virginia. He wrote to *The Adelphian* that, when the great fire in Baltimore occurred, he was sent there to take advantage of the sit-

---

[13] Note the spelling.

uation by selling lumber. Every lumbering company in the Eastern States had the same objective and sent their representatives along. About 300 of them arrived in Washington by the same train, only to be told that the next train would not leave for five hours. While all the others went to hotels to pass away the time, Thomas hired a motor car for $75, and was soon racing towards Baltimore at the rate of 25 miles per hour. Arriving in Baltimore almost two hours before the others, he already had orders for almost three million feet of lumber at 35 cents over the market price by the time they arrived.

In April 1905, the Catholic Cadet Corps was re-activated, the Christian Brothers having agreed more or less to sponsor it by forming a company in each of their three schools: St. Bon's, St. Patrick's Hall, and Holy Cross. The College officers were Lieutenants Fenelon, Meehan, Burke and Hiscock. Captain Carty was in overall command.

In June of 1912, Brother Culhane had reached the canonical time limit as Superior of the College community. Consequently, he vacated the position of President of the College but remained a member of the community and acted as Sub-Superior. He did not remain long in this capacity, however; his abilities were too much in demand.

While the successes of St. Bon's were mounting, St. Mary's College in Halifax was experiencing difficulties similar to those that St. Bon's had faced in the 1880's with falling enrollments and financial insecurity. Archbishop McCarthy of Halifax, aware of the Brothers' success in St. John's, wrote the Superior General in Ireland asking him to take over the management of St. Mary's. The latter agreed and, in 1913, Brother Culhane was transferred from St. Bon's to serve as the first Brother President of St. Mary's. Thus ended an era in the history of St. Bon's rarely equalled for its success. On the occasion of his departure, one of his ex-pupils wrote in the local paper:

> There is not one of my generation who studied with him can think of him but with affection. He was with us in every way, whether in sport or in study.... We felt that whatever he said was right – and invariably it was. Towards his ex-pupils his interest was as keen as his guidance was wise. When success fell to their lot, his congratulations were tempered with admonitions for the morrow, and when disappointment or reverses were their portion, his heart and hand went out in deep-felt sympathy.... He possesses that fine sturdy, hopeful spirit, keen foresight and indefatigable energy needed for a pioneer movement.

Chapter 13

THE DOGS OF WAR

I am a proud man tonight that, thanks to us,
two hundred men will go over the top tomorrow
with the consolation of their religion.

– John Edens (at the front, 1917)

𝔍n other ways, too, 1914, marked the end of an era for St. Bonaventure's. On October 15th, Archbishop Howley passed to his eternal reward at the age of 71. He had been one of the first pupils of the College from 1856-1863 and had always been its great supporter. The College, together with the whole Catholic community, mourned his passing.

The replacement for Brother Culhane as President of the College was Brother John Berchmans Ryan, who had been on the school staff since 1903. Born in Co. Tipperary in 1875, Brother Ryan as a youth was highly respected by his companions as being a kind but shy lad with an exceedingly sensitive conscience. Having joined the Christian Brothers in 1891 at the age of 16, he taught in Ireland and England before being sent to St. John's to replace Brother Downey. To fill the gap left by Brother Culhane's departure for Halifax, Brother O'Sullivan was brought back from New York where, in order to receive medical attention, he had been transferred the previous year.

Br. J. B. Ryan
14th President

The College staff now (1914-15) consisted of Brother J. B. Ryan, Superior/President; T. A. Prendergast, J. C. Fennessey, P. V. Strapp, P. H. White, J. A. Kelly, V. M. O'Sullivan, J. T. Perry, W. K. O'Connell. Brothers W. P. Smithwick and W. C. Walsh, domestic Brothers, were in charge of the house arrangements. Professor P. J. McCarthy was responsible for instrumental music; Mr. Charles Hutton for singing and elocution; Mr. Harwill for physical education. The last was assisted by the leaders of the St. Bon's division (No. 3 company) of the Catholic Cadet Corps which was now in vigorous operation, with a membership of 73 captained by Patrick V. Burke, with Frank Summers and Thomas Halley as lieutenants.

The enrolment of the College was climbing steadily. In 1911, there had been 369 students (79 boarders). In 1912, it rose to 385; in 1913, to 416; and in 1914, it stood at 437. In 1916, it would reach 480.

In October 1914, the new and enlarged boarders' dining room was opened, proving to be a great asset. In December, came the glad news that Edward Crawford was the Rhodes Scholar for 1915.

In February 1915, there was great rejoicing in the College when the announcement came that Monsignor E. P. Roche was to be the next Archbishop of St. John's. Monsignor Roche had been educated, first at St. Patrick's Hall and then at St. Bon's and was a firm supporter of both. He was consecrated in the Cathedral on June 29th by the Papal Delegate, Monsignor P. F. Stagni. The following morning, the St. Bon's Alumni Association hosted the new Archbishop and his guests at their Annual Meeting. Among those present was Brother Culhane who had returned from Halifax for the occasion. The proceedings began with High Mass in the College chapel at 8 a.m., celebrated by Archbishop Roche, followed by Benediction of the Blessed Sacrament given by the Papal Delegate. Charles Hutton presided at the organ, with a choir of ex-pupils conducted by Brother Fennessey. The morning was capped by a gala breakfast in the Aula Maxima,[1] at which Sir Edward Morris, Prime Minister of the colony and President of the Alumni, gave a sparkling and erudite address.

The following day, July 1st, the College students gave an entertainment for the new Archbishop and his guests in the T. A. Hall, the students' Address on the occasion being delivered by Patrick J. Kennedy. Later that evening, the College hosted the new Archbishop and a galaxy of distinguished guests at a dinner in the Aula Maxima.

THE WAR BEGINS

Soon, however, all these celebrations began to fade into insignificance as the war in Europe stretched its deadly tentacles towards the Island. Curiously, when one considers its devastating impact on the College and the country in its later stages, there was little notice taken of it in the College Annals in these first years. The first mention of it in the Annals of either St. Bon's or Mount St. Francis is a casual note on October 31, 1915, that the Brothers coming from Ireland were afraid of submarine attacks.[2] The second that in July 1916, Brother White, returning to Ireland, sailed on a troop ship, the *Silician*, with 500 volunteers. Yet much war preparation was in process.

On August 8, 1914, Governor Davidson wired the Secretary of State in England for permission to raise a Naval Reserve of 1000 men. He noted also that several hundred men with "efficient local brigade training" had offered themselves for service abroad. Action on the Naval Reserve was postponed, but the second proposal was accepted, and a few days later the Executive Council, presided over by Sir E. P. Morris, met with the heads of the various Cadet Corps to decide how to implement it. On August 21st, as a consequence of their recommendations, the Governor called for 500 volunteers. Within a week, this number was filled, mainly

---

[1] The menu for the occasion was grapefruit, oranges, bananas, fillet of cod, salmon steak, Saratoga chips, lamb chops, broiled kidneys, ham sauté, hot rolls, toast, buckwheat cake, marmalade, tea, coffee, cocoa. – quite a breakfast!

[2] Ironically, the submarine was invented by a former Christian Brother, John Philip Holland (1841-1914).

**Fr. Tom Nangle
Newfoundland Regiment
chaplain**

from young men from St. John's, more than half of whom were members of the various brigades.

They were given some basic training, and, on October 4th, the "First Five Hundred" sailed for Europe on the H.M.S. *Florizel*. After some months of intensive training in England, their numbers having been brought up to battalion strength, the Newfoundland Regiment set sail on August 17, 1915 for the Dardanelles where fighting had been going on since April with little success and where the major offensive was now over. The Regiment remained there for some months. Before the decision to evacuate the area was taken at the end of December, it had suffered many losses, more through dysentery and its related diseases because of the appalling conditions rather than through gunfire, but had conducted itself remarkably well and gained a high reputation.

How was the College involved in all this? *The Adelphian* of March 1915 lists the names of the ex-pupils who had "joined up." Sixty had joined the Newfoundland Regiment, eight others had volunteered for Canadian Regiments. By the June issue of the same magazine, the number of those in the Newfoundland Regiment had risen to 73; the number in Canadian Regiments had jumped to 16, while five more, presumably from St. Pierre, had joined French Regiments. John Fox ('10),[3] the 1910 Rhodes Scholar,[4] had been made a lieutenant. Father Tom Nangle ('09) had been appointed chaplain to the Regiment with the rank of Captain.

The first casualties were reported; John F. Chaplin ('10), one of the First Five Hundred, had died in Scotland on New Year's Day, 1915, age 18; on February 25th, Patrick O'Brien ('11) of the Royal Naval Reserve was lost on H.M.S. *Clan McNaughton*, age 19. The last weeks of 1915 and the beginning of 1916 brought grimmer news, for the next engagement of the Newfoundland Regiment was at Gallipoli from September 1915 to January 1916. A terrible storm from November 26 to 28 caused such tremendous havoc, mainly through frostbite, that less than half the men were fit for action when it was over.

In all, the Regiment sustained 39 deaths. St. Bon's suffered more than its share; five ex-pupils were killed in action: Buchanan Freebairn ('09) died of dysentery at Malta on October 23rd, age 22; John MacDonnell ('11), one of the First Five Hundred, died of the same disease on October 29th in Alexandria, age 22; David Walsh ('08) of the Canadian Expeditionary Force[5] was killed in action in France on November 11th on his 25th birthday; while his great friend, Hubert Meehan ('09), of the 26th New Brunswick Battalion, Signal Corps, was killed just a week later,

---

[3] The date given here, as throughout the book, is the year the student left St. Bon's.

[4] He had received permission to postpone taking up the scholarship until the war was over.

[5] He had been living in Edmonton.

on November 18th, age 23. John FitzGerald ('01), of the Army Medical Corps, was killed on December 21st when he left the trenches to attend to a wounded fellow soldier. He was 31 years of age.

This sad news, however, does not appear to have discouraged enlistments. The June 1916 issue of *The Adelphian* lists 109 as serving in the Newfoundland Regiment, 28 in Canadian forces, together with the five in the French forces. There were no further deaths reported but Cuthbert Channing ('11) had been invalided home, age 21. Three of the ex-pupils had been a awarded medals: Lieutenant James J. Donnelly ('00) was awarded the Military Cross (M.C.)[6], the first member of the Newfoundland Regiment to be so honoured. He received the medal personally from the King on May 20th. Thomas (White) McGrath, ('13) was awarded the Military Medal (M.M.). William Gladney was awarded the Distinguished Conduct Medal (D.C.M.).

Redeployed to France in 1916, the Regiment took part in several battles there, beginning at Beaumont Hamel on July 1, 1916, where it suffered terrible losses, more than any other unit engaged. Of the 900 men involved, 100 were reported killed, 210 missing, and 374 wounded. Once more, St. Bon's did not escape. The issues of *The Adelphian* of December 1916, and March 1917, listed Captain Frank Summers ('07), Sergeant Allan Cleary ('09), Lieutenant William Grant ('09), Private Michael Kennedy ('07), and Private Donald Templeton ('12) as having been killed in that fatal drive. Lieutenant Grant was 25 and Captain Summers was 26; the others were 22. Private Ignatius Butler ('13) was reported 'missing in action' but was later officially declared dead. Captain James Ledingham ('06) was among those severely wounded in the battle.

The second battle in which the Regiment was engaged was at Gueudecourt on October 12, 1916. James Donnelly, M.C, now raised to the rank of Captain, was killed while leading his men, age 34. Lieutenant Stephen Norris ('11) and Private Thomas McGrath, M.M. ('13) were killed simultaneously when a shell blew up the trench which they were occupying, age 24 and 22 respectively. Thomas was a member of the medical corps. Later, Sergeant Patrick Tobin ('08) died of his wounds at Ayr, Scotland, age 21.

At home, the Ladies Auxiliary, having been asked to focus their attention on the war effort rather than raising funds for the College, responded accordingly. During the year, they knitted and sewed 1,000 pairs of socks, 418 pairs of mitts, 21 rifle covers, 25 suits of pajamas, 85 flannel shirts, 90 hospital bags, and 100 housewives.(i.e., small sewing kits) for the men overseas.

The President of the College, Brother Ryan, in his annual report on Prize Day on November 17, 1916, revealed that over 160 ex-pupils had volunteered, 16 of

---

[6] The details of Donnelly's award are as follows. On the night of November 4th, he led a patrol of eight men sent to occupy a ridge midway been the two lines. Just as it reached the ridge, it was attacked by a far larger group of enemies. The patrol held the ridge all night even though every man was wounded, some several times, and eventually the enemy retired. The following day, the Regiment advanced and set up machine guns on the ridge, afterwards called appropriately *Caribou Hill*. The Military Cross was awarded to Donnelly for "conspicuous gallantry and determination."

whom had died, while eight were "missing in action." Archbishop Roche, in his remarks on the same occasion, noted: "The toll of death amongst the students of the College has been heavy, and their roll of honor is a long one.... We recall to-day with pride, tinged it may be with sadness, their heroic devotion to duty, the bravery they have shown, the distinctions they have won, and, at the same time, we pay a sad and reverent tribute to the memory of those who have fallen gloriously on the field of honour."

THE WAR CONTINUES (1917-18)

After some weeks' recuperation and reinforcement, the Newfoundland Regiment returned to the front lines at Les Boeufs at the end of January 1917. The first casualty among the St. Bon's ex-pupils in this arena was Private Gordon A. Mullings ('14), killed on January 20th at the age of 18. He and his close friend Jack Oliphant ('15), had joined up together, fought together and been wounded together in France. When Gordon was recovering in hospital in Scotland, he found that Jack was returning to France and immediately asked to accompany him to the battlefield where, at his friend's side, he was killed three weeks later.

At the annual Alumni Dinner on July 14, 1917, it was noted that 181 ex-pupils had joined the armed forces, of whom 58 had become officers. Of them, 14 had been killed and nine were missing in action. Joining the ranks of those killed was Private Gus Meehan, ('06). Living in Edmonton, Gus joined the Canadian Expeditionary Forces and was killed on April 9, 1917, age 30. He was a brother of Hubert Meehan who had been killed in November 1915. Others were Private William Power ('11), killed April 23rd, age 23; Vincent Carew, ('07), died July 10th, age 26; Corporal Edward Grant ('09), killed August 16th, age 24; Private Patrick Farrell ('15), died of pleurisy on October 1st, age 19. Among those "missing" were Lieutenant Samuel Smith ('11), Sergeant James Gear ('11), Sergeant Louis Coughlan ('10), Roger Callahan ('05), M. O'Flynn ('08), Patrick O'Brien ('11), Gerald Byrne ('11), (Canadians), John Ellis ('06), Michael Jackman ('11).

A particularly poignant case was that of Private Leo Shortall ('13). Leo had been seriously wounded in the battle of Monchy, April 24, 1917, and been sent to Wandsworth Hospital in England where he lingered on for some months His mother, learning that he had expressed his plea to see her once more, set out for England. She had reached as far as New York and, in spite of the danger, was about to sail for England when she was informed that he had expired on April 29, 1918, age 19.

The ex-pupils had won further military honours: Sergeant Thomas Lambe ('09), of the Canadian Expeditionary Force had been awarded the M.M. Captain Kevin Keegan ('12) and Lieutenant Gerald Byrne ('11) had been awarded the M.C., Lieutenant Bert O'Reilly ('12), the R.A.M.C., Lieutenant James Howley ('01), the C.Q.M.C.

Meanwhile, at home, the College was pursuing "the even tenor of its ways" with the usual prize debates, intercollegiate games, Sports Day, Distribution of Prizes, and other school activities. The school continued to excel in the public exams. Harold Knight had been elected Rhodes Scholar for 1917 but had been permitted to postpone taking up the scholarship until after the war. Charles Fox was the only candidate in the Island to pass the Senior Associate[7] and was awarded the Jubilee Scholarship, now worth $1,200. In the public exams, the College won eight of the 18 open scholarships offered, and achieved first place in nine subjects. In Junior Associate, William Sullivan won one of the two scholarships awarded; in Intermediate, Ronald McD. Murphy and John O'Mara (both future Monsignors) won two of the six scholarships available; Frank Jackman also won an award. Three newly ordained priest ex-pupils were welcomed: Fathers Thomas Devereux, Thomas DuBourdieu and Robert St. John. Several new Directors of the College were appointed: the Honorable P. T. McGrath, President of the Legislative Council; Mr. J. J. McGrath, B.L, an ex-pupil; Mr. F. L. Doyle, who had taught at the College in the mid-seventies; Mr. W. J. Carroll, sub-Sheriff of Newfoundland, another ex-pupil.

There were changes among the Christian Brothers too. In 1916, Brother White had been transferred back to Ireland and his place had been taken by Brother P. B. Doyle. The spread of the Congregation in North America had prompted the Superiors to designate this section of the Brotherhood as a separate unit or "Province," with headquarters in New York, and Brother Culhane had been appointed one of the new Province's Consultors. A novitiate had been set up in New York, the first three candidates being John Donnolly of St. Bon's, John Keane and Thomas Murphy from St. Patrick's Hall Schools.

However, the war and its horrors continued unabated. During 1917, the Newfoundland Regiment was involved in several heavy engagements and the St. Bon's ex-pupils continued to suffer for their bravery. On September 20, 1917, Lieutenant Richard Taylor ('07) of an English Regiment was killed, age 26. At the battle of Ypres on October 9th, the Regiment lost 50 men, with another 130 wounded and 14 missing. Captain James Ledingham ('06), who had previously been severely wounded in the Battle of Beaumont Hamel, was killed while leading his A Company. He was 28 years of age. Captain Kevin Keegan, commanding C Company, led his men with such bravery that he was awarded the Military Cross and Bar. Fortunately he survived. Some days later, on October 14th, Bertram Collins ('11) was killed, age 21. He had enlisted at the age of 17.

The next engagement in which the Newfoundland Regiment was involved was the Battle of Cambrai which began in the early hours of November 20th and continued for two weeks. So gallantly did the Regiment perform that it was granted the title "Royal," but it paid a heavy toll for this privilege: 79 killed, 43 missing and 340 wounded. Among the dead, St. Bon's mourned the loss of: Lieutenant John Edens ('12), age 21; Lieutenant James Tobin ('08), age 24; Victor Carew ('07), age 23; John Fry ('09), age unknown. In the last days of the battle, on December 3rd, George Kane ('04) was also killed.

---

[7] The Senior Associate was now being taken instead of the London Matriculation.

Victor Carew was the brother of Vincent Carew, whose death was mentioned earlier. In 1916, After being in the trenches for nine months and hearing that Vincent was in England, he obtained furlough to meet him only to find that his brother had sailed for France on the previous day. Victor returned to France to find him, and they were side by side in the firing line when Vincent was mortally wounded. Victor consoled him in his last moments and attended his funeral which was conducted by Father Nangle in Poperingue, Belgium. Both Victor and Vincent had always been staunch in their faith and received confession from Father Nangle the day before Vincent's death.

George Kane was one of the First Five Hundred. He was badly frostbitten in Gallipoli and invalided to England. Several times offered promotion, which he refused, he took part in every engagement with the Regiment and came through without a scratch until the fatal Battle of Cambrai. He is buried in the Seranvilles cemetery near the scene of the battle.

Typical of the attitude of the St. Bon's soldiers was that of Lieutenant John Edens. In his last letter home just a few hours before the battle, he wrote to his parents:

"I have just come from confession and I feel perfectly happy. Walter Green and I got busy and found a priest who was attached to another Division (Father Nangle was away at the time). *I am a proud man tonight that, thanks to us, 200 men will go over the top tomorrow with the consolation of their religion."*

Another death at about the same time was St. Bon's first tribute to modern warfare. Walter Petrie ('09) had been one of the First Five Hundred but when the demand for trained marine engineers grew pressing, he resigned at the end of his year's enlistment and obtained a position on one of the transport ships. On October 8, 1917, on its way from England to Galveston, Texas, his vessel was sunk by a torpedo and he, with most of the crew, lost his life, age 23.

War was not the only enemy to thin the ranks of the ex-pupils at this time. The loss of the *Florizel* in March 1918, sent shock waves throughout Newfoundland. The editor of *The Adelphian* seemed to be traumatized as he wrote:

The awful and stunning news of the Florizel *disaster came upon us in such unexpected horror, as nothing else has done since the days of the sealing disaster of 1914. Shortly after leaving St. John's on 24 March, 1918, a blizzard sprang up and the ship grounded on a reef near Cappahayden and, in a short time, became a total wreck. Of the 139 people on board, only 45 were saved. Among those drowned were six ex-pupils of St. Bon's: Michael O'Driscoll, ('93); John Connolly ('01), brother of Frank Connolly, winner of the Jubilee Scholarship in 1892. He was traveling with his father who was also killed: ex-Lance-Corporal Joseph Mullowney ('01), who had been one of the First 500 and had been invalid-*

ed home after suffering intensely from frost-bitten feet at Gallipoli; Gerald St. John ('16), who was attending St. Mary's College, Halifax and was returning there from a visit to his parents in St. John's; Edwin "Teddy" Berteau ('16) who was preparing to enter the Aviation Corps; Francis Chown ('16) who was also traveling to join the same Corps.

One would have expected that, by 1918, the war-weary armies would be experiencing a lull in the conflict. But the overthrow of the Tzar in Russia and the consequent withdrawal of Russia from the war meant that many battle-hardened German troops were released for action on the Western Front. So, at the beginning of 1918, the fighting grew more intense, and the Allies were forced back by superior German forces. By this time, also, the Newfoundland authorities were finding it more difficult to keep the Regiment up to strength as enlistments slackened. The very popular Father Nangle was enlisted in this effort and succeeded in raising the level of recruitment considerably. Still on May 11, 1918, the Newfoundland Government felt it necessary to pass a "Military Service Act" establishing selective conscription. This move came, however, too late, to be of any benefit to the war effort. In any case, the Regiment had been so decimated that it had to be taken out of the line and placed in reserve.

The relative inactivity of the Newfoundland Regiment during the last year of the war meant that there were fewer casualties among the ex-pupils. Nevertheless, there were further bitter losses. Lieutenant Leonard Edens ('08), brother of John who had been killed in 1917, died on March 8, 1918, just four months after his brother, age 27. Leonard was probably the first ex-pupil to gain his "wings" as a member of the Royal Flying Corps. He was lost while flying over enemy lines and is buried at Hooglede. Frank Furlong ('99), who had joined the Canadian Army, was killed on June 3, 1918, age 33. Lieutenant Frank Burke ('08) was killed while leading his men into action on October 14, 1918, age 30. Michael O'Brien ('16) of Witless Bay was killed on October 23rd. Michael was the brother of Patrick O'Brien, R.N.R., who had gone down with the *Clan McNaughton* in 1915. Christopher Kelly ('13), who was living in New York, joined the American Army and died of influenza in France shortly before the Armistice was signed. One of the last victims of the war to become known to the College authorities was Jean Lassus ('06), age 32. A member of the French army, he had been killed at Flanders during one of the engagements. The last death which *The Adelphian* reported was that of Lance-Corporal Gordon Armstrong ('06). He survived the war but, suffering from its effects, he died on June 2, 1920.

Old Boys of the College were receiving distinguished honours from both Church and State. On January 1, 1918, Sir Edward Morris, who had resigned as Prime Minister to join the Imperial War Cabinet in London in July 1917, was elevated to the peerage and became Lord Morris. On October 5, 1918, Sir Michael Cashin, who had been a student at St. Bon's in the 80's and was presently both a member of the College Board of Directors and President of the Alumni Association, was made a Knight Commander of the British Empire (K.C.B.E.).

During the year 1919, one of the Board of Directors of the College, the Hon. J. D. Ryan, member of the Legislative Council and President of the Benevolent Irish Society, was made Knight Commander of St. Gregory (K.C.S.G.) by His Holiness Benedict XV.

THE MEMORIAL PLAQUE

At the close of the war, plans were set in motion to commemorate those ex-pupils of the College who had served in the armed forces. It was decided that the most suitable monument would be a bronze plaque in the College foyer. The obstacle was the cost - $1000, and this Sir Michael Cashin generously offered to provide. Consequently, on January 13, 1921, in a very impressive ceremony in the Aula Maxima, the plaque was presented to the College by Sir Michael and accepted by Brother J. B. Ryan, the College President, in the presence of His Excellency, Governor Charles A. Harris, Archbishop Roche, Bishop Renouf, and many other dignitaries. After Archbishop Roche had spoken, extolling the courage and dedication of those men, the Governor unveiled the plaque and, in his speech pointed out that among them were two[8] Rhodes Scholars, Jack Higgins[9] and Reg. Knight. Among the dead, he noted particularly Captain Donnelly who had shown such courage in Gallipoli and had lost his life in France; Captain Ledingham, whose courage and abilities he had frequently heard extolled, and Captain Summers, "one of the best Quartermasters." He alluded to the Edens family, three of whose sons had joined up and two of whom had been killed. "Their whole history," he said, "has been one of the tragedies of war." Among the living were Captain Byrne, M.C., Colonel Carty, Captain Kevin Keegan, M.C. with Bar, "who took part in one of the most remarkable feats of the War," Colonel Sullivan, and Father Nangle who was now engaged in preparing suitable monuments for the graves of the Newfoundlanders who had died. The C.C.C. band provided suitable music for the event.

This bronze plaque can still be seen in the foyer of the College, a constant witness to the loyalty and bravery of the ex-pupils of St. Bon's, and asking a prayer from those who enter its portals for those who gave their lives. There are 273 names immortalized on it,[10] including 51 who died during the war, nearly a fifth of all those who had enlisted.[11] Included are 56 Commissioned Officers and 68 non-Commissioned Officers. 201 ex-pupils had enlisted in the Royal Newfoundland Regiment and 72 in the British, French, Canadian and United States Regiments.

---

[8] He did not know that another College Rhodes Scholar– Sydney Herbert, the 1st Newfoundland Rhodes Scholar, had served in the American Army.

[9] Jack Higgins, after completing his law degree at Oxford and having joined a law firm in St. John's, tried to enlist but was refused because of his poor eyesight. Later he joined the hospital corps of the Canadian Expeditionary Force and served on the European Front.

[10] One name had unfortunately been overlooked. It is that of Captain Robert Kent ('06) who joined a Canadian Regiment and received the Military Cross.

[11] One of the distressing results of so many dead young Newfoundland men was the long list of unmarried young St. John's women. In one family, for instance, of five girls, only one was able to find a husband.

The group gained five Military Crosses, one Military Cross with Bar, two Distinguished Conduct Medals, four Military Medals and one Croix de Guerre. Thus one of the most heroic, yet saddest, events in the history of the College found its closure.

The Roll of Honour of the St. Bon's ex-pupils who served, and those who died, in the First World War.

Chapter 14
PEACE BETWEEN WARS

Under the very capable direction of Captain O'Grady,
lessons in physical drill are given twice each week.

– Annual Report, 1921

On the world stage, the period between the end of the First World War in 1918 and the beginning of the Second World War in 1939 was marked by increasing turmoil, mainly because of the economic dislocations caused by the First World War which culminated in the Bank Crash of 1929 and the subsequent Great Depression. Newfoundland suffered uniquely from the effects of these disasters because its inability to finance its activities[1] forced it to surrender its sovereignty and to accept a new form of Government — Government by Commission, with six Commissioners, three from England and three from Newfoundland — all appointed by the British Government, with the Governor as chairman.

The 1920's also were a time of great political ferment in Ireland, and St. Bon's, with its Irish background and largely Irish staff, was naturally affected. In October, the College gave a rousing welcome to a Miss Hughes, who was touring North America on behalf of the Irish crusade for independence, when she spoke to the students in the Aula Maxima about the Irish right to freedom. The annual Alumni Meeting on St. Bonaventure's Day, July 14, 1922, featured a fiery speech by J. J. O'Donnell, B.A., on "Ireland's Claim to Self-determination."

The years 1920 and 1921 featured one valuable property gained and another lost. Directly across from the main entrance to the College is a fine house, surmounted by an observatory, which belonged to the Delaney family, one of whom had been Postmaster General. Mary, his daughter, died in 1920 at the age of 96 and, by her deed, the house became the property of the College, which maintained it for many years before finally disposing of it. It is still (2006) in fine condition and has been designated a historic building. February 19, 1921, witnessed a spectacular fire, fortunately not in the College itself. But the nearby residence of the Archbishop and priests, the "Palace" as it was known, was completely destroyed.[2] Fortunately, there was no loss of life, and the fire did not spread to the Bishop's Library with its valuable collection of books and paintings, but many church records were destroyed. The Cathedral priests took up temporary residence at the College.

By this time, the ex-pupils of the College were beginning to make their mark on the world stage. Nick Duchemin, who had achieved Associate Scholarship standard in 1914 but had been unable to take it up because of his American

---

[1] The root of its financial difficulties was the massive expenditure the support of the Newfoundland Regiment in W.W.I. required.

[2] The cause of the fire, apparently, was a visiting priest who was smoking in bed and fell asleep. He required treatment but fortunately escaped serious injury.

St. Bonaventure's

She is our Mother on a cross-crowned hill.
The light about her where she stands sublime.
Beams Faith undying down the Vale of Time
On all who know her and who love her still.
Now pay we homage on her festal hour
And weave a laurel wreath for this our Queen.
Vainly seeks she not, but she has been
Each good we prize. Let Terra Nova Shower
New Praise, while throughout her throbbing veins
The blood of Alma Mater courses true
Unto each noble urge that yet remains
Revered amid the ways that men pursue.
E'er may with Faith by sons of Erin taught
Sound Science stand to soothe an age distraugt.

L.E.F. English
1930 Adelphian

citizenship, had joined the American Flying Corps in 1917, the first from Newfoundland to do so. He was now working his way up through the ranks of General Electric Company until, in 1924, he became General Manager of that prestigious American Company. J. W. McGrath, who had emigrated to the United States to study law, had become secretary to President Theodore Roosevelt for some years, and was now manager of the famous Fulton Fish Market in New York. Tom Lamb had moved to Australia as manager of the Ford Company there. The Rev. Doctor Browne had won renown for his scholarship and had become editor of the *Catholic Historical Review*.

In 1921 Brother J. B. Ryan's canonical term of office terminated. Before retiring as President, however, he had the satisfaction of knowing that two recent St. Bon's ex-pupils, William J. Browne and Sebastian Young, had been elected Rhodes Scholars, Browne for 1918 and Young for 1921, while Gerard Strapp had won the Jubilee Scholarship ($1,500) for 1920. In 1920, he saw Ronald Murphy, George Bartlett, and Frank Jackman off to All Hallows in Dublin to study for the priesthood. He could note also that in sports, the College remained pre-eminent. In football, for instance, since the Inter-Collegiate League was established in

1899, St. Bon's had won the trophy 13 times; the Methodist College, seven times; and Bishop Field College, twice. In his last Annual Report on Prize Day, March 10, 1921, he noted that "under the very capable direction of Captain O'Grady, lessons in physical drill are given twice each week." Thus, beginning in 1920, one of the College's most enduring and most beloved instructors helped mold the lives of generations of students until his regretted retirement in 1959.

Captain J. J. OGrady
Physical Instructor
1920 - 1959

In the "changing of the guard" in October 1921, Brother J. B. Ryan was replaced as President of the College by Brother J. E. Ryan, which move caused as little disturbance to the school or the religious community as did the change in the name of the President. Brother J. B. Ryan remained on the staff, continuing to be responsible for the senior mathematics.

Brother John Evangelist Ryan* was born in Doon, Co. Limerick in 1871. Having entered the Christian Brothers' Congregation, he taught for some years in Ireland before coming to St. John's in 1892 to teach at St. Patrick's Hall Schools as a member of the Mount St. Francis community. Unfortunately, a month before his arrival, a terrible fire had destroyed much of the city, including St. Patrick's Hall, thus

Brother J. E. Ryan
15th President

leaving the children without either a place to learn or, in many cases, a home to live in. For more than a year, the Brothers sheltered and fed homeless boys in the Monastery while instructing the St. Pat's students in a temporary structure erected on the Parade Grounds. Brother Evangelist was possessed of tremendous energy and determination and, when assigned to teach the senior boys, even in these primitive surroundings, he achieved results comparable to those obtained at the Colleges. In 1900, though only 29 years of age, he was appointed Superior of Mount St. Francis and Principal of the restored and improved St. Patrick's Hall Schools. In 1915, he was appointed the founding Superior of St. Louis College in Victoria, B.C. Returning to Mount St. Francis in 1918, he was appointed, three years later, to succeed Brother Berchmans Ryan at President of St. Bon's.

The College staff at this time (1921-22) consisted of Brother J. E. Ryan, President; Brother P. V. Strapp, Sub-Superior; Brothers P. B. Doyle, J. B. Ryan, W. K. O'Connell, J. T. Perry, M F. Ryan, T. I. Murphy, with Brothers W. P. Smithwick and W. C. Walsh as domestic Brothers. This was a very experienced staff, and the continuity of skilled teaching doubtless contributed greatly to the College's sustained success. The numbers on the Roll reached 507 of whom 84 were boarders.

In his first yearly report, June 1922, Brother Ryan could report that the results were "the best in the history of the College." Six students had passed in Senior Associate (all in the honours division), 23 in Junior Associate (20 in the honours division), 39 passed Intermediate (21 with honours), 38 passed Preliminary (11 with honours).

THE FORUM

Soon after his arrival, Brother Ryan began a project, often mooted but always delayed because of the expense involved — the construction of an ice hockey rink. On October 3, 1922, ground was broken for the new rink and work proceeded so well that on January 23rd of the following year, it was opened for the enjoyment of students.[3] The cost was about $10,000. The official opening, on February 6th, was a gala occasion, with the rink decorated, the students in carnival attire, and speeches from the Governor Sir W. Allardyce, Monsignor McDermott, the Vicar General, and many others. Dubbed "The Forum," the rink was responsible for the domination of St. Bon's in local hockey circles for many years until the other Colleges finally erected rinks of their own. It, or rather its successor, for it burned down in 1979 and was restored in 1980, still continues to serve the students well. In conjunction with the rink, Brother Ryan also built a new stable for the dairy herd which provided milk for the school.

---

[3] Over the protests of the other members of the staff that it was too small, Brother Ryan, who could carry determination to the point of stubbornness, insisted on its present dimensions which make it too small for senior students but ideal for the younger players. Originally, there was a skating area around the hockey rink, but this arrangement proved unsatisfactory, and the skating area was transformed into a place for spectators. At the same time, the hockey rink was lengthened somewhat by removing the skating area at both ends.

Cricket Champs - 1908.
(Seated) M. Power, J. Higgins, T. Nangle, T. Lambe, J. McGrath.
(Standing) F. Pumphrey, J. Rawlins, L. Edens, M. Pike, L. O' Dea, F. Maher.

Amateur Champs - 1928.
(Front Row) E. Ryan, Pat Brown (cox), Gordon Higgins (stroke).
(Back Row) Art Hamlyn, Pat Hanley, Jim Daley, Stan Ryan.

First St. Bon's Boyle Trophy Winners - 1928.
(Front Row) Frank Graham, Ashley Graham.
(Second Row) Gordon Higgins, Gordon Halley, Edmund Phelan,
Thomas Sutton, William Kendall. (Third Row) Paddy Keegan (Mgr.),
William Cotter, John Higgins, (Pres.), Mike Monaghan, Eric
Robertson (Coach), John Wood, Robert Furlong.

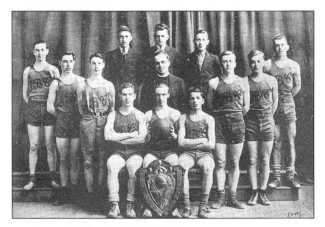

Junior Basketball Champs - 1939.
1st. Row: James Darcy, Charlie Doyle (Capt), George Earle. 2nd
Row: George Gamberg, Robert Madigan, Charlie Power, Br. Carroll
(Coach), Fred Cahill, Frank Foran, Charlie Stamp. 3rd Row: Robert
Murphy, Donald O'Driscoll, Alec MacKenzie.

The rink was not Brother Ryan's only physical improvement to the College. In 1925 he erected an ornamental iron fence around the grounds, incurring the displeasure of the Archbishop in doing so, since he enclosed some Episcopal property[4] in the process. In 1927, in his final year as President, he bought *Oak Farm* on Carpasian Road which served both to supply milk for the College and provide recreation for the students. Having a farm also entailed having someone to manage it, and the College was fortunate in obtaining the services of Mr. Jim Kavanagh to take care of the farm in the summer and the furnaces in the winter. For many years, Jim served the College faithfully in his own quiet, unostentatious way. The lowing of the herd of cows as, under his urging, they went to the farm in the morning and returned to the College in the evening was a familiar sound in St. John's.

Brother Ryan's years in charge were not without incident. In the early hours of the morning of March 8, 1922, he awoke with a premonition that something was awry. Proceeding at once to the dormitories with a flashlight in hand, he was horrified to discover on the stairs the prostrate form of a 13-year old boy, Robert Comerford, lying unconscious. Apparently, the boy had got up to go to the bathroom on the nearby landing and had tripped on his bathrobe, striking his head violently on the stairs. The school doctor, Doctor Scully, and the College chaplain, Father Flynn, were summoned, but the lad died without recovering consciousness. He is buried next to the Brothers' plot in Belvedere. The shock to Bother Ryan, as well as to the whole College community, was shattering.

Later, in February 1924, he had another painful experience. In his typical self-sacrificing approach, he was accustomed, in the coldest part of winter, to rise at 2 a.m. to stoke the furnaces so that the Brothers and boys would have some warmth when rising. One morning, when he opened the furnace door, there was an explosion, and his face was badly burned. Fortunately, there was no permanent damage, but he was out of action for some days and, to his chagrin, was unable to attend the annual Prize Giving.

There were changes also among the Old Boys. At the annual meeting in July, 1923, a new executive was elected consisting of W. R. Howley, President; J. G. Higgins and Father Joseph Pippy, Vice-Presidents; J. G. Muir, Secretary; and T. S. McGrath, Treasurer. In 1927, the St. Bon's Athletic Association came into existence with J. G. Higgins as President. It replaced the St. Bon's Hockey Club.

In September 1924, **Brother J. V. Birmingham***, who was to have a long association with the College, joined the staff from St. Mary's College, Halifax, replacing Brother P. F. O'Sullivan, who was once more transferred to New York. There were various other changes of staff, including the departure of Brother J. B.

---

[4] The property in question was that in front of the Bishop's Library.

Ryan for New York, thus severing a link which went back 20 years, and the arrival of Brother J. A. King, another doughty addition. So, for 1925-26, the staff consisted of: Brother J. E. Ryan, President; Brothers Fennessy, Strapp, Doyle, Birmingham, Perry, M. F. Ryan, Donnelly, G. J. Power,[5] Hamill, King; with Brothers Smithwick and Walsh as domestic Brothers, and Captain O'Grady in charge of physical training. Brother Perry was to be transferred in August, 1926, after serving the College with great dedication for seventeen years, having arrived at St. Bon's in August 1909.

On January 20, 1925, Methodist College burned to the ground to be reborn as Prince of Wales College. On April 21, 1926, Mount Cashel Orphanage did likewise, and for some time the College housed over eighty of the boys in the Aula Maxima, using mattresses generously supplied by Mr. John Henley from his mattress factory.

The year 1925 witnessed two unusual spiritual events. On October 6th, Father William McGrath, ex-pupil and member of the Canadian Foreign Mission Society (Scarboro Fathers), spoke to the student body on his experiences in China[6] and the tremendous challenges facing the Catholic Church in attempting to spread the Gospel in that vast country. Three days later, the College was presented with a relic of the True Cross[7] of Christ, gift of the Superior General of the Christian Brothers. The following year, 1926, was similarly spiritually gifted when five ex-pupils of the College were ordained to the priesthood. They were: Fathers Gibbs, Power, O'Mara, Curtis, and Wall.

Statue of St. Bonaventure.

On June 12, 1927, Brother Ryan presented his last addition to the College before the expiration of his canonical term of office — a marble statue of St. Bonaventure[8], the gift of several ex-pupils in memory of deceased ex-pupils. The statue was carved in Paris at a cost of $800.

In September 1927, Brother J. E. Ryan was replaced as President by another member of the College staff, Brother P. B. Doyle. At the same time, Brother Strapp was appointed Superior of Mount Cashel Orphanage. Although in the classroom, the latter could be replaced, in other ways he could not, and for the next three years, the publication of *The Adelphian* became erratic and the collection of College scrapbooks inadequate, for both of which records of the College's activities he had been responsibile. Brother P. R. Kielley, who had been on the staff for

---

[5] Brother Power was a brother of Greg Power, also an ex-pupil. Greg was a noted poet and athlete, later Minister of Finance with the Smallwood government.

[6] In 1935, the now Monsignor McGrath published a book entitled *The Dragon at Close Range* describing his experiences in China.

[7] This Cross with its certificate of genuineness is now (2006) in the chapel at Mount St. Francis Monastery.

[8] The statue was first placed in the foyer of the College, then outdoors at the corner of the present Holland Hall, and finally at its present location in front of Mullock Hall.

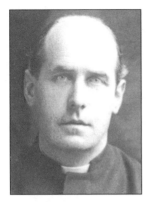

Br. P. B. Doyle
16th President

some time, was also transferred to Holy Cross Schools. To replace those departing, Brothers M. C. Ahern and J. C. Collins were transferred from St. Patrick's Hall Schools.

Brother **Patrick Berchmans Doyle**,* who had joined the staff of the College in 1916, was a native of Waterford, Ireland. He was a brilliant classic scholar, blessed with a photographic memory, a kindly teacher with a whimsical sense of humor and beloved by his students for his fairness and his interest in their welfare. Very unusually for his time, he had obtained his B.A. degree from Queen's University in Belfast[9] in 1914, majoring in Latin and taking Irish, French and English as well. While at St. Bon's, he translated from the Irish, Father O'Leary's *An craos deamhain*, (The Demon of Gluttony) parts of which can be found in various issues of *The Adelphian* of his era.

Unfortunately, none of this protected him when he came in conflict with his ecclesiastical superiors. The College Annals note that, at the Prize Day on December 17, 1927, "through some unaccountable circumstance, Archbishop Roche and priests were not present!" Whatever the cause,[10] this disagreement must have been short-lived since at the banquet celebrating the first Boyle Trophy victory of the ex-pupils hockey team in April 1928, the Archbishop, Msgr. McDermott, the Vicar General and the priests of the city and nearby parishes were present! The warming of the temperature between the Brothers and the Archbishop may well have been caused by the decision of his superiors to transfer Brother Doyle for, on August 29, 1928, word was received at the College that he was being appointed Superior of Vancouver College, Vancouver, B.C. In later years, Brother Doyle was often heard, when describing his removal, to relate humorously and without rancor, how, at St. Bon's, he had "received a belt of the crozier."[11]

---

[9] That University was then a hotbed of sectarian bigotry.

[10] Memorial University College was opened in 1925 with Doctor Paton as its first President. It seems that one reason for Brother Doyle's coming to Newfoundland was that he would teach at the University. However, it appears that the Archbishop was not in favour of Catholics attending or being connected with the University. Hence the tension between him and Brother Doyle.

[11] The crozier is the staff which a Bishop carries during liturgical functions.

Chapter 15
OF MANY THINGS

The founding of the College was the outstanding event
of Bishop Mullock's episcopacy.
– Archbishop Roche, speech at the
Sixtieth Anniversary of the College

Brother Ahern
17th President

It may, or may not, have been significant that Brother Doyle set sail for Ireland on July 2, 1928, and that Archbishop Roche presided at the Annual Sports Day on the 14th. In any event, on September 2nd, word was received at the College that **Brother Michael Christopher Ahern*** was appointed its 17th President. Brother Ahern had come to Newfoundland from Ireland 24 years before, had taught successfully at Holy Cross Schools for several years, and had been Principal of St. Patrick's Hall Schools from 1919-1925. He had been on the College staff for one year. A native of Co. Cork, he was 42 years of age at the time of his appointment. Musically gifted, though self-taught, he was a deeply spiritual person and very self-effacing. Unfortunately, he suffered greatly from stomach ulcers which limited his capacity to attend to his duties.

Nevertheless, the College did extremely well in the yearly public exams. Eleven of the 12 candidates in Senior Matriculation were successful. By contrast, the newly formed Memorial University College, which presented the only other candidates, passed 19 of 57. Richard McGrath won the Jubilee Scholarship.[1] Twenty-one of the 27 candidates from St. Bon's for Junior Matriculation passed, 11 with honours.

As might be expected, given the nature of the man, Brother Ahern's term of office passed quietly. However, there were some notable events. One was the arrival of Brother J. P. Keane in September 1929, joining Brother J. X. Dunphy who had been on the staff since September 1926. Another was the defeat, in February 1930, of the Prince of Wales College hockey team by a score of 11 to 0 in the Prince's Rink — the seventh year in a row that St. Bon's had won the championship, thereby demonstrating the effectiveness of the new College rink. On November 18th, the College organized a concert for the relief of the victims of the historic tidal wave which had destroyed several settlements on the south coast of the Island. On

---

[1] It is worth noting that he was the second member of his family to do so. His sister, Helena (Frecker) having previously achieved this distinction. Richard became Bishop of St. George's, and his older brother, William, Vicar-General of the Scarboro Missionary Fathers. Helena was the first graduate of Memorial University College where she later lectured.

January 3, 1930, Francis J. Doyle, the oldest ex-pupil of the College died. Some years earlier he had given the College several acres of land on Thorburn Road.

The custom was begun, during the winter months, of having free Sunday night concerts for the students in the Aula Maxima. Sir Charles Hutton, for instance, gave a masterly rendering of excerpts from Shakespeare on February 15, 1929, and Tom O'Neill gave readings on March 9th. It was a custom which lasted for many years and gave endless enjoyment to the students while helping develop their cultural appreciation.

As of September 1929, the College staff consisted of Brothers M. C. Ahern, President/Superior; J. C. Fennessy, Sub-superior; J. V. Birmingham, J. C. Collins, M. F. Ryan, J. P. Keane, J. A. King, J. X. Dunphy, G. A. McNally, J. J. Enright, J. G. Smith, with the ever-present Brothers Smithwick and Walsh as co-adjutor Brothers. Captain O'Grady continued to take care of physical education. In the following year, Brother Strapp, having completed his three-year term of office at Mount Cashel, returned to his accustomed place in the College community, somewhat annoyed that things had been disturbed in his room while he was absent.

Early in 1930, the community was joined by Brother L. S. Forde who replaced Brothers Smithwick and Walsh, both of whom had reached retirement age. For the next 13 years, Brother Ford quietly and efficiently took care of the 'temporalities' of the College while adding greatly to its aesthetics by the beautiful flowerbeds he cultivated in the College grounds.

Brother Birmingham
18th President

One inspiring event during these years occurred on July 10, 1929 — the simultaneous saying of three Masses on the three altars in the College chapel by three clerical ex-pupils, members of the same family: Father William Murphy, Parish Priest of King's Cove; Father Aidan Murphy, C.Ss.R., and Father Gerald Murphy, C.Ss.R. Another such occasion was the ordination of Father Alphonsus Chafe in Toronto, the first ex-pupil of the College to be ordained for the Chinese mission.[2] He was soon to be joined by Fathers Hugh McGettigan and Charles Strong. In 1931, Father William McGrath was appointed first Prefect Apostolic of Chuchow, China. Still another was the presentation of a thurible[3] for the College chapel by the student body, James Higgins making the presentation on behalf of the day boys, and Bill Hodge for the boarders.

In 1931, ill health forced Brother Ahern to retire after only three years of office. His successor was **Brother John Vincent Birmingham**;* Brother Ahern remaining on the staff as Sub-Superior. Brother Birmingham was born in 1892 in Cork, Ireland, and hence was just 39 years of age at the time of his appointment. He had

---

[2] Father William McGrath had been ordained in 1921 for the St. John's Archdiocese but soon afterwards transferred to the Chinese mission.
[3] A thurible is the vessel for holding the incense at liturgical functions.

entered the Brothers' Congregation in 1906 and, after teaching for some years in Ireland, had formed part of the pioneer community when the Brothers took over St. Mary's College, Halifax, in 1913. He had joined St. Bon's staff in 1924 teaching languages and maths. Very different from his predecessor, he possessed a flamboyant personality which expressed itself in great enthusiasm for all school activities, particularly sports and cultural events. Though not a particularly gifted teacher, nor, it must be said, a particularly organized administrator, during his term of office, the College won more Jubilee and Rhodes Scholarships than at any other comparable period in its history. Very interested in improvements and renovations, he added the organ gallery to the chapel and placed a large, beautiful stained glass window[4] behind the main altar; both altar and window having been donated by Dean McGrath, P.P. of Bell Island. He renovated the rink, prepared the Aula Maxima for basketball, built two handball alleys at the rear of the school, and constructed a tennis court on what had previously been known as "Brother Strapp's playground." A violin class was formed under the care of the talented Mrs. Kitty (Ryall) Ryan. It was during his presidency, too, that the class pictures along the walls where artistically reset by Brother M. F. Ryan.

A College orchestra came into existence at this time under the enthusiastic direction of Brother Dunphy. It consisted of pupils and ex-pupils as well as other talented musicians. It quickly gained a name for itself. Public radio was just coming into use, and the College orchestra achieved a "first" when it presented a radio broadcast, entitled "An Irish Night," from the Newfoundland Hotel. Brother Birmingham gave an eloquent address for the occasion and introduced the various items on the program.

On April 27, 1932, the College celebrated its Diamond Jubilee. The festivities began with Solemn High Mass in the Cathedral, presided over by Archbishop Roche and with many priests in attendance. In the evening, the ex-pupils gathered at the College and, after Benediction in the Chapel, proceeded to the Aula Maxima where there were many speeches and where they presented a beautiful Monstrance[5] to the College. Two evenings later the pupils performed Shakespeare's *Julius Caesar* to a capacity audience. At the end of the school year, the students presented to the College a pair of fine brass candelabra made in Dublin. On July 2nd, work began on the new organ gallery under the direction of Mr. Charles McCarthy,[6] who had been one of the architects of the chapel itself. In 1933, Mr. Louis Cuddihy donated a fine new organ for the Chapel.

Inter-Collegiate sports, among both present pupils and ex-pupils, were going strong. Usually St. Bon's won the inter-collegiate championship, but they did not always have their own way. In 1932 there was a hiatus described by ex-pupil and

[4] The window was built by Earlay and Co. of Dublin, Ireland.
[5] Monstrance is the sacred vessel in which the Blessed Sacrament is placed for Exposition.
[6] When the organ gallery was being restored in 2004, a bottle was found in the floor containing a message that Mr. McCarthy had built it with the assistance of one of his relatives.

115

radio commentator Aubrey MacDonald,[7] who incidentally depicted the difficult conditions for playing hockey before the advent of artificial ice.

> *In 1932, St. Bon's boasted a terrific College team, but they suffered the biggest upset of that era and therein lies a story. Jack "Jiggs" Monahan was attending St. Bon's and, after an altercation with his superior, left in a huff and a puff, and went to Prince of Wales. Then came the championship game between that College and St. Bon's. The Prince's Rink was bulging at the seams: fans were hanging from the rafters, the game scheduled for eight, couldn't get going till nine. By then the natural ice was mostly water. Heat had taken its toll and the cigarette smoke hovered over the ice surface like an impenetrable pall.*
>
> *"Jiggs" played left wing, opposite the late Doctor Bernard Maher; the late Phil Veitch was in goal for St. Bon's, with Dick Furlong and Ned Fowler on the defence, Bob Godden, center. The game began. Through the pall of steam and smoke you could see the red light come to life over the St. Bon's goal. "Jiggs" Monaghan had scored again. They passed the puck to Monaghan, and he was away; his skates were wings of speed. Final score, three to nothing for Prince of Wales with "Jiggs" accounting for two.*

ACHIEVEMENTS OF EX-PUPILS

A glance through *The Adelphian* of this time (1934) reveals how widely the ex-pupils had become dispersed and how influential they had become. Three ex-pupil priests had achieved their Jubilees: Golden Jubilee in the case of Father Tarahan, P.P. (1857) of Trinity, and Silver Jubilees in that of Father Joseph Pippy ('02), P.P. of St. Joseph's, Hoylestown, and Father Gough, (1893), P.P. of Portugal Cove. Father P. W. Browne, Ph.D., D.D. (1870's), professor at The Catholic University of America in Washington, D.C., had paid a short visit to his Alma Mater. Father Pat Kennedy ('15) was the devoted College chaplain. Four ex-pupil priests were labouring on the China mission, Msgr. William McGrath ('14), Prefect Apostolic of Chuchow, Fathers Alphonsus Chafe ('25), Hugh McGettigan ('27) and Craig Strang ('28). Father S. St. Croix (1894), was P.P. of St. Albans and had established a Co-operative Society there. Michael Connolly ('32) had entered All Hallows Seminary in Ireland.

Archbishop Roche (1892), Monsignor Kitchin (1897), Justice James M. Kent (1889) were honoured guests at Sports Day at which Leo E. English ('06), a well-known Newfoundland writer, donated a medal for the winner of the one-mile walk. Hugh O'Neill ('24), Cecil Duff ('24), James Bradshaw ('25), and Claude Fraser ('20) had just been admitted to the Bar. In Hugh's first case, ex-pupil Judge Frank S. Morris ('18) congratulated him on his achievement. Leonard Burke ('09) a vet-

---

[7] "My Song of Sport," *Book of Newfoundland*, Vol. 4, p. 276.

eran of the War, had been appointed Magistrate at St. George's. Ambrose Buckingham ('06) had been appointed General Inspector of the Mechanical Department at the Paper Mill in Corner Brook. Doctor John Walsh ('16) had just set up practice in St. John's after serving in the Newfoundland Regiment during the war and pursuing medical studies in Edinburgh and elsewhere. John Barry of Curling, R. S. Furlong, B.L. ('20), W. S. Dunphy (1860's), and High Sheriff W. J. Carroll (1870's) had made generous contributions to the College library. William Howley, K.C. (1892) had been appointed a member of the Commission of Government recently set up to govern the country. He had been one of the three College students to place in the First Division of the London Matriculation in 1892. Among the offices he had held were: President of the Newfoundland Law Society, member of the House of Assembly 1900-1913, past President of the St. Bonaventure's College Alumni Association (1920-1926). He was a brother of James Howley, F.G.S., and nephew of Archbishop Howley.

Fred MacNamara ('25) had completed his studies in Germany and had set up his optician office in St. John's Doctor Charles Howlett ('02) had graduated in dentistry at McGill, carrying off the Stuart prize;[8] Doctor A. Larkin ('23) had obtained his medical degree from Queen's University. Doctor Charlie Fox ('07), winner of the Jubilee Scholarship, had been promoted to the rank of Surgeon-Lieutenant-Commander and attached to the cruiser H.M.S. *Danae* in the British navy. He was a brother of Mr. Cyril Fox, K.C. ('06), one-time speaker of the House of Assembly. Arch MacNamara ('29) had passed his second year exams in Dublin. Peter Nicholls ('33) had joined the Hudson Bay Company in Cartwright. Gerard Jackman, B.Com., ('24) was a member of the staff of St. Mary's College, Halifax. Louis Bown ('27) and Stan Carew ('24) had been elected President and Vice-President respectively of the Engineering Society at Dalhousie University where Louis Petrie ('32) won first place in engineering and drawing. At the same university, Cyril Byrne ('26) had passed his second year medical exams; John Bernard McEvoy ('17) had won the Carswell prize for first year law; Jack Ashley ('32), Jubilee, and later Rhodes, Scholar, had won the Entrance Classic Scholarship.

Captain Leo C. Murphy ('10) had been appointed representative for Newfoundland for the firm of Samuel French, one of the oldest play publishers in the world. Thomas Mott ('06) held a responsible position with the First National Bank in Boston; Gerald Byrne ('07) was a radio announcer with the Edison Company of Boston. Tom "Dynamite" Dunne ('24), was a champion wrestler in the U. S.; W. Halley, B.Sc., ('24) of Petty Harbour, was a qualified engineer. Cyril Carey ('24), of Montreal, had been elected an Associate Member of the Engineering Institute of Canada and had received the Civil Engineering Diploma of that Institute. Frank Keating had become a successful commercial artist in New York; Michael Morris ('15), son of Lord Morris, had been made a partner in the law firm of Thorp, Saunders and Thorp in London, England. Gordon James ('27) had

---

[8] He later became one of the most respected mayors of St. John's, but unfortunately died before his term of office was complete.

117

received his First Officer's ticket and had joined the *S.S. Dominica*. Alister Mars ('24) was a midshipman on H.M.S. *Norfolk*. Ron Taaffe ('26) had been appointed General Agent of the Confederation Life Assurance Company in Corner Brook. Bert Morry (1898) was a highly successful building contractor in Victoria, B.C., and Grand Knight of the Victoria Council of the Knights of Columbus. Felix Parsons (1912) held an important position with the Canadian Bank of Commerce at Halifax. Henry "Mac" Hearn ('17) was with the Western Union Telegraph Co. in New York, where Terence F. Foley (1891) was Superintendent. F. R. Clarke, (**??**), Newfoundland Manager of Sun Life of Canada, had been presented with an award for the largest amount of insurance secured by new agents.

Hubert Langton ('04) had written a fascinating letter from California describing his trip across the United States in a Chrysler Sedan which he had purchased for $200, encountering a tornado on the way. He had spent some years in Paris studying art and one of his productions had been accepted by the French Academy of Art. He was now settling in California where his family owned property.[9] James S. McGrath ('18) had held the position of manager of the Chicago branch of the Wall Street Journal with a staff of 450 under him since 1930 and was now Vice-president and Director of the Illinois Telegraph News Co. in Chicago. Captain Kevin Keegan, of Military Cross fame ('12), had visited his Alma Mater.

The Adelphian obituary list for 1934 contained the names of Father James Joy (1886), P.P of Port-au-Port; Father John O'Reilly, D.D., (1885) who had established a night school for the poor boys of St. John's and had written 'The Last Sentinel of Castle Hill"; Charles Eagan, ('11) an outstanding athlete, who had entered the seminary in Toronto but been forced to leave because of ill health; Thomas McCarthy Murphy (1880), Barrister and Solicitor, elected for St. John's in 1886 with the Whiteway Government, Minister of Fisheries, "It is doubtful whether Marconi would have come here to try his first wireless work over the Atlantic if T. J. Murphy had not been Minister of Fisheries" — so reads the obituary account; Thomas Walsh (1865) a West-end merchant, "as honest as the sun"; David Courtney, (1885) Meat Inspector and government Cattle Appraiser — "chiefly instrumental in the establishment of the S.P.C.A. Infirmary"; James Clancy (1860's) — caretaker of the Club Rooms of the Total Abstinence Society; James "Big Jim" Connors ('09) of Bell Island, one of the first boarders to occupy the new dormitory. "In his life-story is written the history of sport on Bell Island for quarter of a century"; Bernard McGrath (1880's), a graduate of St. Francis Xavier College in Antigonish, who taught in the high school at King's Cove — his "advanced and modern ideas in school work have been reflected in the careers of his numerous ex-pupils"; Joseph Downey (1850's), representative for St. George's from 1908 to 1928, Minister of Agriculture and Mines, "he was practically the pioneer of the fresh fish industry of the country, shipping fresh fish to Canada by the old *Bruce* from Channel... during his long political career he did much to preserve

---

[9] At Brother Strapp's request, he had agreed to design a cover for *The Adelphian*, and his work adorned *The Adelphian* for several years beginning in 1936.

the forests of the island and to improve the breed of sheep and cattle in the out-lying districts by the distribution of high grade stock…his wide charity was only equalled by his deep embarrassment at being found out, and he took great pains to cover the trail of his good deeds… his ménage has been known to include a young bear and a baby eagle"; William Smith ('13), one of three brothers who enlisted in the Newfoundland Regiment; he became a non-commissioned officer. His brother Sam became a Lieutenant and was killed at Monchy in 1917; his other brother Stephen was also an officer in the Regiment. Richard Dwyer, J. P. (18**??**), a native of Harbour Grace, "the oldest and best known teacher in the country, President of the Newfoundland Teachers' Association, Principal of Holyrood High school from 1893-1924, father of Father M. P. Dwyer, P.P. of Harbour Main"; William Taaffe (1890's), manager of the Humber Pharmacy in Corner Brook; Michael O'Toole (1887), Magistrate of Harbour Main; Leo Summers (1909), businessman in Montreal.

The same issue of *The Adelphian* displayed the literary talents of the pupils and ex-pupils. There were poems by Brian Cahill and David Howley (both Grade Eleven), another longer poem by ex-pupil Leo English on "Viking Blood." There were prize essays by Michael Harrington (Grade Eleven) of later literary fame, David Howley (Grade Ten), Douglas Darcy (Grade Nine). There was a lengthy article on Cardinal Newman by Archbishop Roche, written when he was P.P. of Manuels; a sermon by Father Pat. Kennedy on the 100th anniversary of the coming of the Presentation Sisters to Newfoundland; an article on the relation of the Papacy to the Italian Government by Father P. W. Browne, D.D., Ph.D.; a lecture by the President, Brother Birmingham, on Gerald Griffin, the Irish novelist and Christian Brother; an article by Father St. Croix, P.P. of St. Albans, on the Co-operative Movement; another on Natural History (posthumous) by James Howley, F.G.S.

All this in one year! Any university would have been proud of publishing such a periodical.

The year 1935 was another eventful year. The staff at this time consisted of Brother J. V. Birmingham, President; Brothers M. F. Ryan, P. V. Strapp, J. P. Keane, A. J. King, F. X. Dunphy, T. B. Regan, P. C. Fleming, W. P. Murphy, M. G. Reilly; with Brothers Smithwick and Walsh now in retirement, Captain O'Grady, continuing to take care of the physical education and Mrs. Kitty (Ryall) Ryan of the violin class. Doctor Leo Sharpe, who had been taking care of the Brothers and boarders for many years, was named Superintendent of the General Hospital, and his place at the College was taken by Doctor J. B. Murphy. Mr. Charles Ellis, who had acted as Field Captain of Sports Day for 25 years also retired from that position.

On May 5th, the College was honoured by a visit from the Apostolic Delegate, Monsignor Andrea Cassulo, who was suitably welcomed by the student body, inspected the school, and lunched with the staff. James Howley (1929) was elected Rhodes Scholar and Douglas Darcy won the Jubilee Scholarship — the first student in Newfoundland to do so at the first attempt. At the beginning of September, a new commercial class was established for those who had completed

Grade XI and wished to prepare for commercial life. Brothers Egan and Dunphy were responsible for conducting the courses. The senior library was enlarged and improved with the addition of 100 new volumes. The year 1936 saw the Golden Jubilee of Brother Fennessy. The event was suitably celebrated at the College.[10] The College students had also participated, with the other students of St. John's, in the 25th Jubilee celebrations for King George V in the spring of 1935.

The College was not slow to take advantage of the increasing popularity of the radio. On March 21, 1936, the College orchestra and choir gave the first of an annual series of musical broadcasts over VONF from the College. A special music room was set up on the top flat of the school for the use of the orchestra. Future broadcasts would be given from this room, the first of which took place on April 15, 1937. The orchestra, under the direction of Brother Dunphy, was acquiring a fine reputation for itself, though it was not until January 1940, that it made its first public appearance in the Pitts Memorial Hall. It consisted of about 30 members and included pupils, ex-pupils and other interested musicians.

The College continued to fulfill one of its essential functions when seven ex-pupils were ordained in 1936. They were Francis Maloney, Philip McCarthy, Richard McGrath, Michael Kinsella, Leo Drake, Gordon Kent, and Leo Burke. In sports, the College reached the zenith of its success, winning the Inter-Collegiate Championships in hockey, football, senior and junior basketball. The ex-pupils hockey team won the city, Avalon Peninsula and Newfoundland championships, their track team won the N. A. A. sports' trophy. In May, one of the students, Harry Whitten, was decorated by the Scouts for his bravery in rescuing two children from a burning house. In 1937, John Ashley was chosen as Rhodes Scholar. There was little doubt that St. Bonaventure's College, in its mature years, was fulfilling all the functions that Bishop Mullock had envisaged for it.

[10]As a memorial of his jubilee, the ex-pupils presented a stained glass window for the chapel, containing the image of St. Columba, Brother Fennessy's patron saint. Brothers

Chapter 16
WAR AGAIN

Might it be that we have
Reached the end of things...?

– Michael Harrington

Brother W. K. O'Connell
19th President

hen Brother Birmingham's period of office was completed in 1937, he was succeeded by **Brother William Kevin O'Connell,*** M.A., another former member of the staff. A classical scholar with a brilliant intellect, a voracious reader, and possessing a talent for writing that made each of his letters a gem to be treasured, Brother O'Connell was an inspiring teacher but with a capacity for sarcasm which, when his anger was aroused, could be intimidating. He was born in County Cork in 1885 of a comfortable farming family. Having joined the Brothers in 1899 at the age of 14(!), he taught for ten years in Ireland and England, was then transferred to All Hallows High School, New York, in 1910 and, a year later, to St. Bonaventure's College. Here he taught successfully for 12 years until transferred in 1923 to St. Mary's College, Halifax, and then, in 1925, to Butte, Montana. In 1929, he was appointed Superior of O'Dea High School in Seattle. After a year "back in the ranks" in 1936-37 at Leo High School in Chicago, he was appointed to succeed Brother Birmingham as President of St. Bonaventure's. If ever there was a peripatetic teacher, it was he! By now, however, having become quite corpulent,[1] and, handicapped, among other ailments, by abnormally high blood pressure, he was not really equal to the responsibility.

Still he was blessed with a competent staff and the school did not suffer, rather it maintained its high standard of scholarship. In 1938, Bruce French won the Jubilee Scholarship, having scored the highest mark ever recorded in this competition. There were few major innovations, except that, in deference to technological advances, a cabinet filing system was installed to contain the records of the students, replacing the time-honoured Register which had been in use since 1889. To assist Catholic young men wishing to attend the Teacher Training Program at Memorial University College, they were accepted as boarders at St. Bonaventure's and a special dormitory set up for their use.

There was, however, one important development. After an absence of many years, Senior Associate (now renamed Grade Twelve) was re-established, particularly for those students who wished to continue their higher studies but were unable to attend Memorial University College. This class proved particularly helpful for

---

[1] His nickname among the boys was "Tubby."

those young men who wanted to study for the priesthood but who had not studied Latin, a necessary requirement for entrance to a seminary. Grade Twelve had always proved a matter of debate between the College and the University authorities. The Christian Brothers believed that, having finished Grade Eleven (which was then the graduating year), the students were, in the main, not mature enough to accept fully the personal responsibility which university life demands. For this reason, the Brothers continued to press the University to grant credit for Grade Twelve courses done in the high schools, but, for various reasons, the University was reluctant to agree.[2] Consequently, in 1940, to obtain official recognition for the Grade, the College associated its Grade Twelve with the Common Examining Board of the Maritime Provinces and Newfoundland. This move proved highly successful, particularly when represented by such brilliant students as William Carew, Francis Carter, and Brian Maloney, all of whom did extraordinarily well. Later, the Newfoundland high school program was altered to add Grade Twelve, apparently vindicating the Brothers' view of the matter, while the University itself, finally accepting the reality of the problem, established a preparatory year for its entering students.

St. Mary's College, Halifax, had become a popular destination for students seeking university degrees, possibly because the students were familiar with the Christian Brothers teaching there. In 1938, for example, there were ten ex-pupils attending St. Mary's of whom five passed in Arts and five in Engineering. Dermot O'Keefe - the future Monsignor - won the gold medal for first place in the College.[3]

Brother Fennessey

On March 31, 1939, the St. Bon's staff lost one of its stalwarts when Brother Fennessy, who had been ailing for some years, passed away. He had joined the College staff in 1896 and faithfully taught the junior students for many years. He had also taken care of the Cathedral altar boys and the College theatricals. In honour of his passing, the local radio station, VONF, cancelled its usual programs and played commemorative music for the entire day. In June, the College student body took an active part in the welcome of King George VI and Queen Elizabeth to St. John's, the first time a reigning English monarch had visited Newfoundland.

---

[2] Later, when Regina High School was opened in Corner Brook with Brother A. F. Brennan as first Principal, agreement was reached with St. Francis Xavier University in Antigonish, N.S., to grant first-year credit for some of Regina's Grade Twelve subjects, thus smoothing the entrance of the Regina students to University life.

[3] In 1940, disagreement between the Brothers and the Archbishop of Halifax led to the Brothers leaving the College and moving the staff to New Rochelle, N.Y., where they opened Iona College which is still flourishing.

Ignatius Rumboldt

In October of the same year, 1939, one of the students was involved in a dramatic rescue of two fellow pupils. In the late afternoon, three Grade Ten boys, Edward Grace, Peter O'Mara and Cyril Nurse, climbed down from Cabot Tower to the Pigeon Caves below. After exploring the caves, they found themselves, as dusk overtook them, marooned on a ledge. In the darkness, Edward launched himself from the ledge to another across a ravine which ran sheer down to the ocean, and climbed the rugged cliff to the top. How he managed to do so, no one afterwards could explain. At any event, he reached the top safely, and the wireless operator at Cabot Tower summoned help from the police and firemen. By 10:30 p.m., the other two lads were safely rescued though with great difficulty. Edward was duly proclaimed a hero.

In 1939, Fabian O'Dea ('34) was elected Rhodes Scholar and, in 1940, Douglas Darcy ('35) was selected for the same honour. Since James Howley and John Ashley had been similarly honoured in 1936 and 1937 respectively, this meant that, in five years, the College had won this prestigious scholarship four times; the only interruption in the series being in 1938, when it was won by Moses Morgan of Prince of Wales College. Moses later became President of Memorial University.

This year also brought losses and gains. In June, Brother Strapp finally retired from the classroom which he had first entered in 1893. He still continued, however, as editor of *The Adelphian.* On the plus side, in September of this year, 1939, Ignatius Rumboldt brought his ebullient personality and outstanding musical talent to the staff as choral instructor. Ignatius had been a pupil of Sir Charles Hutton and continued the tradition of operettas begun by the former while bringing the College choir to new heights. The College will not soon forget his contribution to its cultural life.

Archbishop Roche celebrated the Silver Jubilee of his Episcopal Consecration on June 29, 1940; Archbishop Ildebrando Antoniutti, the Papal Nuncio to Canada, and Newfoundland, came from Ottawa to attend the celebrations. Both Archbishops were welcomed on the College campus by the Catholic students of St. John's. The Annual Old Boys' Association Mass took place on July 1st, followed by a reception by the Jubilarian for the citizens of St. John's on the College Campus.

Vocations to the priesthood and the religious life continued unabated. On July 7th, ex-pupil Father John M. O'Neill was consecrated Bishop of Harbour Grace. McDermott Penney, Eric Lawlor, Robert Moore, Joseph Moriarty, John Burke, Joseph O'Brien, Loyola Lacey, Edward Shea, Edward Walsh, Dermot O'Keefe, William Carew, James Fennessy, Thomas Connolly, John O'Deady, James O'Dwyer, Brendan Quigley, Leslie Kearney were all in various seminaries. Dermot Nash had entered the Christian Brothers Congregation.

THE SECOND WORLD WAR

But, through all these years, the threat of war had again provided an ominous undercurrent. Communism's seductive doctrines had spread throughout Europe; Nazism and Fascism, had grown strong in Germany and Italy. The "war to end all wars" had failed badly in its purpose. In 1935, as reported by *The Adelphian*, Eamonn de Valera, President of Ireland warned the Assembly of the League of Nations that "Today, before the mangled bodies of the youth of this Continent have yet been mercifully assimilated with the clay…, we are here awaiting the result of an eleventh hour attempt to postpone the opening of a conflict which may set the people of the world mutilating and destroying each other again…" In the same year, Mussolini invaded Abyssinia. In 1936, the Spanish Revolution broke out with all its bloody carnage. In the 1939 issue of *The Adelphian*, Monsignor William McGrath, now Prefect Apostolic of Lishui in China, described a terrifying Japanese bombing attack on the town. In spite of Chamberlain's "peace in our times," another world war was only a hair's breadth away.

What was the reaction of the students of St. Bon's to the threat? The age of innocence had faded with the first World War, and with it the shimmering fantasies of the glorious chivalry of battle which had impelled so many to their death in the earlier conflict. Young people now were more cynical, more confused, more reluctant to become involved. Perhaps, their attitude could be best depicted by a poignant poem by Michael Harrington ('34) on the situation entitled:

NESCIENCE — Thoughts of Youth on a Barbarous Epoch. (See Inset).

Nevertheless, as the last verse of this poem indicated, the young men of St. Bon's were prepared "to do their duty."

> *The faith entrenched within*
> *Assuring we stay steadfast,*
> *Helping us to stand fast*
> *To battle and conquer.*

The building of the Gander airport in 1937 and the centrality of Newfoundland in air travel, had attracted young Newfoundland men to the Royal Air Force and to the adventure of flying. The first to enlist in the R.A.F. was Ted Henley ('35) who began his training in this year and was to end the war as a Wing Commander.[4] Others who joined the R.A.F. were Frank Smith ('34), John Dobbin ('37), and James Kieley ('41). Still others kept up Newfoundland's naval tradition. Stan O'Brien, ('31) for instance, was engaged in mine-sweeping with the Royal Navy. In the issue of January 1942, *The Adelphian* lists the names of 215 ex-pupils who had joined the armed forces. This is an extraordinary total. If one considers that an average graduating class would have 30 to 40 members, this would mean that the equivalent of five or six entire graduating classes had enlisted.

---

[4] In 1939, he was sent to Canada as a flying instructor.

NESCIENCE — *Thoughts of Youth on a Barbarous Epoch.*

Thick palls the smoke above
   And we remember;
That we are alone, unarmed,
    In a garden of evil,
    In a forest of shadows,
    In a desert of ignorance.
    No stars, but many false planets,
      To guide us;
      To light our uncertain path
      To doom and dishonour.

Here our petty delusions
Arise and o'erwhelm us;
    Here in the darkness,
    The blanched fate o'ertakes us.
    Know not we lies from truth,
    Nor canons of honour:
    No standard is shown here
    But evil's criterion.

Where are the red days of old,
The chivalrous knighthood,
The lists and the accolade,
The loves so undying,
So vital, so splendid...
Now is none, all vanished;

No blood that shivers on
    The silver swordblades
Of truth and righteousness;
      No hearts that beat forlorn,
Quickened by hopes long gone;
    No loves unquenchable,
    Pure and enduring;
    No sacrifice beautiful:

But terror and horror and lust and madness,
That breaks hearts of sawdust,
    Splits heads of stone.
Might it be that we have
Reached the end of things;
The foul world wallowing
In a mire of rottenness,
The idols of greed
And power and circumstance —
Man — reared and worshipped —
    Standing on feet of clay.

This be our prayer then:
That the light be vouchsafed us:
The grief thrust upon us
To purge us of sinfulness;
The faith entrenched within
Assuring we stay steadfast,
Helping us to stand fast
    To battle and conquer.

By Michael Harrington

St. Bon's Cadets on Parade, led by Captain Maurice Quinlan.

Contrary to its practice during the First World War, *The Adelphian* devoted much space to war concerns. The 1942 issue provides a lengthy description of the air-raids over Bristol, England, as undergone by Brother J. B. O'Sullivan[5] at Prior Park College, Bath. Brother O'Sullivan, it may be remembered, had been one of the first to enter the fledging novitiate at St. Bonaventure's under Brothers Slattery and Crehan in 1894 and had taught for many years in South Africa before returning to Europe because of declining health. The situation at Bath could not have been helpful in this respect. The same issue contains a poem to Brother O'Sullivan by L.E.F.E. (Leo English). There was an essay on "British War Aims" by Ronald Ryan of Grade Eleven, and an article on "The Post-War World" by W. J. Browne[6] ('15). Greg. Hogan (Grade Ten) won the class prize for his essay on "Poppy Day— Its Origin and Meaning." The students were being encouraged also to buy War Savings Certificates.

There was another problem which directly concerned the College. When the British Admiralty had given Bishop Power the land across from the College on which the Brothers' monastery, Mount St. Francis, was to be built, one of the stipulations had been that, in case of war, it could be reclaimed. Now the Newfoundland Government, searching for places to train its militia but not wishing to disturb the Monastery, asked that, instead of this property being reclaimed, Shamrock Field be given instead. This was agreed, and for the duration of the war and for some time afterwards, St. Bon's lost the use of its football field which became covered with tents and other army installations. Generally, however, except for a strictly enforced "black-out" which severely curtailed night activities, Government rationing of sugar, eggs, and other commodities, lessons in first aid for the members of the staff, and buckets of sand in the attics in case of an incendiary bomb attack, the College continued peacefully on its way.

However, one member of the staff, Brother Dunphy, was involved in an incident which, though amusing in retrospect, was frightening at the time.[7] Brother Dunphy, who was an American, used to invite musicians from Fort Pepperrell, the U. S. army base, to join the College orchestra. Some of these were soldiers; others were civilians. On one occasion, one of the civilians informed Brother Dunphy that he was about to visit the States and asked him to take care of his movie camera and projector while he was away. Brother Dunphy agreed and placed these machines in a cupboard in the College music room. It appears that, on his way back to the States, this man was arrested as a German spy and, supposedly, shot. Brother Dunphy was summoned before the American authorities at Fort Pepperrell and quizzed as to his involvement with the culprit. Fortunately, he was able to convince them of his innocence but it must have been a traumatic experience. Though the incident was kept very quiet, it

---

[5] At some stage, Brother Sullivan had changed his name to O'Sullivan.
[6] Rhodes Scholar, 1918.
[7]The writer was a member of the staff at the time but, since he is writing from memory and has no written documentation, some of the details of this incident may be incorrect, though the incident itself did, indeed, take place. The equipment in question remained in the music room cupboard for several years afterwards.

First Communion, Spring, 1941.
(Front Row) Gerald Ottenheimer, Edward Dillon, John Wadden, Robert Shapter, Alan Frecker, David McCormick, Gerard Walsh, Thomas Manning. (Second Row) Donald Noah, Paul Bryant, Francis Neary, Francis Clift, Adrian Cahill, David Molloy, Robert Colford, Henry Byrd. (Third Row) Br. Darcy, Michael Hogan, Pierce Phelan, Robert Whelan, Francis Duff, Francis Crotty, Aidan Ryan, Henry Carew. (Fourth Row) Cyril Greene, John Wallis, Philip Lewis, John Kelly, Peter Linegar, Michael Walsh, David Fox.

St. Bon's Orchestra, 1952-53.
(Front Row) Peter Oliver, John Savage, Kevin Walsh, Arthur Knight, Michael Walsh, Gerald O'Mara, Gerard Conran, Joseph Bowe, Noel Veitch, Michael Kennedy. (Second Row) John Lawlor, Benedict Hatfield, John Marshall, Gordon Laws, Gordon Buckingham, Donald Walsh, Frank Slattery, John Kavanagh, Robert Martin, Robert Kavanagh. (Third Row) Brother Draney, Robert Linegar, Ronald Ozone, Thomas Devereux, Kelvin Grant, David Molloy, Kevin Ryan, Michael Conran, Thomas Byrne, Brother Fleming.

may not have been a coincidence that, in August, Brother Dunphy was transferred back to the United States to the great loss of the music program in the College.

There was extensive news about ex-pupil members of the armed forces: David Howley ('35) and John Dobbin ('37) had joined the R.A.F.; Jim Kielley, also serving in the R.A.F., had been promoted to Sergeant. He had been injured in a crash but had recovered and was now serving with the R.A.F. in Ceylon. His brother John ('38) had enlisted in the Home Defence Force. Dr. Arthur Knowling ('24) had resigned his position as house doctor at the Sanatorium and had joined the Royal Canadian Medical Corps; Joseph (Josh) O"Driscoll ('16), had been promoted to Captain of the Newfoundland Militia. His son Donald ('39), a Sergeant Pilot in the R.A.F., had been wounded while taking part in bombing raids over Germany and was in hospital; Sub-Lieutenant Fabian O'Dea, R.C.N.V.R., had been appointed instructor in torpedo training for new officers. There was relief that Gunner Joseph Kearney ('39), who had previously been reported missing in the Middle East, was now known to be a prisoner of war. Gerry Halley ('21), the College's champion sprinter, had been appointed Sergeant in the Royal Canadian Artillery; Jack Lee ('26) had been promoted to Second Lieutenant; Larry Furlong ('23) had enlisted in the Royal Montreal Regiment and was in training at Aldershot. To honour these volunteers, on April 11, 1940, the Old Boys held a card party and dance in the Knights of Columbus Club Rooms. Fifty-one members of the Royal Navy and Royal Artillery were present.

The sad, but not unexpected, news of the first war casualty was not long in arriving. Dermot Trainor ('29), a member of the Artillery, was killed in action, the only St. Bon's casualty in 1940. The next, in 1941, was Captain Alban Cleary ('04) of the Royal Navy Reserve. After leaving school, Alban had safely survived the entire First World War, ferrying ships across the Atlantic. Now while bringing his ship from London to Buenos Aires, he was killed on June 6th. The third casualty was Sergeant Frank Smith of the R.A.F., mentioned above. On July 7th, Pilot Officer Richard Howley was reported missing while in action over the south-east coast of England.

There were other deaths not connected with the war. Bishop Renouf ('86) of St. George's had died and been succeeded by Bishop M. F. O'Reilly. Brother Smithwick, the long-serving domestic Brother, having joined the College staff in 1911, died on November 18, 1941, at the age of 83, and was buried in the midst of a howling blizzard; Alexander White ('21) was on the Bell Island ferry when it collided with another vessel; he and another 25 people were drowned.

By 1942, Brother O'Connell's deteriorating health forced him to resign as President and his predecessor became his successor; i.e., Brother Birmingham returned for a second term in this office; it proved to be an adventuresome one. The reality of war was soon to brought home to the people of the Island. To the horrified shock of all Newfoundlanders, on October 14th, the ferry S.S. *Caribou,* en route from Sydney to Port-aux-Basques, was sunk by a German submarine with the loss of 137 lives. St. Bonaventure's was involved in this disaster only indirectly. Brother P. J. Ryan, a member of the Provincial Council of the Brothers, had been in St. John's visiting the schools. He was on his way to take the ferry when it was destroyed. Returning to St. John's, he thought it safer to take a plane back to New York.

Three days earlier, there had been a joyous occasion. On October 11th, 140 Knights of Columbus had assembled in the College chapel for a Mass celebrated by the newly consecrated Bishop O'Neill and followed by a sumptuous breakfast in the College refectory. They could have had no inkling of the disaster in which they were soon to be involved. The K. of C. hostel was located on Harvey Road, just a few hundred yards away from the College. It was the custom to hold weekly Saturday entertainment there for the servicemen and their friends. On Saturday, December 12th, while some 400 young people were enjoying themselves at the concert, a fire broke out. It caused the death of some 100 of those present, many crushed in the stampede to reach the doors. To add to the horror, the music was being broadcast, and the shouts and screams of the panic-stricken victims could be heard by all those listening to the radio. It was the greatest tragedy in the history of St. John's.

Among the dead were two ex-pupils of St. Bonaventure's and one present pupil. John St. John ('01) was acting as accountant for the hostel. Instead of fleeing when he noticed the fire, he first went to warn the people in the dormitories, thus helping them to escape. Then, on his way to safety, he stepped aside to let a young girl pass, was overcome by the smoke and burned to death. Gerald Corbett ('24) was also working in the hostel. He had escaped the fire through a window, but, missing John St. John, who he thought was behind him, went back again to help him to safety. He was trapped and died. The third death was especially tragic. It was that of Henry Walsh. Harry (as he was called) was a student at the College, a member of the senior football championship team and captain of the junior championship team. An active scout, he was volunteering in the cloakroom of the hostel when the fire broke out and he was unable to escape. The school was shocked at his untimely death. On January 19, 1943, a memorial Mass was celebrated in the College chapel for the three St. Bonaventure's victims in the presence of their parents and relatives.

Besides the victims of the K. of C. fire, four others ex-pupils died in 1942, all in the R. A.F.: Sergeant Pilot Thomas Delaney ('37), Pilot Officer Brendan Lacey ('39), Sergeant James Oakley ('38), Sergeant Ralph O'Keefe ('40). For all of these, their religious training had stood the test in their time of trial. Brendan Lacey, for instance, was a deeply religious young man. Writing home to his parents, he mused: "Last week I was on dawn patrol. It was so peaceful flying away up there above the clouds that I just sat back and thought — I thought of how close I was to God." On another occasion, he wrote to one of the staff: "The one thing which sometimes worries me is that I cannot get to Sunday Mass and Holy Communion. Make it up for me, Brother.... Don't worry about me. God always came first and He always will."

The following year, 1943, brought still worse news; 11 new names of ex-pupils were added to the war dead. Their duties had taken them all over the world.

Sergeant Gerald Bown ('28), R.A.F., and Sergeant Gerald Russell ('40), R.A.F., were killed over Italy; Sergeant Gerard Cantwell ('39), R.A.F., over England; Bill Collins ('36), R.A.F., crashed in Bermuda after making more than 20 ferry flights across the Atlantic; Gunner John Gamberg ('35), R A.F., died of malaria in Tunisia, Private Brendan Kenny ('27), of the U. S. Amphibian Force, was killed in the invasion of North Africa; Staff Sergeant Theodore Tooton ('32) also died in the African campaign; George MacDonald ('39), R.C.A.F., perished in Burma; James Sinnott ('31), of the Royal Artillary, died in Twillingate of wounds caused by a bomb explosion while in action in England; James Stick ('38), R.C.A.F., died over Europe; John (Honor) Veitch, ('38) was killed on the last day of the year in Italy. Honor was quite deaf but had succeeded in enlisting by lip-reading what was said to him. On the day of his death, he and some comrades were outside their trench when a mortar whistled overhead. The others immediately ducked into the trench for protection, but Honor, not hearing the sound, remained where he was and was killed.

On March 31st, the school Annals reported that "A severe snow storm raged today and 'drifts' were twenty feet high in some places." The Annalist noted that the "majority of students could not get to school" – no thought of a school closing in these hardier days! The statue of St. Bonaventure began its peregrinations and, on July 16th, was moved to a spot near the tennis court (now Holland Hall.) After a hazardous journey through Europe and across the Atlantic, the recently ordained Fathers Joseph O'Brien ('35) and Loyola Lacey ('36) arrived safely in St. John's on August 28th with many a story of their harrowing escapades along the way. On September 28th, the long-serving Brother Strapp celebrated his Golden Jubilee as a Christian Brother. The staff, pupils and ex-pupils joined in honouring him. On November 3rd, Brother W. C. Walsh passed away. He was the last of the little group that had formed the original Christian Brothers' novitiate in the College during Bother Slattery's regime.

The war continued relentlessly. *The Adelphian* for 1943 reported that in all, 324 ex-pupils had enlisted and that 29 of these had "made the supreme sacrifice." In 1944, more names were added to "The Roll of Honour." Pilot Officer Robert J. Fitzpatrick ('39), R.C.A.F., was reported "missing" on May 13th when the Lancaster in which he was flying over Belgium was shot down. A year later he was listed as "presumed dead." Next was Lieutenant Commander Dermot F. English ('26), R.C.N.R. Lieutenant Commander English had served in the destroyer H.M.C.S. *Hamilton* and then commanded the minesweeper H.M.C.S. *Mulgrave* before assuming command of H.M.C.S. *Valleyfield* which was torpedoed on May 16, 1944, the first Canadian frigate to be sunk in the war. He, 12 other officers, and 107 sailors lost their lives. Flight Lieutenant Thomas Jackman,[8] ('29), R.C.A.F., was shot down over the English Channel. Pilot Officer Kevin Evans, ('36), R.A.F., having fought over Germany for four years without incident, had then been appointed an instructor only to meet his death serving in that position on

---

[8] His uncle, Lieutenant Stephen Norris, was killed in W.W.I.

September 16, 1944. Kevin possessed great musical talent and, besides being a prominent member of the College orchestra, had often entertained the student body with his beautiful violin playing. Flight Sergeant Myles Murphy, ('38), R A.F., was killed on July 28th, though only listed as "among the missing" until the following year. Also listed among the dead was William Hynes ('38), R.C.A.F. William had been declared missing after a training flight almost two years earlier, but was only now officially declared dead. In November 1944, word came to the College that Brother Crehan, one of the original band members who had taken over the College in 1889 and who had been President for a very brief period, had also died.

The year 1945 was no better. No sooner had it begun than, on January 5th, Sergeant J. Bonaventure Thorburn ('28), R.A.F., met his death. At the end of the same month, on January 29th, Sergeant Joseph F. Fitzgibbon ('41), R.C.A.F., also perished. By a strange irony, Gunner William Garland ('37) of the 166th Newfoundland Royal Artillery Regiment, after surviving all the perils of the front on numerous occasions, slipped and fell from a bridge near Halifax while on his way home. He was the first Newfoundland soldier of WW II to be buried in Belvedere Cemetery. Writing of him in the *Daily News*, a friend stated that "many an erring one (*among his comrades*) may thank the example of Bill Garland for bringing him back to the true fold." Gerald T. O'Connor ('44) was with an infantry regiment of the 3rd Armored Division, United States Army, when, towards the end of the war, it pushed forward into Germany in April 1945. As it advanced, it met with increasing opposition and suffered severe casualties. Among those who fell on April 16th was Gerald. He had been an outstanding athlete at the College; in June 1943, he had placed first in three senior events.

By the time the war came to a close in the second week of May 1945, 348 ex-pupils of the College had served in the armed forces, and forty of them had paid the supreme price.[9] Even after the war was over, casualties continued to trickle in. One such was Francis Jones ('16). Francis joined the Canadian Army after leaving school in 1916 and served with it until 1919. When WW II began, he once more joined up, this time with the First Canadian Division, until he was hospitalized in 1944. He lingered on until July 1, 1946, when he passed to his reward.

---

[9] It is to be regretted that the heroism of these ex-pupils has not been commemorated in the College halls as has that of the veterans of World War I. A list of those who died can be found in Appendix 4.

Chapter 17
CONTRASTS IN LEADERSHIP

*Is it true that a well-known figure protested to the headmaster
of a prominent school on a hill about the manner
in which his sons were being harassed by their companions
because of his political activities?*

– Anonymous newspaper article

Brother A. M. Knight
21st President

The year 1945 was to bring other changes to the College. Brother Birmingham had completed his three-year term of office, and his place was taken by **Brother Alan Marcellus Knight,*** whose appointment marked a distinct change of policy on the part of the higher Superiors. Brother Knight was a Newfoundlander,[1] the first graduate of St. Bonaventure's to assume responsibility for the College since Father William Fitzpatrick had done so in 1871. Born in 1906, Allan Knight had entered St. Bon's in 1919 at the age of 13, having previously attended Holy Cross Schools where he had performed as one of the "three little maids from school" in the *Mikado*, a fact difficult to visualize in the light of the corpulence of his later years. A brilliant student and an excellent musician,[2] he had graduated in 1919 with distinction before joining the Christian Brothers that same year. After teaching at All Saints School and Iona Prep. in New York and Leo High School in Chicago, he formed one of the original staff of Iona College, New Rochelle, when it was opened in 1940. From here he was appointed to St. Bonaventure's in 1945.

His regime began on a sad note. During the summer, one of the Grade XI students, Charlie Shapter, while celebrating his graduation with his family at Three-Mile Pond just outside the town, was drowned in spite of the heroic efforts to save him by his sister, an excellent swimmer. He and his two brothers were popular students and the whole College was thrown into shock at his loss.

Otherwise things started well. Gerald S. Doyle, O.B.E., once more displayed his munificent generosity to the College by awarding a $500 scholarship annually. It first holder was Kevin Barron[3] who had placed second in the Island in the June exams. In the same exams, Paul Fardy, of the same class, was awarded the King George V Jubilee Scholarship. In September, the finances of the College were substantially increased when it received an award of $20,021.70 to compensate for the

---

[1] There is some surmise, supported by the other appointments to the other Brothers' schools in St. John's at this time, that, in view of the political situation, Archbishop Roche was urging the Superiors to appoint Newfoundlanders in charge of the various schools.
[2] His favourite amusement in later years was to read the score of some classical symphony.
[3] Kevin became an eminent neurosurgeon in the United States.

confiscation of the College farm for a housing development. But 1946 began on a somber note. On January 16th, the worst blizzard in years closed down for a week, not only the schools, but the entire town, with snow piled high in the College avenue as elsewhere. Things improved, however, when, on June 14th, "Victory Day" was celebrated with great éclat in St. John's, and two ex-pupils were honoured by the British government: Dr. Vincent Burke with an O.B.E., and Leo F. English with an M.B.E.

But another war was soon to begin; a war, not of guns, but of words. The time for Newfoundland to recover its self-government had now come, and there was bitter disagreement as to the best way forward; specifically, whether to return to responsible government or to join Canada as one of its provinces.[4] It is not part of our story to relate the pros and cons of this debate, but it is indicative of the influence which St. Bonaventure's College ex-pupils now exercised in the Island that, when a National Convention met on September 11, 1946, to determine the future of the country, the presiding chairman, Judge Cyril J. Fox, and ten of its 45 members were St. Bon's ex-pupils. These were: Major Peter Cashin ('06), Michael Harrington ('35), Gordon Higgins ('25), David Jackman ('18), Thomas Kennedy ('34), Willliam Keough ('32), John McCormack ('23), Leonard Miller ('27), Edmund Reddy ('22), and Dennis Ryan ('36). Michael Harrington was the youngest member of the Convention.

But to return to the College itself: regrettably, Brother Knight's impressive gifts were intellectual rather than administrative, and his term in office was not a particularly effective one. So, perhaps it was fortunate that, like Brother Doyle before him, Brother Knight, having seen the advantages for the students of an affiliation with Memorial University and, being unaware of the opposition of the Archbishop, had investigated the possibilities of some such relationship. In those sensitive times, the result was, perhaps, to be expected — a request from the Archbishop for his transfer. Consequently in August 1947, he was appointed Superior of O'Dea High School in Chicago — a position which he occupied for only a few months before resigning. He was happy to return to normal teaching duties.

There is one story about him during his time at St. Bon's, however, which should not go unrecorded. He was a great procrastinator, seeing all possible sides of any question and thus finding it difficult to act. One evening, a Brother rushed into his room crying that there was a fire upstairs in the boarders' trunk room. "Oh!" exclaimed Brother Knight, "What should we do?" Exasperated, the other retorted: "Well, you can do one of two things. You can either call the fire department or let it burn!" Needless to say, Brother Knight opted for the former of these two alternatives.

Brother Knight's successor, **Brother Patrick Cathal Fleming**,* was of a different stamp. A native of Westmeath, Ireland, he was born on May 14, 1913, joined the Christian Brothers at the age of 15, and came to Newfoundland in 1931 when only 19. After teaching for two years at St. Patrick's Hall Schools, he was

---

[4] For those not familiar with the history of Newfoundland, the supporters of Confederation were largely Protestant, while the Catholics favoured self-government.

Brother P. C. Fleming
22nd President

Maurice Quinlan

transferred to St. Bonaventure's where he spent 10 happy and successful years before being transferred to New York. After four years at Blessed Sacrament High School in New Rochelle, N.Y., he received the unexpected appointment as President of St. Bonaventure's College at the early age of 34. Brother Fleming was an enthusiastic teacher, an excellent organizer and administrator, blessed with prudence beyond his years. Before long, the College was "in top gear" again, while many needed physical improvements were made to both school and residence.

The next few years required all the prudence Brother Fleming could muster, for feelings grew higher and higher as the time for deciding the future of the country drew near, and those few among the College students whose parents supported the Confederation side found life difficult at school. On one occasion, for instance, a local tabloid asked, "Is it true that a well-known public figure protested to the headmaster of a prominent school on a hill about the manner in which his sons were being harassed by their companions because of his political activities?" The incident was untrue and Brother Fleming decided to ignore it, but it is also true that the "sons" in question were having a difficult time.

Fortunately, he was blessed with a strong staff. It consisted of Brothers J. P. Keane, G. A. Kealy, B. A. O'Quinn, J. G. Shea, P. N. Synan, J. B. O'Connor, A. F. Brennan, E. B. McInerney, M. D. MacCullough, C. J. Avendano, W. G. McIntyre, G. R. Bates, and T. P. Draney. Brother Strapp continued to act as archivist and editor of *The Adelphian*, and Brother D. I. Hipditch was the domestic Brother responsible for maintenance. Captain O'Grady continued to take care of the physical education program. Mr. Ignatius Rumboldt directed the choral music, while Brother Draney, who was a talented musician, trained and directed the orchestra. In October, in another break with tradition, Brother Fleming hired Mr. Maurice Quinlan as a high school teacher, the first time since the Brothers arrived in 1889 that a layman had occupied such a position. Mr. Quinlan continued for many years to give great service to the College, not only as a teacher but as football coach and Cadet Commander. He was noted for his teaching ability and his keen interest in the welfare of his students.

Like that of Brother Knight, Brother Fleming's administration started on a favourable financial note. In November 1947, he received a cheque of $25,000 from the Government for the restoration of Shamrock Field, though it must be stated that it took considerable pressure on the part of friends of the College to obtain this compensation. In the following month, two sets of stained glass windows, which had been ordered by Brother Birmingham, arrived for the chapel. They had been created by Earley & Co. of Dublin. One set, representing *The Apparition of the Sacred Heart to St. Margaret Mary Alacoque*, was donated by Gerald S. Doyle, O.B.E. Of the other set, *The Coronation of the Blessed Virgin*, one window was donated by John A. Barron; the other by Larry Cashin. Both sets added greatly to the devotional beauty of the chapel.

Under Brother Fleming's firm direction, the College continued to excel in every aspect. Some idea of its activity can be drawn from the following list of activities from February to July, 1949. In February, the Glee Club under Ignatius Rumboldt and the Orchestra under Brother Draney gave a recital in the new St. Patrick's Hall auditorium before a capacity audience. Both senior and junior hockey teams won their respective championship. The seniors won easily but the juniors had a close call being forced into overtime in the final game by Bishop Feild College.

In March, the Old Boys' hockey team won the All-Newfoundland Championship. The annual high school students' retreat began on the 1st with Father Haungs, S.J., as director. On the 15th, the senior debate was held on the practical topic: "The City Council should implement the means of providing an artificial ice hockey stadium for St. John's." The winning team was the affirmative: John Lewis, Peter Hatch, and Tom Whelan. Brother Keane was the moderator. The next morning, the entire student body assembled in the Aula Maxima for the presentation of the hockey trophies by the victorious teams.

The Annual Distribution of Prizes had been caught up in the political turmoil of the time. Postponed several times, it was finally held on the March 24th, but, at the request of the Archbishop, it was a purely private affair with no official guests invited. The College Annalist noted that this was "due to the friction between the Archbishop and the civil authorities. The impending Confederation with Canada was the cause of the trouble." The formal Confederation with Canada was to take place at the end of the month. Oddly, there is no other mention of this historic event in the College Annals.

In April, the Inter-Collegiate hockey team traveled to Grand Falls for a three-game series with the Grand Falls Academy team. Perhaps as an augur of things to come, the College team lost all three games — but "the boys had a wonderful time" — so says the Annalist. At the end of the month, the seniors presented a three-act play entitled *Career Angel* under the direction of Brother English.

The activities of May and June were no lighter. In May, the College Glee Club and Orchestra gave their annual Spring Concert before another capacity audience. From the 18th to the 20th, the Grammar Grades presented a series of plays. On the 19th, Sir Edward Emerson, ('01), Kt., K.C.S.G., died.[5] He was Chief Justice for Newfoundland and for many years President of the Old Boys Association and a member of the Board of Directors of the College. On the 28th, the primary students, all 54 of them, received their First Holy Communion. Held on June 1st, the Annual

---

[5] He was succeeded as Chief Justice by Sir Albert Walsh. ('16)

Sports Day was successful though the day was, not unexpectedly, "cold and sunless." The turkey teas were prepared as usual by Mrs. J. W. Allan and her Ladies Auxiliary, and tastefully presented in the Aula Maxima.

All this, however, did not mean that studies were neglected. On June 20th, 160 students began their C.H.E. examinations with, according to the President's Report, the "usual satisfactory results."

While the boys were away during the summer, the activities continued. The Annual Old Boys Reunion was held on July 17th, Father Patrick Kennedy being guest speaker. On the 29th, Alphonsus Penney, Richard Woodford and Daniel Murphy were ordained to the priesthood.

Meanwhile, extensive repairs were being made to the buildings and grounds. A new fire escape was erected at the rear of the College, and repairs made to the exterior walls and roof. The second tennis court was removed to provide a larger play area in front of the Forum, while the other court was increased to regulation dimensions. The main gate was widened by several feet.

The school year 1949-50 was another eventful one. For the first time, the numbers on the roll exceeded 600. Shamrock Field was back in use after a ten-year hiatus. On September 1st, Coadjutor Archbishop Thomas J. Flynn ('11) died, to the great grief of the Catholic community — he was very popular and had been expected to succeed Archbishop Roche who was now quite ill. In October, the Honourable Francis Forde, Australian High Commissioner to Canada, who was an ex-pupil of the Christian Brothers in Australia, visited the school. In February 1950, news was received that Father Patrick Skinner ('22), C.J.M., had been nominated Auxiliary Bishop of the Archdiocese.[6] Father Skinner was, at the time, Rector of Holy Heart Seminary in Halifax. He was consecrated Archbishop at that seminary on St. Patrick's Day, March 17, 1951, and came to St. John's immediately afterwards.

In January 1950, the Annual Distribution of Prizes returned to its normal public setting, with the new Lieutenant Governor, Sir Leonard Outerbridge, presiding. On the first day of February, the Catholic Church in Newfoundland, and St. Bonaventure's in particular, lost one of its most eminent members when Sir Charles W. Hutton, O.B.E., K.S.G., passed away in his 88th year. Sir Charles had taught music and elocution at the College from 1901 to 1918, when overwork forced him to resign. He had been organist at the Basilica for over 60 years. His protégé, Ignatius Rumboldt, was now carrying on his work at the College.

Sports Day this year presented Brother Fleming with an unusual problem, once more forcing him to use all his well-known tact. The new Premier, Joey Smallwood, was anxious to have himself acknowledged by the Catholic authorities. He came to the Sports as a private individual, paying his entry fee like anyone else and circulated among the crowd. Brother Fleming recognized what he wanted, and the possible embarrassing situation which might occur for most of those invited to the Marquee, since the College Directors were, for the most part, anti-confederates.

---

[6] It will be noted that Father Skinner was nominated as Auxiliary, not Co-adjutor, Bishop; that is, he did not have the right of succession to the See as had Bishop Flynn.

Yet, as head of the Newfoundland Government, Premier Smallwood could hardly be ignored. So Brother Fleming spoke to those in the Marquee, telling them that he intended to invite the Premier to the Marquee and to the tea afterwards. Forewarned, those who wished made their escape inconspicuously and Joey made his entrance in tranquility.

During the summer of 1950, to meet the burgeoning enrolment, the school library,[7] on the second floor of the residence, was turned into a classroom and the library moved to the lower floor which it shared with the Grade Twelve classroom.

Early in the following school year, 1950-51, an eminent ex-pupil and three former Presidents of the College died. Archbishop E. P. Roche (1892) passed away on September 23rd after a lengthy illness. The entire school attended his funeral obsequies, which were celebrated by the Apostolic Delegate, Archbishop Ildebrande Antoniutti. Archbishop Roche was the last bishop to be interred in the Basilica crypt.

In September, Brother J. E. Ryan, who had been President of the College from 1921-27, died in New Rochelle, N. Y. In October, Brother P. J. Culhane passed away. A Solemn Requiem Mass in his memory was celebrated in the College Chapel and attended by a large number of his ex-pupils. He had been President of the College from 1903 to 1912. Brother W. K. O'Connell passed away on December 3, and the College Chapel was the scene of a similar Mass for the repose of his soul. He had been President from 1937 to 1942.

In January 1951, Mr. P. F. Halley, newly appointed to the College Board, had offered a scholarship fund, capable of providing $100 annually in honour of his deceased son, Arthur. Mr. Nicholas Duchemin began the practice of donating $500 annually for the purchase of new books for the library.

In May, under the auspices of the St. Bon's Athletic Association, a new event was added to the traditional races with the introduction of a five-mile marathon for the senior students and a three-mile marathon for the juniors. The senior event was won by Gerry Emsley; the junior, by Len Coughlan. By June, the new handball alleys were ready for use, replacing the old ones which had been blown down during the previous winter.

Archbishop Skinner returned from Rome on June 21st, having received the pallium, the emblem of his office as Archbishop. As part of his reception, the school children lined the city streets from the railway station to the Palace. The College students were very impressive as, dressed in their sports uniforms, they marched to their position on LeMarchant Road to the beat of the drummers. As a fitting ending to the school year, ex-pupils Fred Cahill, Tom Moakler and Francis McNeilly were ordained in the Cathedral, having made their preparatory retreat at the College.

In the following school year, September 1951- June 1952, the College staff lost one of its longest serving and most valued members when, on March 20, 1952, after

---

[7] This room, on the 2nd floor of the old building, had served as the College chapel for some 50 years until the new building was opened in 1909.

a prolonged illness, Brother Strapp passed to his eternal reward. It is difficult to assess his importance to the College, not just for his many years of teaching nor for his coaching of the College teams, but for the link he provided between the former students, even those of previous generations, and the present day. His careful attention to preserving the history of the school through *The Adelphian*, the College Annals, and various other ways, was irreplaceable. His remains were waked in the College chapel on Friday, Saturday and Sunday and were visited by hundreds of ex-pupils and friends. Archbishop Skinner celebrated the Funeral Mass on Monday, and Bishop O'Neill presided at the Absolution. The Vicar General, Monsignor Rawlins, read the prayers at the graveside. Perhaps it had been an omen of his passing that, just a month previously, the senior hockey team had lost the championship to Prince of Wales College for the first time in twenty years.

At the suggestion of Archbishop Skinner, the Cadet Corps, now under the auspices of the Canadian Army, had been re-activated earlier in the year under the direction of Mister Quinlan. The response of the students was enthusiastic and about eighty boys signed up. The first inspection was held on May 16, 1952.

The year 1952-53 was the last year of Brother Fleming's Presidency. In recognition of his abilities, he had been appointed a member of the new Provincial Council of the Brothers. Fittingly, the Senior Hockey trophy returned to the College while the Junior remained in its care. Both Senior and Junior basketball teams won their championships under Brother Rohan's expert coaching. Before leaving, Brother Fleming received many gifts from the students, the Old Boys' Association, ex-pupils, the Ladies Auxiliary and the St. Bon's Athletic Association. The College Annals summed up his services thus:

> *During his term of six years, he has accomplished extraordinary work. The reading of these Annals... will give some idea of the amazing number of improvements for which he has been responsible.*
>
> *Keeping pace with these material improvements in the College, the spiritual and scholastic tone of the institution has been quickened. A wonderful spirit of discipline is found within the school because of his able administration.*
>
> *The relationship of the Brothers with the Archbishop and the clergy is pleasant, and great cooperation between them is evident. This is due, in large measure, to his tact and foresight.*
>
> *Brother Fleming could well be proud of what he had accomplished for the betterment of the College during his six years of office.*

The little and the great.

Chapter 18
TUMULTUOUS TIMES

We must of necessity make a drastic cut
in the size of our entering class each September
for the next few years... Relief in some form must come soon."

– Brother H. P. Tarrant

Brother H. P. Tarrant
23rd President

Brother Fleming's successor in office in September 1953 was **Brother Hugh Pius Tarrant**,* a native of St. Lawrence and a former boarding student at St. Bon's, the third ex-pupil to take up the reins of office. The community now consisted of: Brother Tarrant, President; Brother J. P. Keane, Sub-Superior; Brother E. A. English, Bursar and Councillor; Brother A. F. Brennan, Councillor; Brothers M. E. Stoyles, M. N. Kent, G. R. Bellows, T. P. Draney, D. I. Hipditch, E. B. Wakeham, J. L. Heathwood, G. B. Rohan, M. D. Walsh, R. J. Lasik, E. G. French and J. J. McCarthy. The lay members of the Staff were: Captain J. J. O'Grady, M. J. Quinlan, and I. A. Rumboldt. There were 693 boys on the roll. An outbreak of polio in the city forced the postponement of the opening of the schools for three weeks, to the delight of the boys, at least those not affected by this dread disease.

In November 1954, a shrine to Our Lady of Fatima[1] was erected in the grounds of the College near the main entrance. On May 27th of the following year, the Portuguese fishermen brought to St. John's a similar statue of Our Lady of Fatima. It was a thrilling spectacle to see these rugged fishermen marching through the streets of the city, singing hymns to the Madonna, on their way to present the statue to the Cathedral where it is now enshrined. June 1955 witnessed spectacular celebrations for the one hundredth anniversary of the consecration of the Cathedral in which the staff and students of the College took an active part. Cardinal McGuigan of Toronto came to St. John's for the occasion. As part of the celebrations, the Cathedral was raised to the rank of a Basilica.

When school re-opened in September 1955, there were 720 boys on the roll and two more teachers on the staff: Mr. Edward Sexton and Mr. Michael Woodford. Pressure on available space was becoming acute, and word was being received of a proposed new regional high school for St. John's. In his first Annual Report, Brother Tarrant warned that the College accommodations were so over-taxed that "we must of necessity make a drastic cut in the size of our entering class each September for the next few years... Relief in some form must come soon."[2]

---

[1] The Blessed Virgin had appeared to three poor shepherd children in Fatima, Portugal, on several occasions during the year 1917.
[2] *The Adelphian,* 1953, p. 14, CBASJ.

Brother J. B. Darcy
24th President

Meanwhile, talented members of the staff, Brothers Bellows and Heathwood, resurrected the tradition of Gilbert and Sullivan performances with the operetta *H.M.S. Pinafore,* the high standard of which was widely praised. Mr. Richard O'Brien built and supervised the painting of the stage sets. Brother Heathwood published a special 50th anniversary edition of *The Adelphian.* The College was specially blessed when Monsignor Anton Fyme, having retired from his parish of Merasheen because of age and ill health, took up residence in the College as its chaplain.

Brother Tarrant's term of office expired in 1956, but before leaving, he caused extensive improvements to be made to the building, notably a complete renovation of the Aula Maxima. The woodblock floor was replaced by terrazzo flooring, the walls paneled, and the stage renovated. The cost was $23,000. He replaced the old coal furnaces with oil furnaces, had new desks and cabinets constructed in the chemistry lab, and improved the physics lab. A tiled floor was laid in the boarders' dining room. Perhaps the most important improvement, however, was the installation of an artificial ice plant in the Forum. This last was initiated by the ex-pupils, headed by Mr. Alec Henley. The cost was approximately $25,000.

On the debit side, the College was greatly pained to lose the services of Mr. Ignatius Rumboldt as choir director. For some time, Mr. Rumboldt had been increasingly uneasy in his position as Cathedral organist and choir director. The Cathedral authorities desired greater emphasis on Gregorian chant, while Mr. Rumboldt's training had been in the classical tradition of such immortals as Bach and Mozart. Eventually, Mr. Rumboldt decided to resign from all church positions and begin a new career in the secular field, in which endeavour he proved eminently successful. His place was taken, both as organist at the Cathedral and as music director at the College by Mr. Rainer Reiss, a former German paratrooper who had lost both an eye and a leg in the war. He was an exceptionally capable musician but lacked the buoyant personality which made Mr. Rumboldt so successful.

HOLLAND HALL

Brother Joseph Bertrand Darcy, (1956-60), Brother Tarrant's successor, was also a former student of the College (1925-36) and a member of the staff (1940-47). He found immediately on his arrival that the pressure for admittance had become intolerable; about twice as many boys were seeking admission as there was space available, and most of those applicants had fathers and grandfathers who themselves had been pupils of the College. Moreover, all the other schools were filled and there was nowhere else for them to go. With the approval of the Provincial and of the Archbishop, he decided to erect a junior school building on the site of the tennis courts. It was impossible to obtain a bank loan,[3] but with the help of a government loan of $125,000[4] and loans from friends[5] of the College, it was possible to proceed. After the plans had been approved, ground was broken for the new building in August 1957. The architect was Mr. Fred Colbourne.

Meanwhile, makeshift arrangements were made to accommodate more classes while, in a dramatic break with tradition, female teachers were employed for the junior grades. Grades One and Two were put on a half-day schedules, the stage in the Aula Maxima was turned into a classroom, as were the Episcopal Library (with the permission of the Archbishop), the school library and the Brothers' library. The first female teachers were Mrs. Mollie Hann, Mrs. Arnott, Mrs. Alma Firth, soon joined by Mrs. Sara Sexton (wife of Edward Sexton). For the first time also, a school secretary was engaged in the person of Mr. Alex English.[6]

Still, in spite of the difficulties, school activities proceeded as usual. In November, the first ice-sheet was laid in the Forum which was formally blessed by Monsignor Fyme on March 2, 1957. At the end of June, four ex-pupils of the College were ordained for the Archdiocese. Fathers John Maddigan, Philip Lewis, John Wallis, Leo Shea. At about the same time, Father Reginald Collins, C.S.C., another ex-pupil, was ordained in Washington, D. C. The first Gerald S. Doyle Memorial Scholarship of $1,500, donated by his family in his memory, was awarded to James Power of St. Ita's School, O'Donnell's, Salmonier. In the June exams, the College had won numerous scholarships; Stephen Stack was only three marks behind the Jubilee Scholar. When school re-opened in September, enrolment was at a new high, 820, of whom 52 were boarding students. There were 92 students in Grade Eleven, necessitating its division into three classes. In May 1958, there were extensive celebrations to mark the 25th winning of the Boyle Trophy by the College ex-pupils. These celebrations included a motorcade and a reception and dinner at the Old Colony Club. Both daily papers, *The Evening Telegram* and *The Daily News,* ran special supplements commemorating the event.[7]

In what may have been an omen of things to come, word was received from the Archbishop that the membership of the College Board (which had been largely inactive) had been changed. It was now to consist of the Archbishop, Monsignors H. Summers, R. McD Murphy, and D. L. O'Keefe, Sir Albert Walsh, Edmund Phelan, John Ashley, James Greene, Stan Carew, and John Hoskins. The retiring

---

[3] Bank rates at the time were very low and the banks were expecting imminent increases. Meanwhile they were postponing any substantial loans.

[4] A good friend in the Department of Education, Mr. Phil Hanley, had informed us of the availability of this loan. Previously, the government had given a loan of $250,000 to help rebuild Prince of Wales College under the condition that a similar loan be available to the other denominational Colleges for the same purpose. The archdiocesan authorities decided that only half of this amount should be applied for in case the girls' College should wish to apply for such a loan.

[5] These friends were Miss Agnes O'Dea, Miss Margaret Parker, Mr. Jay Parker, Mr. Laurence Cashin.

[6] Alex left soon afterwards and was replaced by Joseph Mulrooney.

[7] A full list of the 26 St. Bon's Boyle Trophy Championship teams is in Appendix 5.

Directors were the Bishop of Harbour Grace, the Bishop of St. George's, Monsignor Rawlins, Doctor Alain Frecker, Messrs. J. G. Higgins, A. M. Duffy and J. A. Barron. This made clear that the College was no longer to be considered a responsibility of the entire Province, but solely of the Archdiocese itself, while the fact that the Christian Brothers had not been consulted carried its own implications.

When school opened in September 1958, the new building was not quite ready but the top floor with five classrooms was available. Added to the female staff now were Mrs. Iris Kendall, Mrs. E. Murray, Mrs. A. M. O'Keefe and Mrs. G. M. Singleton. Mrs. M. Lacey was engaged as substitute for Mrs. Hann who was ill. A few days later, Cardinal Leger, Archbishop of Montreal arrived to bless the new Regional High School for girls named Holy Heart of Mary High School. Brother Darcy, who together with many other Brothers had been active in the Newfoundland Teachers' Association, was named President of the Association and a member of the Board of the Canadian Teachers' Federation. Thirteen members of the previous year's Grade Ten class won scholarships. On October 9th, the College, besides mourning the loss of Pope Pius XII, was shaken by the unexpected death of Doctor Joe Murphy, who had been the College Physician for almost 25 years.

The annual Communion Breakfast of the Alumni was held in the Aula Maxima on November 2nd. Afterwards, the Archbishop blessed the new building and an "open house" was held during the day. On February 16th, a blizzard of unusual intensity descended on the city, with winds reaching 135 m.p.h. Several large windows at the rear of the main school were shattered by the gale, and the following morning the staff was kept busy shoveling snow off the corridors where it had accumulated to a depth of some six inches. To make matters worse, one of the radiators froze and split so that heat could not be restored. For several days, the Brothers and boarders were dependent on a small gas stove in the kitchen for their meals.[8] The city itself came to a standstill since all but essential traffic was banned and all schools closed. A similar blizzard on March 28-29 brought the city to a standstill once more.

At this time, the Newfoundland Government was looking for land on which to build a nurses' residence and asked for some acres of the College farm on Signal Hill Road. The Brothers made a counter-proposal that the Government should buy the entire farm which was of very little use to the College. Because of its site on Signal Hill, the Government was interested and entered into an agreement with the Federal Government to purchase the land for a National Park. On March 13th, a part payment of $66,000 was received from the Newfoundland Government.

UNDER THREAT

While from all external signs, the College was in a stronger position than ever, with a strong staff and bulging enrollment, excellent examinations results, and

---

[8] On one of these days, a parent, Mrs. Margaret Comerford, invited the Brothers to her home for a meal, for which kindness the Brothers were extremely grateful and must have "eaten her out of house and home."

Getting "conkers." (chesnuts)

highly praised cultural and athletic achievements, events were transpiring behind the scene which would threaten its very existence. These came about as follows. In 1956, Archbishop Skinner had written the Provincial Superior of the Christian Brothers, Brother A. A Loftus, informing him that there were plans to rationalize the high school situation in St. John's with two large schools, one for the girls and one for the boys, replacing the existing high schools. The Presentation and Mercy Sisters had agreed to staff the girls' school and to donate their entire salaries to finance it; the Brothers were asked to do the same for the boys' school. The Brothers responded that, while they were prepared to staff the new school, they found the financial request beyond their capacity, but offered to donate one-third of their salaries for the purpose. The Archbishop replied that this was not adequate for his needs, and that the boys' school would have to be postponed for some years.

Nothing further was heard of this proposal for almost three years when, on May 3, 1959, a letter from the Archbishop was read in the parish churches announcing that the Jesuits were coming to St. John's in 1962 to take over the boys' regional high school, which would serve the east end of the city only, while the Brothers would continue to administer Holy Cross "for the present," as well as continuing to take care of the grammar schools.

The Christian Brothers were not prepared to accept this arrangement which constituted a unilateral breach of their contract with the Archdiocese and which would have reduced their professional standing in the Archdiocese to that of grammar school teachers. Over the years, also, the Brothers had prided themselves on the number and quality of priestly vocations which they had fostered in the Archdiocese. Consequently, they were particularly distressed to hear read a letter from Cardinal Pizzardo, Prefect of the Congregation for Seminaries, which accompanied the Archbishop's letter. In his letter, the Cardinal stated that he was happy that the Jesuits would be coming to St. John's so that priestly vocations could be better cared for. It was an indication of the strength of the Brothers' feeling that at a meeting held on June 16th with the Brother Provincial to discuss their future status in the Archdiocese, all but one of those present voted to leave the Archdiocese.

Eventually the situation was appealed to Rome where the Brothers received strong support. Fortunately, the Archdiocese had seriously underestimated the demand for entrance to the boys' high school; in fact two such schools were needed. This made a mutually satisfactory agreement possible. Negotiations between the Brothers and the Archdiocese resulted in the Brothers receiving the new High School (to be called Brother Rice High School) being built on Bonaventure Avenue, while another high school was to be built for the Jesuits. The only bright spot in this gloomy year occurred when school was dismissed two days early in honour of Queen Elizabeth's visit to the Province. Like the mood of the Brothers, the weather was damp, foggy and cold for her visit.

Matters improved somewhat with the reopening of school in September when the results of the public exams revealed that 12 boys in Grade Ten and four in

Brother J. J. Enright
25th President and
1st Principal

Grade Eleven had won Centenary scholarships. Of the Grade Twelve candidates (under the Nova Scotia Board), nine of the 11 who wrote the exams passed. Once more the opening of school was postponed because of a polio scare. To accommodate the still increasing enrollment, the number of boarders[9] was reduced and part of one dormitory was turned into a classroom. The staff for this year was much the same, except that, among the lay teachers, Robert MacKenzie took the place of Mike Woodford who had moved to Nova Scotia. Mrs. Kennedy was engaged as supervisor of the reading program in the primary grades. The study of French was introduced into the lower classes with Mrs. Daphne Collins as instructor.

At Christmas, Captain O'Grady, after 40 years of service and having reached his 80th birthday, decided to retire. A special school assembly was held in his honour and he was presented with a luxurious arm-chair. The following issue of *The Adelphian* was dedicated to him. His successor was Mr. Fred Murphy, an ex-pupil.

During the summer of 1960, the exterior of the main building (Mullock Hall) was painted for the first time in its history at a cost of approximately $7,000. The work was done by Ted Murphy of Clem. Murphy & Son. The result was a great improvement in the appearance of the complex.

The new school year began in September 1960 with enrolment again at a peak. The year was hardly begun, however, when news was received that Brother Darcy had been appointed a Consultor for the American Province of the Brothers and had to depart for New York, leaving to his successor the unenviable task of dismantling the 104-year-old institution.

In November, **Brother Joseph Jarlath Enright**,* a native of New York, arrived to take up the burden of President of the College. Brother Enright had taught at the College from 1929 to 1934 and, consequently, was well known and respected by the local community. One of his first acts was to enlarge the school library so that it could accommodate a full class; new tables and chairs were bought and the whole environment made very attractive.

For the 1961-62 school year, the numbers on the roll were as follows: 667 in the grammar school and 299 in the high school; the total, 966, once more the highest in the history of the College. The staff consisted of: Brother J. J. Enright, President; Brother J. P. Keane, Vice-President; Brother M. E. Stoyles, Bursar; Brothers C. Goodland, B. Molloy, D. Fitzpatrick, D. Walsh, E. Cove, E. Pigott, J. Walsh, A. Rogers, J. Murphy, D. Dugan, M. Barron, V. Hall, A. Manning, M. Withers. Lay-teachers in the high school were: Maurice Quinlan, Edward Sexton,

---

[9] The opening of regional high schools in the rural areas was reducing considerably the need for boarding facilities.

I GRADUATED IN 1961

Noel Veitch, Rainer Rees, Hugh Fardy (coach); in the grammar school: Mrs. Kennedy, A. Firth, D. Collins, M. Hann, I. Kendall, C. Singleton, A. O'Keefe, E. Murray, and Miss R. O'Brien. Miss Teresa Kerivan was librarian, Mr. Fred Dunphy, physical education instructor, Joseph Mulrooney, secretary.

One rather sad feature of Brother Enright's administration was the constant bickering among the Colleges over hockey. The problem was the conflict between the sporting game traditionally played in Newfoundland and the professional approach which was being introduced into the local scene. In spite of many meetings and resolutions, the problem was never really solved until the Intercollegiate League was discontinued when the colleges were closed.

In June 1962, the St. Bonaventure's College Board was dissolved and the 106-year history of the College came to an end. The high school students were dispersed between the new Brother Rice High School and Gonzaga High School, and St. Bonaventure's College became St. Bonaventure's Grammar School.

Chapter 19
DECAPITATION AND DESTRUCTION

... as of September 4, 1962, St. Bonaventure's ceases
to be the Roman Catholic College for Males.
— Archbishop P. J. Skinner, C.J.M.

In July 1962, Brother Enright received the following letter from the Archbishop:

Dear Brother Enright,
*   At a meeting of the Board of Directors of the Roman Catholic College for Males (St. Bonaventure's College), held on Thursday, June 27, 1957, the following resolution was passed: "that on the opening of the Regional High School for Boys, the course of studies at the RCC for M. will not include Grades 9,10,11,12."*
*   I am writing to inform you, Brother, that as of September 4, 1962, St. Bonaventure's ceases to be the Roman Catholic College for Males. It will henceforth be known as St. Bonaventure's Grammar School, and will come under the R. C. Board of Education of St. John's.*

— P. J. Skinner, C.J.M.
Chairman, Board of Directors

Accompanying that letter was another in which the Board stated, as had been previously agreed,[1] that it would take over the remaining debt on the new building (Holland Hall) as of September 1962. This debt consisted of $75,000 on the Government loan and $68,677.18 on the private loans.

Upon until now, the College had led a relatively independent existence, hiring it own teachers and taking care of its own physical needs, but, with the change of status, the school came under the authority of the R.C. School Board, with the advantages and disadvantages which this new arrangement entailed.

While the high school student body at St. Bon's was divided between the two new high schools, the high school staff of the College transferred as a body to the new Brother Rice High School, where Brother G. R. Bellows became its first principal. Those who transferred were: Brothers Keane, Walsh, Goodland, Fitzpatrick, Molloy, Hall and Stapleton. The boarders, while attending Brother Rice, continued to reside at St. Bon's, and the high school Brothers did likewise until their new monastery should be built. The high school section of the College library was also transferred to the Brother Rice under the direction of Miss Teresa Kerivan, necessitating the building up of the grammar school library, which Brother Enright

---

[1] Fortunately, Brother Darcy, when financing the new building, had realized that, if the status of the College were to change, it would not be possible to repay the debt. He had, therefore, before undertaking the debt, arranged with the Archbishop to take it over if this change of status should occur.

quickly set out to do. He was keenly interested in career guidance, and such literature now occupied a prominent place in the school's library.

Brother Enright made many physical improvements in both school and monastery, painting, refurbishing, adding new equipment. The major renovation undertaken during his term of office was the replacement of the slate roof on the main building during the summer of 1963 at a cost of $7,000, an expense which was borne by the school itself, not by the School Board.

However, his activities were not limited to the school. He also found time to lecture at Memorial University and to become President of the Newfoundland Teachers' Association. Under the leadership of Doctor William Higgins, a Scout and Cub movement was organized; a site was obtained for its outdoor activities, and a large building erected upon it.

In February 1963, St. Bon's was both honoured and delighted when one of its outstanding graduates, Fabian O'Dea, Q.C., was appointed Lieutenant Governor of Newfoundland and Labrador, the first ex-pupil of the College to receive this honour.

At the opening of school in September 1963, another "tempest in a teapot" was created when the Board decreed that all students in Grades 1-3 in St. Raphael's and St. Pius X parishes must attend their local schools. This created a very difficult situation for St. Bon's which, though no longer a College, was still not a parish school[2] and accepted students from throughout the city. The problem was accentuated by the fact that, even with the new classrooms, the pressure on enrolment was not completely solved since, for three possible Grade One classes, there were 184 applicants. Brother Enright protested vigorously against the move, even threatening to resign if modifications were not made to the plan.

Brother Enright's term ended in 1966. While he had administered the school efficiently, he was happy to leave since he could never reconcile himself to the change in status of the College from the "glory days" of old. He was replaced by **Brother John Majella McHugh**,* a native of Placentia and brother of Brother Gerald G. McHugh, later Superior General of the Brothers' Congregation, and of Father Richard McHugh. In October of the following year, 1967, in order to provide additional accommodation, the main chapel was dismantled and, controversially, transformed into a classroom. A new, much smaller, chapel was provided on the second floor of the monastery adjacent to the school.

It was decided to unite the living quarters of the Brothers teaching at St. Bonaventure's and St. Patrick's in the Brothers' monastery at Mount St. Francis. While this was partly for financial reason, it was mainly to provide living quarters at St. Bon's for the Brother Scholastics who would be attending Memorial University. The first contingent of nine student Brothers arrived in September 1968 and was soon happily engrossed in university studies.

To provide for this new arrangement, in 1969 Brother McHugh resigned as Principal of the school to concentrate on the duties of Superior and Director of the

---

[2] St. Patrick's Hall was the parish school for the area.

Principals of St. Bonaventure's Grammar School 1962-1998

Br. J. J. Enright
1962-66

Br. J. M. McHugh
1966-69

Br. R. B. Lynch
1969-74

Br. J. I. Gale
1974-78

Br. R. A. White
1978-82

Br. A. R. Estrada
1982-84

Br. D. M. Vaughan
1984-88

Mr. Ron Kieley
1988-90

Mr. Patrick Hogan
1990-1995

Mrs. Nina Beresford
1995-1998

student Brothers, while Brother Barry R. Lynch was appointed to succeed him as Principal of the school. Being under the School Board meant that finances could be obtained for needed major improvements. Of these, the most pressing was the replacement of the exposed and dangerous fire escape at the rear of the main building by an enclosed fire escape which made fire drills much safer.

The school continued without exceptional incidents for several years with numbers continuing to grow. At the opening of school in September 1973, there were 830 boys on the roll. However, by the following September, numbers had dropped to 780, a sign that the "baby boom" was beginning to decline. In September 1974, Brother John I. Gale replaced Brother Lynch as Principal; Brother Lynch having been appointed Principal of Regina High School in Corner Brook. In the same year, Mr. Alec Henley was elected chairman of the R. C. School Board. Under his administration, the school benefited by the addition of a gymnasium which was badly needed since the Aula Maxima, which had traditionally been used as such, was not really suited for this purpose. To help provide suitable gym equipment, the Fathers' Association held a "sweep" which raised $4,500.

September 1975 saw an enrolment of 689 students, and a staff of four Brothers and 25 lay teachers. Besides the four teaching Brothers, there were seven student Brothers in residence who assisted in the classrooms as part of their teacher training. On November 13th, a portrait of Captain J. J. O'Grady was unveiled in the presence of his family and the student body.[3]

In February 1976, a reception was held in the Aula Maxima in honour of the 100th anniversary of the arrival of the Christian Brothers in Newfoundland. Many Brothers who had taught in the Newfoundland schools returned for the occasion, among them Brother J. T. Perry who had been a teacher at St. Bon's in the early 1900's. In October, the Old Boys' Association sponsored a banquet at the Old Colony Club to commemorate the 120th anniversary of the founding of St. Bonaventure's. Approximately 200 ex-pupils, some dating back to the class of 1915, were in attendance.

Numbers of students continued to fall and by September 1977, the roll had dropped to 620. In September 1978, Brother Gale became Principal of Brother Rice High School and was replaced as Principal of St. Bon's by Brother Robert A. White. There were 570 pupils present to welcome his arrival. School proceeded smoothly until March of the following year, 1979, when double tragedies struck. The first took place in the early hours of March 24th when a fire, set by one of the workmen at the Forum (he had a record of psychiatric problems), burned it to the ground. The tragedy was all the greater since the Forum has just recently been completely renovated by the Men's Association with two new dressing rooms, new lighting and exterior siding. The young man responsible was later arrested for arson. The Forum was rebuilt and was re-dedicated on October 29, 1980. Neddy Barron, who had been in charge of the Forum for 20 years, suffered a heart attack and died in April of that year.

---

[3] This picture now (2006) hangs in the corridor outside the chapel.

King Arthur's court.

The Forum on Fire, March 24, 1979.

Sports Day - Preparing the maze.

Sports Day - Junior drill.

Joey Gellately

A still greater tragedy struck three days after the Forum fire, when one of the kindergarten students, Joey Gellately, while on his way to school, was killed on the crosswalk at Bonaventure Avenue. A happier occasion was the installation, on May 31st, of Archbishop A. L. Penney as successor to Archbishop Skinner who had recently retired because of age. Archbishop Penney, like his predecessor, was an ex-pupil of St. Bon's.

For the first time in many years, full-scale musicals began to be staged in the Aula Maxima. In May 1979, *The Emperor's New Clothes,* written by Brother Blackmore and orchestrated by the school band instructor, Mr. Jim Duff, was performed. In May 1980, a second musical by Brother Blackmore, *A Simple Tale of Childhood,* was performed, and in May 1981, still another of Brother Blackmore's musicals, entitled *The Pied Piper of Hamelin,* was staged before a capacity audience at Holy Heart Auditorium, the St. Bon's students being joined by girls from Mercy and Presentation schools in a most successful production. In May 1982, the fourth annual musical was performed in Holy Heart auditorium. Entitled *Resurrexit* and also composed by Brother Blackmore, it was highly successful.

A valuable addition to the school was the acquisition of offset equipment which enabled the school to print its own pamphlets, school magazines, programs and other such material. One result of this acquisition was the publication of *The Oracle,* Vol. I, No. I, the first issue of the school newspaper which was intended to become an integral part of the school life.

On Saturday, May 9, 1981, Mrs. Betty Pyne, the long-time school secretary, died. She had been working in the school until Wednesday, so her death.was most unexpected and a tremendous shock to students and teachers by whom she was greatly loved. Two days later, Mrs. Alma Firth, one of the first lady teachers hired by the College, passed away. She had been a valued teacher at the school for some 20 years.

In April 1982, advantage was taken of Mr. Mike Savage's visit to the school to tape his two-hour reminiscences for future generations. He was the oldest living ex-pupil, having entered St. Bon's in 1899.

The rebuilding of the Forum had placed a very heavy debt on the school and it was decided to establish a special Board to take responsibility for it. Special Sweeps were held in 1981 and 1982 to help pay off this debt. On both occasions, the magnificent sum of approximately $20,000 was raised. The members of the Board were: Brothers White, Holden and Moore; Mr. Bill Gillies (Men's Association) Secretary; Mrs. Elaine Dunne, Mothers' Club; Mr. Myles Furlong, treasurer; and Mr. Kevin O'Regan, Chairman.

June 1982, marked the end of Brother White's period of office. He was transferred to St. Francis High School in Harbour Grace, his place at St. Bon's being taken by Brother René Estrada, an American from California. In 1986, Brother Estrada was replaced by Brother D. M. Vaughan. Both of these Principals administered the school efficiently. The only unexpected event during their term of office occurred in 1987 when a fire in Holland Hall did considerable damage to the building.

In 1988, after administering St. Bon's for 99 years, the Christian Brothers decided that, because of declining numbers in their ranks, they could no longer be responsible for the school. It therefore passed into lay hands; the first lay Principal being Mr. Ronald Kieley, who had been vice-principal for some years. On his retirement in June 1990, he was succeeded by Mr. Patrick Hogan, an ex-pupil of the school. Because of the rapidly declining birth-rate in the Province, the number of students continued to decrease. Consequently, in 1992, the School Board decided to amalgamate St. Bon's with Mercy Convent. Thus, for the first time in its 136-year history, St. Bon's became a co-ed school. Three years later, in 1995, Mrs. Nina Beresford was appointed its first female Principal.

In 1998, as a result of two referenda and of a determined push by the Newfoundland government, the denominational system of education, which had been in place since the 1850's with reasonable success, was replaced by a secular public school system. Secular public school boards were established and one of the first acts of the new Avalon East School Board was to move to close St. Bon's in spite of its continued success and the strong opposition of the parents to its closure. At first the Board intended the closure to be at the end of June, but the parents took legal action, prevented this, and in defiance celebrated the 140th anniversary of the school with a series of events including a dinner dance, an open house, a special Mass and reception, culminating in a traditional Sports Day on June 8th. However, the Board did eventually win the legal battle and succeeded in closing the school at the end of August. St. Bonaventure's was the first and only school closed by the Board in 1998.

Chapter 20
RESURRECTION

With no funds, no staff, no authority, they determined to make the attempt.

In October 1997, after the second provincial referendum had revealed the probable loss of the denominational system, four concerned people met in the library
of Gonzaga High School to discuss the possibility of an independent Catholic
School. They were Father Vernon Boyd, S.J., a teacher at Gonzaga High School,
Doctor Michael Bautista, Elaine Aylward, and Susan Chalker Browne. Although
they had no funds, no site, no staff, no authority, they determined to make the
attempt. Their first objective was to involve other parents in the project, and by
November the group had increased to 20. Seizing the opportunity of a visit of the
Canadian Jesuit Provincial, Father David Nazar, to St. John's, they met with him in
the library of St. Pius X Church and pleaded their cause so eloquently that he agreed
to consider the possibility of Jesuit involvement. He did, however, lay down three
preconditions: there must be adequate expression of interest on the part of parents;
other religious orders must be supportive, and a bursary fund must be established to
ensure that no student was turned away because of financial need. When news of
possible Jesuit involvement spread abroad, interest increased greatly.

In the meantime, another group of parents was making a similar attempt.
However, in spite of determined efforts, this other group was not able to make much
headway. Eventually it disbanded, and some of its members joined with the Pius X
group. As a result of Father Nazar's interest, in the summer of 1998, Father Winston
Rye, S.J., who was just stepping down as Principal of Gonzaga, was assigned to
work with the group. As word of these developments grew, interest increased still
further. The group took its first formal step by becoming incorporated as *The Board
of Directors of the Catholic Jesuit School Trust, Inc.* The Board members were:
Doctor Michael Bautista (Chair), Madonna O'Shea, Father Winston Rye, Yvonne
Steiner, Bill Jameson, Maria Tracey, Ron Hynes, Ed Martin, Janet Henley-Andrews,
Susan Chalker Browne, Charlie Riggs, Mary Mandeville, Cecil Critch, Bernadine
Power, Bon Fagan, Alice Furlong, Lily Abbass, Harry Bown, Jack Parsons, and the
Hon. James McGrath.

The second formal step took place when, in early 1999, since sufficient "expressions of interest" having been obtained to suggest that such a school was feasible,
the Jesuits formally agreed to administer it, "in the Jesuit Tradition," with Father Rye
as President, though as yet there was no building, no funds, no student body. Various
available buildings around the city were examined to decide on the best location.
After much consideration, it was decided that the St. Bon's complex, now empty,
was the most suitable — this in spite of the fact that the Avalon East School Board
had taken most of the school equipment: library books, desks, musical instruments
(much of which had been paid for by the school and not by the Board), and allocated it to other schools. First, however, the Government had to agree to return the
property to the Archdiocese. Eventually the Government did so, and the School

Board made the needed legal transfer. The Archdiocese agreed to rent the premises to the Board of Directors of the school, initially for 10 years, at a cost of $1 a year.

This decision was indeed fortunate, for it enabled the new Catholic school, while establishing its own identity, to benefit from the long tradition of St. Bon's and the esteem in which it had been held and, as well, to have the advantage of the excellent facilities which St. Bon's had built up over the years. September 1999 was set for the opening. Many things had to be decided upon; in particular, a staff had to be hired. Furthermore, there were many contentious issues to be decided, perhaps the most important one being the amount of tuition that would be charged. This proved very difficult to agree upon, and it was only after much discussion and soul-searching that it was decided that the tuition should be in the $3,000 a year range with various deductions. Another decision which created warm discussion was the matter of a school uniform. Eventually it was agreed that a simple uniform should be worn by all students. It consisted of dark pants, white shirt, school tie, and school blazer; for the girls, a skirt was an alternative to pants. Appeals were sent out for the school library and, in a short time, the response more than compensated for the books that had been removed by the Avalon East School Board. A financial campaign was begun to establish a bursary program as well as for general expenses. The result of this campaign were very encouraging. In May 2000, the Committee reported that it had raised the $296,500 needed to repair and equip the buildings and to finance the bursary program for the current year.[1]

The buildings needed considerable face-lifting. Lacking funds to hire people to do this work, a group of parents of prospective students and other well-wishers, under the direction of a Board member, Charlie Riggs, set to work, usually at night after their own day's work was over, to repair, clean, and paint the school. The future students helped as well as they could. This group continues to make major and minor physical repairs and improvements, and it is safe to say that the school would have been much poorer physically without their quiet, dedicated efforts.

An interesting curiosity was that, while the linoleum on the corridor leading to the chapel was being taken up to reveal the hardwood floor beneath, an old letter, dated April 6, 1934, was found underneath it. The letter read: *This linoleum was placed on this corridor during the Easter vacation 1934. The undersigned Brothers were then members of the community. To our successors we extend best wishes for continued development of the sublime work of Catholic Education.* It was signed by all the Christian Brothers then on the staff.

A call to replenish the library was answered enthusiastically by friends and well-wishers. To be useful to the students, all these volumes had to be properly organized and graded, and volunteers Kitty Power, Eileen Wall and Kay Allan spent countless hours sorting, arranging and cataloguing them.

---

[1] In the first year of its operation, the bursary provided about $150,000 in financial assistance to 40% of the student body, thus fulfilling the commitment the Board of Directors had made to the Jesuit Provincial in the previous year.

Father Winston Rye, S. J.
26th President

So, on September 7, 1999, after a one-year hiatus, St. Bonaventure's (now returned to its former status as a College) re-opened its doors, with some 197 students in Grades Kindergarten through Nine. The opening day celebrations were highlighted by a special Mass in the Basilica, presided over by Archbishop James MacDonald and concelebrated by all the Jesuit priests in Newfoundland. Over 1000 parents, relatives and friends joined with the students and staff in what proved a very moving and inspiring occasion.

The staff consisted of Father Winston Rye, S.J., as President; Mr. Cecil Critch, former Principal of St. Patrick's Hall, as Vice-Principal; Brother Joseph Frechette, S.J., Susan Barron, Jaline Kelly, Paul Murray, Eileen Pardy, Cathy Carroll, Kathryn Coffin, Annette Mallay, Jennifer Spurvey, Paula Moyse, Annette Snook, Vincenza Etchegary, and Juanita MacDonald. Carol Noseworthy was engaged as school secretary and Jim Haley hired as maintenance man. Jane McGrath D'eon, an experienced Guidance Counsellor, generously volunteered her services; Carmel Woodford acted as accountant, Sister Elizabeth O'Keefe and Elaine Aylward offered their assistance to the reading program, Mrs. Pat O'Dwyer volunteered to help in the secretarial work.

Father Rye was an efficient and experienced administrator and quickly got the school off to a good start. From the beginning, it was determined that this would be a "school with a difference." Besides the usual academic and cultural subjects, strenuous efforts were made to form the school into a Catholic community. "Respect for themselves, respect for others, respect for their school" were attitudes inculcated into the students. Mass was celebrated each school morning by Father Rye in a temporary chapel erected in one of the unused second floor classrooms. To help bond the various age levels together, a "family" system was introduced, similar to the "house" system in English public schools. Each student was allocated to a family which, on special occasions, sat and ate together, the older members of the house being responsible for the younger ones. A Parents' Auxiliary was formed with Bernadine Power as President, and soon set about raising the money needed for the incidental school expenditures, class equipment, etc.

Music quickly became a distinguishing part of the curriculum with Vincenza Etchegary in charge of instrumental music and Brenda Gatherall and Cathy Carroll in charge of vocal music. Not satisfied with this, the College offered a home to the St. Pat's Dancers who had been without one since the closure of St. Patrick's Hall School. The Dancers' presence gave still another cultural dimension to the life of the College.

Academic subjects, however, were not neglected as shown by the fact that in the Provincial Science Fair held in the spring of 2000, two Grade Nine students and one Grade Seven student won top awards. The school's success continued when a Grade Nine student placed first in the Province in the Pascal Mathematics

Competition. The scientific tradition of the school was also illustrated when an ex-pupil, Kevin Keough, Ph.D., Vice President of Memorial University, was named the first "Science Czar" of Canada by the Federal Government.[2]

In March 2000, a new school emblem was unveiled. It was entitled *The Phoenix*, and the explanation given for its adoption was that the mythical bird, the Phoenix, was supposed to consume itself by fire every 500 years and a new youthful Phoenix would emerge from its ashes. This "resurrection" was exemplified when the new St. Bon's emerged from the ashes of the old school. In commemoration of this rebirth, a musical composition, specially composed for the College by the distinguished Canadian composer, Michael Snelgrove, was presented to the College by him. The composition was entitled simply *The Phoenix*.

The reputation of the College for excellence quickly spread and the new millennium got off to a good start when a second Kindergarten class and a Grade Ten class were added, with an increase of over 70 students. The year 2001 was equally encouraging, with Grade Eleven making its appearance and over 300 students on the roll.

The opening Mass in September 2001, was celebrated in the Basilica by the new Archbishop of St. John's. Archbishop Brendan O'Brien[3]. Archbishop O'Brien continues the strong support given by his predecessor to the College, and this is a great encouragement to the Board and parents.

The excellence of the music program was highlighted when, in the Rotary Musicfest of 2001-2002, six of the College's seven instrumental groups reached Gold Standard[4], and the remaining group, together with the Primary and Elementary choirs, attained the Silver Standard.

However, the College got quite a scare when, in November, Father Rye was rushed to hospital with a suspected heart attack. Fortunately, it proved not serious and he was soon able to return to the College. An historic event was the celebration of the 100th birthday of Mr. Edmund Phelan, Q.C., a highly respected St. John's lawyer and the oldest ex-pupil of St. Bon's. While at the College, Mr. Phelan had been an outstanding scholar and athlete, acting as captain of the football, hockey and track teams. His wife, Margaret, had served as President of the Ladies Auxiliary.[5]

September 2002 marked another significant development when Grade Twelve was introduced and St. Bon's became once more a fully-fledged high school. Registration had now climbed to 322, with 20 teachers and six auxiliary staff (not including volunteers). Another development at the same time was the erection of two large flagpoles in front of the College. These poles had graced the front of St.

---

[2] In 2003, Doctor Keough was appointed CEO and President of the Alberta Heritage Foundation for medical research.

[3] Archbishop MacDonald had retired on reaching the age of seventy-five as required by canon law.

[4] These groups were the Concert Band, the Symphonic Band, the Wind Ensemble, the Brass Quintet, the Dixieland Combo and the Senior Jazz Band. The Junior Jazz band was awarded Silver.

[5] Mr. Phelan died on March 11, 2005 at the age of 102.

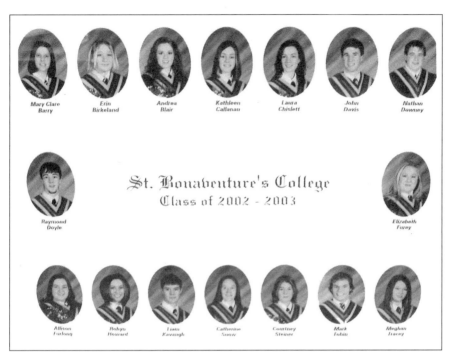

First graduating class of the new St. Bon's.

On retreat.

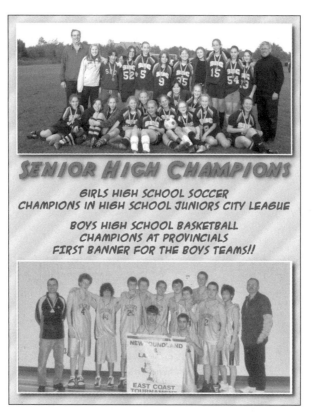

In games.

In concert.

Patrick's Hall School as part of the memorial to Blessed Edmund Rice, the Founder of the Christian Brothers. They were the gift of the Brothers. Another gift, that of Ray and Mary Power, was a beautiful trophy case to house all the historic trophies won by the College. Fittingly, it was placed in the corridor leading to the Aula Maxima where the winning of so many of these trophies was celebrated.

THE CHAPEL RESTORED

In preparation for the first graduation of the revived College in June 2003, the students were very anxious to have the main chapel restored so that the Graduation Mass could be celebrated there. Though they recognized the enormous difficulties involved, from the beginning, the restoration of the chapel had been the ardent desire of all involved. In a great act of faith, this restoration was now undertaken by the volunteer parents and friends led by John Barry with the expert assistance of architect Ron Fougere. The painting of the high ceiling was a hazardous undertaking for amateurs, and the school was fortunate that Mr. Derm Dobbin, an ex-pupil, offered his workmen with the needed scaffolding to undertake this task. The electrical work was done by G. J. Cahill Limited at cost. To meet fire regulations, a second door had to be cut from the chapel into the adjoining classroom. When the chapel itself was ready for use, various groups donated furnishing and equipment. The Archdiocese donated the beautiful, large crucifix which had adorned the now closed St. Joseph's Church in the east end of the city. The family of Helen Kennedy donated the reredos on which it was mounted; the altar and candles were the gift of Father Len Attilia, former principal of Gonzaga High School.

Perhaps the most significant restoration was that of the stained glass windows. It was not possible to use the original windows themselves for these had been sold. However, Mr. Alec Henley, with the assistance of photographer Bob Crocker, with great generosity and skill found a substitute. The original windows were, by an original process, photographed on plexiglass, The resulting copies were then mounted in the windows and could hardly be distinguished from the originals. The cost to Mr. Henley was some $32,000.

Because of the limited access to the organ gallery, fire regulations required that only a few students at a time could be permitted there. The restoration committee therefore, used their ingenuity to build a second staircase so that now the gallery can be used to its capacity. While this was being done, another interesting letter was unearthed, this time enclosed in a bottle. It read that the organ gallery was the work of C. J. McCarthy[6] when he was 76 years of age, with the help of his son Joseph and of Stephen Kerrigan. The enthusiasm of the chapel restoration workers overcame all further obstacles. On June 19, 2003, the chapel was reconsecrated, and a week later, on Thursday, June 26, the Graduation Mass took place. The 16 proud high school graduates were the first such St. Bon's high school graduates in 41 years. Many tears were shed by the older generation as it seemed that the beauty and solemnity of former days was finally being revived.

---

[6] Charles McCarthy was the great grandfather of Father John McCarthy, S.J.

Another proud event of 2003 was the installation of Bishop Raymond J. Lahey, an illustrious ex-pupil, as Bishop of Antigonish, N.S. He had previously been Bishop of St. George's. Still another was the winning of the Rose Bowl at the Kiwanis Music Festival by the College wind ensemble, an incredible feat considering the brief time the band had been in existence.[7] Adding to the joy was the winning of the Junior Rose Bowl for piano by a Grade Eleven student, James Hurley, while the other groups in the competition did extremely well. In the Rotary Musicfest, all six bands received the Gold Standard for excellence. In May, three of the bands traveled to Toronto to compete in the Musicfest Canada in Toronto; each was awarded the Gold Standard. To round off the year, the band instructor, Vincenza Etchegary, was awarded a Certificate of Achievement as part of the Prime Minister's Awards for Teaching Excellence. This award carried with it a prize of $1000 for the school.

In another sphere, Matthew Bown, a Grade Eleven student, was awarded Best Male Actor in the Avalon East High School Drama Festival. The College's cultural program was quickly establishing itself as one of the best in the Province, while to prove that the physical side of the students' education was not being neglected, one of the graduates, Mark Tobin, entered on a hockey career and is now playing in a professional league.

Fr. Vernon Boyd, S.J.
27th President

Father Rye's very successful term of office expired in June 2003 and Father Vernon Boyd, S.J., was appointed to succeed him. To ease the transition, Father Rye remained in charge until mid-October. Hardly was Father Boyd installed than the College received for the chapel the magnificent gift of eight stoneware sculptures of the Canadian Martyrs by the renowned Newfoundland artist, Gerald Squires. Also adding to the beauty of the chapel were newly installed carpeting[8] and lighting. Still later, the original Stations of the Cross were recovered from the museum at Blackhead. A gift of $5000 enabled the purchase of chapel chairs with kneelers. Of interest was the revival of the Old Boys' Association annual dinner, the first of which took place in May 2004. This year's graduating class numbered 20.

The school year, 2004-2005, while continuing the round of success which attended the College, was largely occupied with preparations for the College's 150th anniversary in 2006. December 2005 to December 2006 was declared the anniversary year. It began with a special Mass in the Basilica at which Archbishop O'Brien presided. This Mass was introduced by a Proclamation specially composed for the occasion. The Proclamation gave thanks for all those who had contributed to the development of the College from its foundation by Bishop Mullock in 1856, and asked

---

[7] The wind ensemble repeated this feat in the following year, 2004.

[8] The carpet once more the gift of Mr. Alec Henley.

God's blessing on its future endeavours, in particular that the Holy Spirit would enable the students to "continue to be a light to the world and pledge of the Father's love."

Next, on December 7, was a Gala Dinner[9] in the Fairmont Hotel at which a newly designed school flag was unveiled. In March, a special concert celebrating the history of the College through various musical compositions and oral presentations by the students, with accompanying slides, was held in the Arts and Culture Centre. Pride of place among the compositions was Michael Snelgrove's *The Phoenix*. During March, April, and May, a series of thought-provoking lectures was held in the Aula Maxima on the theme of Religion and Human Knowledge. It featured internationally known speakers and attracted a wide audience. In July was held an alumni weekend centring around the Feast of St. Bonaventure – again recalling a longtime tradition of the College. Finally, to conclude this year of celebrations, another special Mass took place in the Basilica on December 1, 2006.

In September 2006, the structure of the administration of the College was changed somewhat to take account of the wider responsibilities which the President had to accept. Father Boyd remained as College President with over-all authority, but Mr. Cecil Critch, the Vice-Principal, was appointed Principal with responsibility for the day-to-day running of the school. To date, this new system is working well.

Mr. Cecil Critch
Principal
2006-

In the course of its history, St. Bonaventure's College has experienced many ups and downs, but always its innate strength has enabled it to endure. It has been the educational flagship of the Catholic Church in the Province and now that it is the only high school remaining whose teaching is based on religious belief, the College is of more importance than ever as a shining example of true education and as a poignant reminder of what has been lost in the destruction of the religious education system. May it continue to flourish and to provide the Christian leadership which is so urgently needed to surmount the many challenges to Christian values which are presented by today's society. As did St. Bonaventure, may it always remain true to its motto: *Fides et Scientia — Faith and Knowledge.*

---

[9] The Dinner, at $150 a plate, was intended as a fundraiser and was quite successful in this respect.

Chapter 21
EPILOGUE

She stands majestic...
– College Song

As St. Bonaventure's College celebrates the 150th anniversary of its foundation and looks forward to its next century, it is perhaps time to consider why it has prospered when so many similar institutions have fallen by the wayside. One reason indeed is the unique family spirit which has prevailed throughout its lifespan and which has created such a bond between its pupils and its teachers; another is that its impact on society has been far greater than could be expected of such a relatively small school far from the major educational centers of Canadian society.

This latter point is worth examining in detail. In education, for instance, the College was the first successful attempt at higher education in St. John's after the disintegration of St. John's Academy and spurred the other denominations to emulate its success. Again, when Brother Slattery was President from 1889 to 1896, he devised the reformation of the educational system for the Island, including the first common public examinations (the Council of Higher Education) and the proper training and reimbursement of teachers. St. Bon's instituted Grade Twelve when Grade Eleven was the accepted pinnacle of secondary education, and held on to this Grade for many years before the educational authorities, particularly the University, accepted its necessity. The College graduates have held leading positions in the educational world, not only in Newfoundland but throughout the world. Christian Brothers A. F. Brennan ('37) and G. R. Bellows ('43), for instance, were both Superintendents of Catholic schools in Newfoundland;. Brother James Bates ('33) held a similar position in Vancouver; Louis Cuddihy (1880's) in Montreal. John Penney ('06) became professor of English at Harvard University. Brother Brennan became President of both the Newfoundland and Labrador Teachers' Association and the Canadian Teachers' Federation — the first Newfoundlander to be elected to this latter prestigious position.

In scientific education, the College has also been in the forefront as evidenced by the use of X-rays by Brother Crehan only a year after they were invented and their application to hospital use a few years later. The College, through Brother Enright, also introduced to Newfoundland the use of mini-apparatus in the science lab which greatly increased the safely of scientific experiments for high school students. The College can likewise boast of many eminent doctors and scientists: James Howley (1850's) who, with Alexander Murray, made the first geological survey of Newfoundland and, in 1915, wrote *The Beothucks or Red Indians*, still considered the classic work on these vanished people; Kevin Keough ('57), the first "Tsar" of Canadian science and presently CEO of the Alberta Research Fund; Douglas Darcy ('35) who spent his entire scientific career as a member of the Royal Cancer Research Institute in England and made several important discoveries in this field; Kevin Barron ('45), prominent surgeon in New York; John Kelly ('51), surgeon and expert in medical law in Washington, D.C.; John Quinlan, ('34) brain specialist in Toronto; and many other well-known doctors in Newfoundland itself.

In the political sphere, the College has produced two Lieutenant Governors of Newfoundland and Labrador: Sir Albert Walsh ('16) and Honorable Fabian O'Dea, Q.C. ('34); four Prime Ministers/Premiers: Honourable Daniel J. Greene (1860's), Sir Edward Morris (1870's), Sir Michael Cashin (1880's), Honorable Daniel Williams ('72); three Chief Justices: Lewis E. Emerson ('16), Albert Walsh ('16), Robert Furlong ('20); five Federal Senators: Hon. John Higgins ('09), Vincent Burke (1897), Sir Albert Walsh, Gerald Ottenheimer ('51), William Doody ('46); four leaders of Provincial political parties: William Browne ('15), Peter Cashin ('06), James Greene ('45), Jack Harris ('74). Two ex-pupils were mayors of St. John's: Charles Howlett (1860's) and John Murphy ('39). During the National Assembly to decide on Confederation, 10 of the 45 delegates, including the chairman, Hon. Cyril Fox, were graduates of St. Bon's. Not to be forgotten is W. J. McGrath, who became secretary to President Theodore Roosevelt.

On the literary scene, Michael Harrington ('34), Greg Power ('26), Tom Cahill ('45), Paul O'Neill ('48) as well as Archbishop Michael Howley (1850's) are considered important Newfoundland poets, historians and writers. Father Michael J. Ryan, S.T.D., Ph.D., (1870's), won renowned as a church historian. His writings found their way into *The Catholic Encyclopedia* and *The American Ecclesiastical Review* and other prestigious publications. Other graduates, such as Monsignor William McGrath ('14) and Father Leslie Fitzgerald ('17), have made their contribution to our literary heritage.

To be noticed, also, is the success of so many of St. Bon's graduates in the field of business. Beginning with Nicholas Duchemin ('14) who became General Manager of General Electric in the United States, St. Bon's ex-pupils have made their mark in many areas of the world of commerce. Craig Dobbin ('51), for instance, just recently deceased, was the major shareholder in the largest helicopter company in the world; his brother, Basil ('58) has become a major resort developer in Newfoundland; John Kelly ('56) has carved out an important niche for himself in the high tech industry; Gary Mooney ('62) as done the same in the insurance world. Gerard Cahill ('39) is the founder of the largest construction company in Eastern Canada; Danny Williams introduced cable television to Newfoundland.

To enter the Mullock Hall and to study the photographs on its walls is to be made aware of the notable athletic achievements of the College. For many years, its hockey teams reigned supreme, the Boyle Trophy almost always in its possession; its football and basketball teams were invariably either victors or close contenders. Among its never-to-be-forgotten heroes were such outstanding athletes as Billy Cotter ('28), whose pole vaulting record remained unchallenged for many years; Andy Cahill ('30), whose graceful hockey maneuvers were a delight to behold; Pat Kelly ('38), long distance runner supreme; Gordon Halley ('21), unequalled at the 100-yard dash. Sports Day inevitably brought out unexpected talent as when the unheralded Pat Doyle ('58) easily defeated the College's star athletes in the five-mile marathon. But it was the sportsmanship instilled into the competitors that was most important. Athletes learned to respect both themselves and their opponents, to strive to the utmost of their ability and their endurance, to refuse to admit defeat until the last whistle had blown, but to refuse to cheat in order to gain advantage.

However, it is as a vehicle for spreading the message of Christ that St. Bonaventure's has, perhaps, made its greatest contribution. It has given eleven Bishops and Archbishops to the Catholic Church in Newfoundland: Archbishops Michael F. Howley, Edward P. Roche (1892), Patrick J. Skinner ('22), Thomas J. Flynn ('12), Alphonsus L. Penney ('41); Bishops John M. O'Neill ('21), Michael F. Power (1898), Henry T. Renouf (1880's), Richard T. McGrath ('28), John March (1880's), Raymond J. Lahey ('47). Well over 100 priests and Monsignori are also among its ex-pupils. On the missionary field, the Canadian Missionary Society (Scarboro Missions) counts a considerable number of St. Bon's ex-pupils among its ranks, priests who laboured in China and the West Indies, notably Monsignor William McGrath, Prefect Apostolic of Cuchow, China, who was also, in his later years, noted for spreading devotion to Our Lady of Fatima throughout North America. Another outstanding ex-pupil, Archbishop William A. Carew, ('40) after spending many years at the Vatican Secretariate of State, served as Papal Representative to Rwanda-Burundi, to Palestine and finally to Japan. Monsignor James Doody ('47), Fathers John Maddigan ('43), Charlie Conroy ('44) and other priest graduates served in South America, principally in Peru, where Father Charlie was actually elected mayor of the town of Monsefu but died in a tragic car accident. Father Leslie Kearney, S.J, ('33) has spent his priestly life ministering to the people of Guyana; Father John Whelan, S.J, ('47) did the same for the people of India. Other graduates have served and are serving in the Catholic schools in the West Indies, Christian Brothers John Holden ('60) and John Buckingham ('56) are training African Brothers as teachers in Cape Town, South Africa. Several graduates and members of staff are the recipients of honours from the Pope because of their services to the Church: Dan Ryan, Charles Hutton, Honourable J. V. O'Dea, Patrick Halley, Frank O'Leary, Edmund Phelan.('21), James Higgins ('31) Robert Furlong ('20), Alec Henley ('41), Robert Connolly ('18) and Doctor Kevin Tracey ('41).

Even such a summary glance at the achievements of the graduates of St. Bonaventure's College as this gives an indication of the school's ability to develop the human and spiritual gifts of its students as well as demonstrating how important the school has been for the wider community. Doubtless there have been failures; fallen human nature always leaves its mark, clashes of personality or other unfavourable conditions may have hindered the development of some students. Our prayers and regrets go with those for whom St. Bonaventure's did not succeed in being the support that is its aim. But, especially, our prayers go to those students who are at present enjoying the advantages of the education which St. Bon's provides as well as to those who will enter its portals in the years to come, that they may strive to emulate and even to surpass the achievements of their predecessors in advancing the kingdom of God and the welfare of their fellows. Eventually may we all be gathered together again with the Lord to enjoy the eternal reward for our labours.

THE VOICE WE SHARE

From where I stand tonight,
balanced on the edge
of a tomorrow I am destined to travel
and the yesterday that carried me safely here

I am beyond words
Language fails me.

But the Grace that is this moment
is a voice,
a voice not formed in words
but in the silent mystery
of the simplest prayer –

the voice we share.

We hear it in the seven silent chords of the rainbow
and the quiet trickle of rain.
We are called to it by the whispers of the Holy
and the gentle light of the Nazarene.
We know it in the absolute stillness of God.

And this simplest prayer,
our voice beyond speech,
moves in quiet strength
where language cannot reach;

To children whose pure words are seldom heard.
To the broken, the lonely, who can only whisper.
To the hungry, the sick, whose eyes speak a silent pain.
to the conflicted, the oppressed, whose ears hear only
fear.

From where we stand tonight,
balanced on the edge
of a tomorrow entrusted to our care
and the yesterday that gently showed us how,

From where we stand,
this moment
and forever,

our life,
our voice,
is prayer.

James Albert Stockwood
2007 Graduate

BIOGRAPHICAL NOTES

Ahern, Brother M. C. In September 1934, Brother Ahern was transferred to All Hallows Institute, New York. In the following year he was appointed Provincial Consultor while teaching at Iona Prep., New Rochelle, where he died on November 16th of that year.

Ahern, Father William. After leaving St. Bon's, Father Ahern served for three years at the Cathedral in St. John's before returning to Brooklyn in 1892. He served as assistant priest at St. Joseph's Church for seven years and then, in 1899, founded St. Gabriel's Church in east New York which he turned into a flourishing parish. He remained pastor of this church until his sudden and untimely death on July 27, 1907, at the age of 47 just as he was preparing to return to visit his friends in Newfoundland.

Birmingham, Brother J. V. After completing his second term of office as President of St. Bon's, Brother Birmingham moved to Vancouver College. Two years later he was transferred to Leo High School in Chicago. For a brief period he taught at St. Edward's College in Liverpool, England, and then returned to Leo High School where he remained for some 14 years. Then, having retired from the classroom, he moved to St. Laurence High School in nearby Oak Lawn. On May 15, 1969, while on a vacation in Ireland, he passed to his eternal reward.

Carfagnini, Most Rev. Enrico, O.S.F. After leaving St. Bon's, his future career was tumultuous. After wandering for some time on the mainland, he moved to Harbour Grace at the invitation of Bishop Dalton and there designed and supervised the erection of Bishop Dalton's cathedral. In 1870, after the latter's death, Carfagnini became its Bishop, much to the consternation of the majority of the priests and people of that diocese. His episcopate was marred by increasing controversy, and in 1880 he was transferred to the Bishopric of Gallipoli in Italy where he presided until his retirement in 1898. He died February 12, 1904.

Crehan, Brother J. J. After returning to Ireland and serving for brief periods in various schools, Brother Crehan was transferred to Christian Brothers College in Cork where he taught with eminent success for five years before being appointed secretary of the educational committee of the Brothers in Ireland, a post which he held with distinction for the next twenty years. He died in Dublin, October 10, 1944.

Culhane, Brother P. J. Brother Culhane left for Halifax on July 3, 1913. After 27 highly successful years at St. Mary's, he was, in 1930, appointed Provincial Superior of the American Province, which office he held until 1942. He died at the Brothers' Novitiate in West Park on October 20, 1950.

Downey, Brother J. J. After his return to Ireland, Brother Downey was stationed at Christian Brothers College, Cork. Subsequently he was appointed Superior of the Brothers' school in Dun Laoghaire, Dublin. In 1918 he was appointed Superior of Christian Brothers College but soon became ill and died on June 4, 1919.

Doyle, Brother P. B. After two years of great financial difficulty in Vancouver (the Brothers wryly referred to the College as "Mortgage Hall") Brother Doyle resigned and was transferred to O'Dea High School, Seattle. Three years later he moved to St. Mary's College, Halifax, as professor of classics. When the Brothers left St. Mary's in 1940 to open Iona College in New Rochelle, N.Y., Brother Doyle began the most fulfilling part of his life as professor of Latin in this rapidly growing institution. Perhaps the most treasured part of his apostolate was equipping young men with the Latin they needed to enter Dunwoodie Seminary in N.Y. At one time during Brother Doyle's sojourn at Iona, more students entered Dunwoodie from Iona College than from the New York minor seminary itself. He remained the beloved soul of the College until his death there on May 8, 1961.

Enright, Brother J. J. After leaving St. Bon's in 1962 and returning to the United States, Brother Enright continued to have an active teaching career. First he was appointed head of the science department at All Hallow's Institute, N.Y. Only a year later, he was transferred to St. Laurence High School in Chicago with the same function. Here he remained for 25 years until deteriorating health necessitated his semi-retirement. In 1978, he was appointed Provincial Bursar of the Western American Province of the Christian Brothers. Shortly afterwards, diabetes began to take its toll and he had to undergo an operation for the removal of a leg. After a lengthy illness, he was transferred to St. Joseph's Care Residence in New Rochelle, where he died on February 10, 1989, on his 78th birthday.

Fitzgerald, Father William. After leaving St. Bon's, he joined the Brooklyn diocese where he had a long and notable career, achieving the rank of Monsignor, before dying on March 20, 1936, at the age of 82.

Fleming, Brother P. C. That Brother Fleming's success at St. Bon's was no accident is shown by his subsequent career. After completing a six-year term of office on the American Provincial Council, he was elected to the Brothers' General Council in Rome. Here he was equally successful, being re-elected for another six-year term which ended in 1972. During this time, he was largely responsible for resolving a serious dispute between the Brothers and the Archdiocese of St. John's which almost resulted in the Brothers leaving the Archdiocese. He then returned to the United States and taught at Essex Catholic High School in New Jersey for three years, following which, in 1975, he became a member of the staff of Catholic Memorial High School in Boston where he taught very enthusiastically and successfully until, having suffered a heart attack, he retired in 1987. He continued to reside at Catholic Memorial until ill health forced his removal to the

Brothers' care residence in New Rochelle, N.Y, where he died on March 15, 2001 at the age of 88.

Flood, Brother J. B. After leaving St. Bonaventure's and spending a short time in Ireland, Brother Flood moved briefly to South Africa and then to Australia where both his health and his talents flourished. He died in Launceston, Tasmania, on November 30, 1940, at the age of 86.

Howley, Father Richard, D.D. After leaving St. Bon's, continued to serve in the Cathedral and as hospital chaplain for three more years during which time he attended Bishop Mullock on his deathbed. In 1870 he moved to Canada and then to the United States where he died in Albany, N.Y. on September, 3, 1912.

Knight, Brother A. M. After a short time at O'Dea High School, Brother Knight returned to Iona College in New Rochelle where he taught happily until his death on February 2, 1971. Like his confreres, he is buried in the Novitiate cemetery of the Christian Brothers in West Park.

Lavelle, Brother G. B. After leaving St. Bonaventure's and returning to Ireland, Brother Lavelle joined the staff of the Brothers' prestigious school in Synge Street, Dublin (Jame Joyce attended this school for a short time.) In June of that same year, he was elected to the General Chapter of the Brothers, as he was again in 1905 and 1910. In 1906, he was appointed a member of the Education Committee of the Congregation of which he remained a member for the next 20 years; so there can be no doubt of the respect in which he was held by the Brothers. In 1903, he returned to Waterpark College as Superior and again achieved exceptional success. He is next found in Wexford where, as Superior, his results were equally outstanding. In 1909, he was transferred to his native Tuam in the west of Ireland where he laboured for the next 11 years. His last assignment was as Superior of the Brothers' school in Dundalk where he spent the last 19 years of his life. While in Dundalk, he invented a new system of shorthand particularly adapted to the Irish language but was not to see it in print. Here, too, he became so crippled by the rheumatism which had afflicted him in Newfoundland that he could only walk with the aid of two sticks. Eventually, he moved to the Brothers' home for the aged in Baldoyle where he died on May 13, 1940.

Lovejoy, Father J. R. was born in Ireland in 1840, ordained in 1866. Upon leaving Newfoundland in 1872, he moved to the Albany Diocese, N.Y. where he died on June 11, 1874, at Stephentown. *The Adelphian* identifies him as a Franciscan, but this seems to have been a mistake as there are no other indications that such was the case.

McCarthy, Brother P. D. Patrick McCarthy had a long and distinguished career as a Brother. Leaving St. John's in November 1896, he entered the Brothers' novitiate at Baldoyle, Dublin, where he received the religious name, Brother Dominic. After teaching for almost 20 years in various schools in Ireland and obtaining his B.A. degree from Queen's University in Belfast, he was assigned to St. Mary's College, Halifax, for which the Brothers had assumed responsibility two years earlier with Brother Joseph Culhane as its first Brother President. In the notorious "Halifax explosion" of 1916, Brother Dominic lost the sight of one eye when it was pierced by a splinter of flying glass. Undeterred, he subsequently obtained his M.Sc. degree from Notre Dame University and his Ph.D. from Fordham University. In 1924, he was appointed the founding Principal of the Brothers' high school in Butte, Montana, and later principal of All Hallows School in New York and Leo High School in Chicago. His final assignment was to Iona College, New Rochelle, N.Y., were he taught European history until his official retirement in 1952. Not willing to accede to age, however, he moved back to All Hallows where he taught mathematics for another six years. He died on February 9, 1968, at the age of 88 and is buried in the Brothers' graveyard in West Park, N.Y.

McHugh, Brother J. M. In 1970, after completing his term as Superior of St. Bon's, Brother McHugh spent some time considering the possibility of joining a contemplative order but eventually decided to remain as a Christian Brother. In the following year, 1971, he was appointed Principal of Brother Rice High School in St. John's. After his six-year term in this position, he became consecutively Principal of Brother Edmund Rice Secondary School in Toronto, and then Deputy Provincial of the Canadian Province. He was also Principal of Vancouver College, and finally Principal once more of Brother Edmund Rice Secondary School. While in Vancouver, he was found to be suffering from cancer. Treatment alleviated this for some time, but, when he moved to Toronto, it returned with greater force. While on medical leave, he spent some time with the monks at the Cistercian monastery in Hockley Valley, Ontario; then, his health having improved, he went to the Brothers' school in Dominica in the West Indies to engage in school work there. In July 1989, he participated briefly in the Provincial Chapter at Mono Mills, ON, but quickly became ill and returned to St. John's to enter the Palliative Care Unit at St. Clare's Mercy Hospital. There, surrounded by the Brothers, his family and his close friends, he died on the July 6, 1989, his untimely death mourned by all who knew him.

O'Connell, Brother W. K. After resigning from St. Bon's because of his deteriorating health, Brother O'Connell was transferred to All Hallows School in New York where he had a relatively light teaching load until 1949 when his health force him to resign completely from teaching. He died rather suddenly on December 3, 1950.

Perry, Brother J. T. After leaving St. John's, Brother Perry taught in Butte, Montana, and All Hallows, N.Y., before being appointed Superior of St. Louis College in Victoria, B.C. This last appointment proved unsuccessful, for diplomacy was not one of Brother Perry's many virtues, and he was transferred to

Power Memorial Academy, N.Y., where he served with distinction from 1933 to 1947. After stints in various other schools, he was assigned to the Brothers' Scholasticate in Lakewood, N.J., and then, in retirement, to Iona Grammar School, New Rochelle, N.Y. where he ended his days on March 28, 1983, at the great age of 98.

Ryan, Brother J. B. After remaining on the College staff for the year following his retirement as President, Brother Ryan was granted a year's sabbatical to obtain his Master's Degree in mathematics at Notre Dame University in Indiana, following which he returned to St. Bon's, having in the meantime been appointed Consultor to the Provincial Superior. In 1924, he was transferred to New York, and in 1928 became the first Principal of the newly opened Juniorate of the Brothers in West Park, N.Y. In 1932, he visited St. Bon's on the occasion of its Diamond Jubilee. He died at West Park on February 4, 1936, beloved by all who knew him, not the least by his former students in St. John's.

Ryan, Brother J. E. After a year at St. Patrick Hall Schools, he taught at Iona Prep., New Rochelle, N.Y., and Leo High School, Chicago, before being appointed Superior of Sacred Heart School, N.Y., and then of the Brothers' Juniorate in West Park, N.Y. Following this last assignment, he retired to Iona Prep., New Rochelle, where he passed away on September 30, 1949.

Slattery, Brother J. L. Soon after leaving St. John's, Brother Slattery was appointed Principal of Waterpark College in Waterford. In 1897, at the urgent request of Bishop Howley, he was summoned back to St. John's to open a Catholic Orphanage, one which the government had agreed to finance (an agreement on which the succeeding government promptly reneged). After completing his term of office at Mount Cashel and suffering from serious health problems, Brother Slattery returned to Ireland in 1907 and was stationed at the North Monastery in Cork until his death on November 10, 1910 at the early age of 63.

Slattery, Father P. A., O.S.F. After resigning as President in 1875, Father Slattery returned to Ireland and later moved to Sydney, Australia, where he served as Provincial Superior and built an exact copy of St. Bonaventure's, a type of building hardly suited to the Australian climate. Returning to Ireland, he was appointed guardian of the Franciscan monastery in Limerick. He died in 1914.

Tarrant, Brother H. P. On leaving St. Bon's, Brother Tarrant returned to Iona College and the teaching of English. Shortly afterwards, he was asked to take up again the Office of Dean of the College in preparation for an official inspection by the State of New York. Four years later, he suffered a severe stroke which deprived him of speech and forced him to retire. He continued to live in the College community, giving great edification by his patient acceptance of his handicap, until his death on July 6, 1985.

BIBLIOGRAPHY

Manuscript sources:

Annals of St. Bonaventure's College, 1889, CBASJ.
Feild Papers, collection of the letters of Bishop Feild, AASJ.
Journal of the House of Assembly, various years, PANL.
Minutes of the Board of St. Bonaventure's College, various dates, CBASJ.
Diary, Bishop J. T. Mullock 1863, RCASJ.
Scrap Book, St. Bonaventure's College, 1892, CBASJ.
Slattery Papers (SP), a collection of over 450 letters from the pioneer Christian Brothers in Newfoundland to their Superiors in Ireland, 1875-1910, CBASJ.

Collections:

Centenary Souvenir Book (1855-1955), Archdiocese of St. John's, Robinson, 1955.
    - Higgins, J. G., "Bishop Power."
Christian Brothers Educational Record, an annual journal of the Congregation of Christian Brothers containing articles on educational matters and also the obituaries of deceased Brothers, private printing, CBASJ.
    - O'Connell, Brother W. K., "Brother John Columba Fennessy, 1872-1939," 1940.
    - McCarthy, Brother P. D., "Brother T. A. Prendergast," 1954.
Encyclopedia of Newfoundland and Labrador, Vol. IV, Harry Cuff, St. John's, NL, 1993
The Adelphian, Journal of St. Bonaventure's College from 1904 to 1962. Originally published four times a year but eventually only once. It contains the important events of the life of the College for the year in question, CBASJ.
    - Carroll, W. J., "The Mid-Seventies," Vol. 4, No. 1, June, 1907.
    - Morris, Lord Edward, "Recollections of Old St Bonaventure's," Vol 4, No.1, 1907.
    - Devine, P. K., "*Reminiscences of St. Bonaventure's in '78, '79, '80,*" 1931.
The Book of Newfoundland, Vol. 1, Newfoundland Book Publisher, St. John's, 1937.
    - Burke, Vincent P. "Education in Newfoundland."
    - Wood, R. R., B.A., "Bishop Field College."
The Book of Newfoundland, Vol. 4, Newfoundland Book Publisher, St. John's, 1967.
    - McDonald, Aubrey, "My Song of Sport."
The Newfoundland Quarterly, Vol. 7, No.1, July 1907.

Authors:

Darcy, Brother J. B., *Fair or Foul the Weather,* Creative Book Publishing, St. John's, 1999.
House, Edgar, *Edward Feild, the Man and His Legacy,* Jesperson, St. John's, 1976.
Howley, Archbishop M. F., "Address to the Old Boys of St. Bonaventure's College, *The Evening   Telegram,* July 19, 1911.
————, *Ecclesiastical History of Newfoundland,*Vol. 1, Boston, 1888.
————, *Ecclesiastical History of Newfoundland,* Vol. 2, Terra Nova Press, St. John's, NL, 2006.
Johnson, Paul, *The Birth of the Modern World Society, 1815-30,* Weidenfeld & Nicolson, London, 1991.
McCarthy, Michael, "The Tragedy of Villa Nova," *The Monitor,* August 1978, RCASJ.
O'Neill, Paul, *A Seaport Legacy,* Press Porcepic, Erin, Ontario, 1976.
Rowe, Fred, *The Development of Education in Newfoundland,* Ryerson, Toronto, 1964.

Stockman, Julian, *Artemis*, Scribner, 2002.

Talbot, Thomas, *Newfoundland: or a Letter Addressed to a Friend in Ireland in Relation to the Condition and Circumstances of the Island of Newfoundland, with an Especial View to Emigration*, S. Low, London, 1882.

Tucker, H. W., *Life and Episcopate of Edward Feild, Bishop of Newfoundland,* 3rd edition, 1923.

Newspapers:

Evening Herald, 1896, PANL.
Morning Courier, St. John's, 1850, PANL.
Royal Gazette, St. John's, 1850, PANL.
The Colonist, 1889, PANL.
*The Evening Telegram,*1889, 1911, PANL.
The Herald, 1904, PANL.
The Newfoundlander, 1875, PANL.
The Record, 1860, PANL.

Archives

AASJ, Anglican Archives, St. John's.
CBASJ. Christian Brothers Archives, St. John's.
PANL, Provincial Archives of Newfoundland and Labrador,
Propaganda Fide Archives, Rome, Italy.
RCASJ, Roman Catholic Archives, St. John's

Abbreviations

CBER – Christian Brothers Educational Record
C.F.C. – Congregation of Christian Brothers
C.H.E. – Council of Higher Education
FGS – Fellow of the Geographical Society
HMS – His (Her) Majesty's Ship.
JHA – Journal of the House of Assembly.
KCSG – Knight Commander of St. Gregory
MBE – Member of the British Empire
MHA – Member of the House of Assembly
OBE - Order of the British Empire
O.S.F – Order of St. Francis (Franciscan)
SCRC, America Settentionale – North American Letters to the Congregation for the Propagation of the Faith.
SP – Slattery Papers.

APPENDIX 1

CLERICAL ALUMNI OF ST. BONAVENTURE'S COLLEGE
BY DATE OF ORDINATION

ARCHBISHOPS

M. F. Howley,	1868	Bishop of St. John's 1894-1904, Archbishop, 1904-1914
E. P. Roche,	1897	Archbishop of St. John's, 1915-1950
T. J. Flynn,	1919	Co-adjutor Archbishop of St. John's, 1945-1949
P. J. Skinner, C.J.M.	1929	Archbishop of St. John's, 1951-1979
W. A. Carew,	1947	Papal Pro-Nuncio to Japan, etc.
A. L. Penney,	1949	Bishop of Grand Falls, 1972-1979 Archbishop of St. John's, 1979-1990

BISHOPS

H. T. Renouf	1895	Bishop of St. George's, 1920-1941
John March	1888	Bishop of Harbour Grace, 1906-1940
M. F. Power	1906	Bishop of St. George's, 1911-1920
J. M. O'Neill	1927	Bishop of Harbour Grace/Grand Falls, 1940-1972
R. T. McGrath	1936	Bishop of St. George's, 1970-85
R. J. Lahey	1963	Bishop of St. George's, 1986-2004; Bishop of Antigonish 2004.

PREFECT APOSTOLIC

W. C. McGrath, SFM	1921	Prefect Apostolic of Chuchow, China

MONSIGNORI

John Scott,	1863	Mark P. Dwyer,	1909
E. F. Walsh,	1867	John J. Rawlins,	1909
Joseph V. Donnelly	1870	Edward J. O'Brien,	1910
Vincent P. Reardon,	1872	John P. Kirwin,	1914
William Veitch,	1871	Francis J. Ryan,	1915
John J. St. John,	1874	Michael F. Dinn,	1918
F. D. McCarthy,	1884	William H. Casey	1919
W. J. Browne, D.D.	1887	Patrick J. Kennedy,	1921
Dr. Joseph Murphy,	1888	W. J. Williams,	1922
William P. Kitchin,	1902	Harold A. Summers,	1923
William P. Finn,	1904	John W. McGettigan,	1923
		George F. Bartlett,	1924

MONSIGNORI

James A. Miller,	1924
Ronald McD. Murphy,	1924
Jeremiah C. Stoyles,	1925
John W. O'Mara,	1926
Joseph P. Hogan,	1929
John J. Murray,	1930
Edward P. Maher,	1931
Joseph W. Peddle,	1931
Patrick J. Bromley,	1932
Eric R. Lawlor,	1942
Joseph M. O'Brien,	1942
Dermot L. O'Keefe,	1943
James T. Fennessy,	1944
Albert M. O'Driscoll,	1947
William P. Hogan,	1948
Richard T. Woodford,	1949
Raymond March,	1950
Roderick T. White,	1951
James J. Doody,	1953
David P. Morrissey	1955
John F. Wallis	1957
Edward T. Bromley,	1958

PRIESTS

Richard Dunphy 1860
John Conway, 1862
Denis O'Brien, 1863
Patrick O'Donnell, 1863
John Kinsella, 1867
Dean Nicholas Roche, 1867
Dean William Born, 1867
Dr. George F. Doyle, 1869
Patrick Delaney, 1870
Lawrence K. Vereker, 1870
Dean Wm., Doutney, 1871
William Fitzpatrick, 1872
J. J. Whelan, 1874
Michael O'Driscoll, 1874
Stephen O'Flynn, 1875
Richard Walsh, 1875
William H. Jackman, 1877
John Bennett, C.Ss.R, 1877
James McNamara, 1877
Gregory J. Battcock, 1878
Michael Morris, 1878
Dean Matthew O'Rourke, 1878
Richard J. Phippard, 1880
Thomas Lynch, 1883
Walter M. Tarahan, 1883
Stephen O'Driscoll, 1885
M. J. Ryan, Ph.D., D.D., 1886
Maurice Bonia, C.Ss.R, 1887
Thomas O'Donnell, 1888?

Dean James J. McGrath, 1889
Laurence, Kavanagh, S.J., 1889
Patrick J. O'Brien, 1890
T. A. Fleming, 1892
William H. Jackman, 1892
Dr. John A. O'Reilly, 1892
Dr. Cornelius O'Regan, 1895
M. F. McGuire, 1896
Andrew Jordan, 1898
James C. White, 1898
James Walsh, 1898
John T. Ashley, 1889
Edward Curran, 1900
Alfred J. Maher, 1900
J. H. Scully, 1900
Dr. Stephen J. Whalen, 1901
Alexander R. Howley, 1902
James McNamara, 1902
James J. Coady, 1904
James M. Joy, 1904
William. O'Flaherty, 1906
James Donnelly, 1907
Stanislaus St. Croix, 1908
Thomas Gough, 1908
Joseph F. Pippy, 1908
Peter Kelly, 1909
J. J .Walker, 1909
Edward Wilson, 1909
Joseph W. Donnolly, 1910
Dr. James J Greene, 1910

John S. Kavanagh, 1910
Andrew T. Nolan, 1911
Dr. John Carter, 1915
Patrick Hearn, 1916
Thomas J. Liddy, 1916
Dr. F. J. McGrath, 1916
Thomas D. O'Neill, 1916
Thomas J. Devereux 1917
Robert A. St. John, 1917
Michael F. Dinn, 1918
John Dwyer-Savin, 1918
Adrian J. Dee, 1919
Michael J. Leamy, 1919
William Murphy, 1919
Francis J. Pumphrey, 1919
Edward J. Rawlins, 1919
Augustine Thorne, 1919
Lawrence A. Fortune, 1920
Michael Kennedy, 1921
Joseph Connors, 1922
George W. Battcock, 1923
Leslie G. Fitzgerald, 1923
William V. Sullivan, 1923
Andrew Whalen, 1923
Henry Curtis, 1924
Randal Greene, 1924
Augustine Gibbs, 1925
Jeremiah Howard, 1925
John J. Power, 1925
William Ryan, 1925
John Curran, 1926
John F. Ryan, 1926
John Fleming, 1927
Michael F. Hayes, 1927
Francis Jackman, 1927
Joseph Burke, 1928
Albert McEvoy, 1928?
Gerald Murphy, C.SsR., 1928
Dr. Paul O'Reilly, 1928
Aidan Murphy, C.Ss.R. 1929
Alphonsus Chafe, SFM, 1930
William P. Collins, 1930
J. Ronald Jones, 1930
Cyril S. Egan, 1930

Patrick Miller, O.M.I., 1930
Robert J. Greene, 1931
Albert Slattery, 1931
Richard Carroll, O.M.I., 1932
John A Cotter, 1932
Leo Foley, M.M., 1932
Hugh McGettigan, SFM, 1932
Francis W. Bradshaw. 1933
Craig Strang, SFM, 1933
Alfred H. Bown, 1934
Francis Meaney, 1934
Joseph P. Michaels, O.M.I. 1934
John J. Hunt, 1935
William Young, 1935
Leo J. Burke, S.F.M., 1936
Leo. J. Drake, 1936
Gordon Kent, 1936
Michael J. Kinsella, 1936
Philip McCarthy, 1936
Edward Moriarty, SFM, 1936
Francis Mullowney, 1936
Michael Carey, S.F.M., 1937
Thomas Morrissey, SFM, 1937
Walter Walsh, 1937
Michael Connolly, 1939
Michael Maloney, 1939
William J. Hennebury, 1940
John B. Kent, 1940
Thomas Morrissey, 1940
Brendan Quigley, 1940
Vincent Quigley, 1940
McDermott Penney, 1942
Francis Terry, 1940
J. Loyola Lacey, 1943
John J. O'Deady, 1943
James L. Glavine, CSsR, 1944
Edward Shea, 1944
Robert Moore, SFM, 1945
Joseph Moriarty, SFM, 1945
John J. Murray, 1945
Edward A Walsh, 1945
James A Dunne, 1946
James L O'Dwyer, 1947
William J. Boland, CSC, 1948

Kevin McCarthy, 1948
Gregory Pumphrey, 1948
Daniel P. Murphy, 1949
Francis Burke, 1950
Gregory L Hogan, 1950
Fred J. Terry, 1950
Fred W. Cahill, CSB, 1951
Charles Greene, 1951
Leslie Kearney, S.J., 1951
Francis W. McNeilly, 1951
Thomas J. Moakler, 1951
Michael Hynes, 1953
John Molloy, 1953
Charles O'N Conroy, 1954
Kevin M. Ryan, 1954
Gerard Bates, 1955
John Hanton, 1955
Leonard Kelly, 1955
Patrick McCormack, 1955
Edward Purcell, 1956
Reginald Collins, CSC, 1957
Gordon Grace, 1957
John Maddigan, 1957
Leo Shea, 1957
William J. Browne, S.J., 1958

John McGettigan, 1958
Richard D. McHugh, 1958
Hubert Whelan, 1959
Robert Caul, S.A., 1960
John Collins, 1960
John Whelan, S.J., 1960
Joseph Gash, 1961
Desmond McGrath, 1961
Francis Slattery, 1961
Valentine Power, 1962
Ronald Bromley, 1963
James Beresford, 1964
William Pomeroy, 1964
Patrick J. Kennedy, 1966
Edward Brophy, 1967
Edwin J. Gale, 1966
Dermot McGettigan, 1967
Aidan Devine, 1969
William Ashley, 1970?
Charles Kelly, 1972
William J Ryan, 1973
Francis Puddister, 1977
Brian Quigley, 1977
Douglas Stamp, CSsR, 1980
Raymond Earle, 1986

APPENDIX 2

INSPECTOR'S REPORT OF ST. BONAVENTURE'S COLLEGE, 1890
(Some extraneous matter has been omitted)

The total income was $4,659.48, made up of the annual Legislative grant of $3,465.48 and receipts from fees $1,184. The expenditure, owing to the outbreak of diphtheria among the resident students in December 1889, was unusually large, amounting to $5,734.07. Of this the sum of $970.50 was expended in the purchase of new apparatus for the experimental study of physics together with a collection of mineralogical specimens, anatomical models and a varied assortment of objects intended to illustrate the different processes used in their manufacture. A considerable outlay was also incurred in laying out and improving the College grounds.

Despite the alarm occasioned by the outbreak of diphtheria in the College, the attendance for the past school year was larger than for any year since 1886. The whole number of pupils enrolled was one hundred and sixteen, of whom forty-one, including twelve pupil teachers, were resident students.

The accommodations provided for the students comprise every arrangement calculated to ensure their health and comfort, the appointments of the dormitories, refectories, recreation-rooms, gymnasium, &c, being all that could be desired. While all possible pains are taken to promote the physical well-being of the students, as well as their intellectual development, no effort is spared to cultivate in them a high standard of manly conduct and to form their character upon sound moral and religious principles. The inner government of the institution is directed with great care; and the discipline throughout, while thoroughly effective, is equally removed from that undue stringency and espionage which generally breed distrust and antagonism and that laxity so conductive to the growth of careless or vicious habits. That such a system of discipline, firm yet gentle, vigilant yet unobtrusive, together with the example of high Christian character constantly before them in the teachers themselves, can fail to exert a most salutary influence upon the subsequent career of these young men, it is impossible to believe.

With respect to the scholastic work of the past year, which I had the opportunity of testing just before the Christmas vacation by a careful examination extending over four days, it affords me pleasure to be able to speak in terms of unqualified satisfaction. The admirable organization of the schools, the excellent discipline maintained, and the well-directed enthusiasm of the teachers were reflected in the orderly behavior of the pupils and the eager interest which they displayed in their work. The students were grouped in five classes. The work of the fifth class (lowest) embraced a knowledge of English grammar as far as syntax, elementary parsing, analysis and composition, reading and spelling in fourth book, the compound rules and simple proportion in arithmetic, the outlines of geography with particular reference to the British Isles and Newfoundland, the outlines of Newfoundland history, and elementary drawing.

The fourth class was doing more advanced work in the same branches, with the fifth reader instead of the fourth, and had begun the study of French. Several of the pupils in this class were particularly quick and intelligent in their answering.

The third class read with careful enunciation in sixth book, had a good knowledge of etymology and syntax, as set forth in the Christian Brothers' class-book, together with the analysis of simple sentences and more advanced exercises in composition. In arithmetic, considerable facility was shown in vulgar fractions and interest. The work of this class in French was a stage more advanced than that of the last-mentioned, comprising about eighty exercise of Ahn's first book. At this stage the study of book-keeping, by simple entry, and elementary algebra was introduced, and the history of Newfoundland gave place to that of England. This class on the whole, were well up to the mark in all the branches and bore themselves with creditable self-possession.

The second class, numbering twenty pupils, read with pleasing expression in the sixth book, had attained a more advanced knowledge of grammar and analysis, with more ambitious efforts in composition and a more minute acquaintance with the geography of Great Britain and America and the history of England. In arithmetic, the class had mastered vulgar and decimal fractions and the different rules involving the principle of percentage, such as Profit and Loss, Stocks, &c. The work in algebra had been extended to embrace a knowledge of all the simple rules from an elementary text-book and, in book-keeping, to double entry. The study of French, from Ahn's first book was continued, about one hundred exercises having been gone over. While their pronunciation would not perhaps come quite up to the Parisian standard, they were thoroughly familiar with the grammatical construction of sentences, as far as they had gone, and showed considerable facility in the correct rendering of easy English sentences into French and *vice-versa*. In this division, the study of Latin was taken up, pupils being well-grounded on the first part of Smith's *Principia*, to the end of Passive Voice; and natural philosophy was also introduced. I was pleased to observe in the work of this class, as a whole, an evidence of talent and power of sustained application which promise well for their future success.

The students of the first class, six in number, under the special care of Rev. Brother Crane (*sic!*) a gentleman of extensive experience as a teacher in some of the most advanced schools of the Christian Brothers' Order in Ireland, were following the programme of the London University matriculation examination for June 189I. At the time of my examination of the class in December, they had already made gratifying progress in the course. The work in Latin was particularly thorough. Recognizing the fact that a knowledge of Latin does not consist in mere ability to translate, the teacher had aimed with success to impart to his class an intelligent grasp of the syntactical principles of the language and facility in composition. I trust some of the members of this class will be encouraged to present themselves at the examination for matriculation in the London University to be held in June next, when the Newfoundland Jubilee Scholarship (value $480 per annum for two years) will be open to competition.

I was pleased to note that drawing was taught to all the classes in the College; and that the study of vocal music according to the Tonic Sol-Fa system was pursued with much zest under the direction of Rev. Brother Flood. St. Bonaventure's was thus the first educational institution in the country to introduce this new and popular system....

I have every confidence that under its present management, the institution will maintain a leading position among the educational establishments of the Colony and continue to place within reach of our youth the means of acquiring a liberal education upon the solid basis of morality and religion.

APPENDIX 3

ST. BONAVENTURE'S RHODES SCHOLARS

1904 – **Sydney M. Herbert.** Herbert worked with the Imperial Tobacco Company in England and the United Tobacco Company in South Africa. He served in WWI, and died in 1957.

1906 – **John J. Penney.** Penney taught at the Naval College in Halifax, at Esquimalt in British Columbia, and at Harvard University. He died in 1963.

1909 - **John G. Higgins.** Higgins became a lawyer and was active in the Responsible Government League. He was selected as a Progressive Conservative for St. John's East, became Leader of the opposition, and was appointed to the Senate. He died in 1963.

1911 - **John E. J. Fox.** Fox served with the Newfoundland Regiment in WW1. Later he worked as a stockbroker, controller and senior investment officer in London, Montreal and New York. He did in 1977.

1914 – **Edward H. M. Crawford.** Crawford served in both World Wars. He became a lawyer, practicing for twenty years in Winnipeg, and later in St. John's. He died in 1972.

1917 - **Harold S. Knight.** Knight served with the Royal Newfoundland Regiment and was wounded in action in France. He later practiced law in St. John's for 35 years. He died in 1965.

1918 – **William J. Browne.** Browne was a lawyer, politician and author. From 1924 to 1965 he was elected as a Conservative both provincially and federally, at one point serving as Solicitor General of Canada. He died in 1989.

1921 - **Sebastian P. Young.** Young practiced medicine in Nova Scotia until his death in 1934 from a heart condition. He was 37.

1936 - **James T. Howley.** Howley became an electrical engineer, worked in firms across Canada. He died in 1995.

1937 - **John B. Ashley.** Ashley taught at Memorial University, eventually serving as head of the Classics Department. In 1982 he was named Professor Emeritus by the university. He died in 1991.

1939 - **Fabian A. O'Dea.** O'Dea served in WWII, practiced law in St. John's and was Lieutenant Governor of Newfoundland during the 1960's.

1940 – **Douglas A. Darcy.** Darcy studied zoology at Oxford and joined the Royal Cancer Research Institute in London, England, where he did research in cancer until his retirement.

1949 - **James J. L. Greene.** Greene practiced law in London, England, and St. John's. In 1959, he was elected as a Progressive Conservative for the Provincial seat of St. John's East, and later became party leader.

1952 - **Cyril J. Fox.** Fox is a journalist and author who has worked with the Canadian Press and Reuters in London, Paris and Brussels. He lives in London, England.

1954 – **John Lewis** Lewis has practiced medicine in St. John's and Uganda. He is presently residing in St. John's.

1957 - **Arthur M. Sullivan.** Sullivan taught at Memorial University as Head of the Psychology Department, Dean of Junior Studies, and principal of Sir Wilfred Grenfell College in Corner Brook.

1962 - **Robert J. Kelly.** Kelly has worked as a business analyst with American Express and other companies in the United Kingdom.

1963 - **Neil A. Murray.** Murray worked with the Newfoundland Arts community as a writer, critic, editor and radio host. He suffered from asthma and died from respiratory failure in 1988 at the age of 44.

1966 - **Adrian J. Fowler**. Fowler worked with the English department at Memorial University, eventually becoming Principal of Sir Wilfred Grenfell College in Corner Brook.

1969 - **Daniel E. Williams.** Williams practiced law in St. John's, was owner of Cable Atlantic and is currently (2006) Premier of Newfoundland and Labrador.

1971 - **Augustus E. Lilly.** Lilly practices law in St. John's and is secretary for the Rhodes Scholarship Selection Committee.

1973 - **Robert J. Joy.** One of the founding members of the theatre group Codco., Joy has had leading acting roles on Broadway, in television, and in major Hollywood films.

1975 - **Timothy J. Whelan.** Whelan studied internal medicine with a sub-speciality in radiation oncology. He currently practices in Hamilton, Ontario.

1982 - **William H. Devlin.** Devlin is a cardiologist who practises and teaches in Michigan.

1987. **Sean P. Connors.** Connors is a cardiologist at the Health Sciences Centre in St. John's.

2000 - **Jason T. Stanley** Stanley completed a Master of Philosophy degree at Oxford. He's co-authored a book entitled, "The Healthy College Cookbook."

- compiled by Susan Chalker Browne

APPENDIX 4

ST. BONAVENTURE'S COLLEGE
WAR DEAD - WORLD WAR I

Butler, Ignatius
Berteau, Edwin
Burke, Frank, Lieut.
Byrne, Gerald
Coughlan, Louis, Sergt.
Callahan, Roger
Cleary, Allan, Sergt.
Collins, Bertram,
Chaplin, John
Coultas, Norman
Carew, Victor
Carew, Vincent
Chown, Francis
Donnelly, J. J. Capt., M.C.
Edens, John, Lieut
Edens, Leonard, Lieut.
Ellis, John, Corpl.
Farrell, Patrick
Freebairn, Buchanan
Fitzgerald, John, Sergt.
Furlong, Francis
Fry, John
Gear, James, Sergt.
Grant, William, Lieut.
Jackman, Michael

Kane, George
Kelly, Christopher
Kennedy, Michael
Lassus, John
Ledingham, James, Capt.
Meehan, Augustine
Meehan, Hubert, Corpl.
MacDonald, John
McGrath, White, M.M.
Mullings, Gordon
Mullowney, Joseph, Corpl.
Norris, Stephen, Lieut.
O'Brien, Michael
O'Brien, Patrick
O'Flynn, Michael
Petrie, Walter
Power, William
Smith, Samuel, Lieut.
Summers, M. Frank. Capt.
Shortall, Leo, Corpl.
Tobin, James, Lieut.
Tobin, Patrick, Sergt.
Templeman, Donald
Taylor, Richard,Lieut.
Walsh, David

APPENDIX 5

ST. BONAVENTURE'S COLLEGE
WAR DEAD - WORLD WAR II

Bates, Michael
Bown, Gerald
Brownrigg, Garrett
Callanan, Gordon
Cantwell, Gerard
Cleary, Alban
Collins, William
Delaney, Thomas
Dicks, Thomas
English, Lt. Cmr. Dermot
Evans, Kevin
Finn, James
Fitzgibbon, Joseph
Fitzpatrick, Robert
Gamberg, John
Garland, William
Hibbs, William
Howley, Richard
Hynes, William
Jackman, Thomas

Kenny, Brendan
Lacey, Brendan
Larner, Arthur
Maher, Leo
McDonald, George
Murphy, Myles
Oakley, James
O'Connor, Gerald
O'Keefe, Ralph
Penney, Fintan
Pippy, William
Russell, Gerald
Smith, Francis
Sinnott, James E.
Stick, James M.
Strapp, Dr. Gerald
Thorburn, Bonaventure
Tooton, Theodore
Trainor, Dermot
Veitch, John

APPENDIX 6

MEMBERS OF THE ST. BON'S
26 BOYLE TROPHY CHAMPIONSHIP TEAMS
1928-1959

1928 - E. Robertson (M.), E. J. Phelan, (Capt.), G. Halley, (Vice- Capt.), W. Kendall, M. Monahan, G. F. Higgins, T. Sutton, A. Graham, J. Wood, F. Graham, W. Cotter.

1930 - B. White, G. J. Egan, E. Kennedy, G. Halley, T. Sutton, E. English, A. Hamlyn, W. Cotter, A. Graham, E. Phelan, (Capt.), M. Monahan, F. Graham, W. Kendall, J. Quigley, P. Keegan, (M.)

1931 - E. Phelan, E. Kennedy, F. Graham, B. Hutton, G. Halley, A. Hamlyn, W. Cotter, (Capt.), P. Keegan, (M.), T. Sutton, A. Graham.

1932 - W. Cotter, (Capt.), F. Graham, E. Kennedy, T. Sutton, E. English, A. Graham, A. Hamlyn, G. Halley, B. Hutton, P. Keegan, (M.)

1933 - W. Cotter, (Capt.) , F. Graham, E. Kennedy, T. Sutton, E. English, A. Graham, A. Hamlyn, G. Halley, B. Hutton, P. Keegan (Mgr.)

1936 - A. Hamlyn, (Capt.), G. Halley, G. Hanley, R. Furlong, F. Cahill, B. Maher, B. Hutton, E. Brophy, R. Godden, J. Maher, J. Norris, F. W. Donnelly (Coach).

1937 - A. Hamlyn, (Capt.), F. Cahill, G. Hanley, R. Furlong, C. Godden, J. Vinicombe, B. Hutton, E. Brophy, J. Edstrom, B. Collins, J. Maher, L. Walsh, E. Furlong, P. Henley, J. Coffey, E. Berrigan, F. W. Donnelly, (Coach), R. S. Furlong, (Mgr.)

1938 - C. Thompson, P. Henley, R. Simms, B. Collins, W. Byrne, G. Hanley, R. Furlong, B. Hutton, F. Cahill, (Capt.), J. Vinicombe, E. Berrigan, A. Felix, F. Graham, J. Edstrom, K. Brophy, W. Comerford, F. W. Donnelly, (Coach), R. S. Furlong, (Mgr.)

1939 - C. Thompson, K. Brophy, C. Penny, B. Walsh, F. Gamberg, L. O'Reilly, B. Collins, W. Harris, J. Vinicombe, J. Veitch, W. Collins, J. Foley, F. Thompson, W. Byrne, J. Dunne, F. Cahill, R. Furlong (Capt.), F. W. Donnelly, (Coach), R. S. Furlong, (Mgr.)

1940 - F. Gamberg, J. Finn, J. Vinicombe, (Capt.), F. Cahill, W. Harris, J. Veitch, C. Thompson, R. Furlong, J. Dunne, W. Collins, L. O'Reilly, B. Collins, B. Walsh, C. Penny, J. Foley, D. O'Driscoll, F. W. Donnelly, (Coach), R. S. Furlong, (Mgr.)

1944 - W. Harris, (Capt.), J. G. Doyle, J. G. Kielly, C. G. Power, J. J. Reardigan, C. P. Power, H. M. Furlong, C. J. Penny, W. A. Power, T. G. Trainor, N. J. Vinicombe, J. F. Walsh, F. W. Donnelly, (Coach), J. T. Vinicombe, (Mgr.)

1945 - C G. Power, (Capt.), C. J. Penny, F. M. Gamberg, J. G. Doyle, H. M. Furlong, H. C. Fardy, P. O'Mara, T. G. Trainor, N. J. Vinicombe, W. A. Power, J. J. Vinicombe, J. F. Walsh, W. F. Harris, (Coach), J. T. Vinicombe, (Mgr.)

1946 - C. G. Power, (Capt.), F. M. Gamberg, J. G. Doyle, T. G. Trainor, H. C. Fardy, H. M. Furlong, N. J. Vinicombe, W. A. Power, G. E. Gillies, F. J. Murphy, J. J. Reardigan, J. G. Kielty, W. A. Corbett, W. J. Harris, (Coach), J. Vinicombe, (Mgr.), A. Jamieson.

1947 - C. G. Power, (Capt.), W. J. Harris, F. M. Gamberg, J. G. Doyle, H. M. Furlong, T. G. Trainor, H. C. Fardy, E. P. Murphy, E. C. Withers, J. J. Reardigan, F. J. Murphy, N. J. Vinicombe, W. A. Power, F. W. Donnelly, (Coach), J. T. Vinicombe, (Mgr.)

1948 - C. G. Power, (Capt.), W. J. Harris, F. M. Gamberg, H. M. , Furlong, H. C. Fardy, W. A. Furlong, T. G. Trainor, N. J. Vinicombe, E. C. Withers, J. J. Reardigan, F. J. Murphy, W. A. Corbett, E. P. Murphy, H. E. Conway, J. G. Doyle, F. W. Donnelly, (Coach), J. T. Vinicombe, (Mgr.)

1949 - C. G. Power, (Capt.), J. G. Doyle, F. M. Gamberg, H. C. Fardy, H. M. Furlong, N. J. Vinicombe, E. C. Withers, J. F. Ryan, W. A. Corbett, J. J. Reardigan, J. J. McNamara, G. E. Gillies, H. E. Conway, F. J. Murphy, F. W. Donnelly, (Coach), J. T. Vinicombe, (Mgr.)

1950 - C. G. Power, (Capt.), J. G. Doyle, F. M. Gamberg, H. C. Fardy, N. C. Hutton, H. M. Furlong, F. J. Murphy, N. J. Vinicombe, W. A. Corbett, G. E. Gillies, J. F. Ryan, J. J . Reardigan, J. J. McNamara, R. J. Furlong, F. W. Donnelly, (Coach), J. T. Vinicombe, (Mgr.)

1951 - H. C. Fardy, (Capt.), J. G. Doyle, F. M. Gamberg, N. C. Hutton, E. M. Manning, N. J. Vinicombe, W. A. Corbett, G. E. Gillies, J. F. Ryan, F. J. Murphy, J. J. Reardigan, J. J. McNamara, J. Vinicombe, (Coach), J. T. Vinicombe, (Mgr.)

1952 - H. Fardy, (Capt.), N. J. Vinicombe, J. G. Doyle, N. C. Hutton, E. M. Manning, C. Maddigan, J. F. Ryan, G. E. Gillies, J. J. Reardigan, W. A. Corbett, J. J. McNamara, N. Sparrow, C. Greene, M. V. Greene, J. Vinicombe, (Coach), J. T. Vinicombe, (Mgr.)

1953 - G. E. Gillies, (Capt.), J. J. Reardigan, J. Ryan, N. J. Vinicombe, W. A. Corbett, N. Sparrow, F. Fardy, W. Organ, N. C. Hutton, C. Greene, E. M. Manning, J. G: Doyle, M. V. Greene, J. Vinicombe, J. T. Vinicombe, (Mgr.)

1954 - G. G. Gamberg, N. J. Vinicombe, W. A. Corbett, E. M. Manning, N. Sparrow, G. E. Gillies, (Capt.), F. J. Murphy, J. F. Ryan, J. J. Reardigan, H. C. Fardy, N. C. Hutton, M. Greene, C. Greene, J. Vinicombe, (Coach), J. T. Vinicombe, (Mgr.)

1955 - M. Greene, G. G. Gamberg, H. C. Fardy, (Capt.), N. C. Hutton, C. Greene, L. Coughlin, W. Organ, N. J. Vinicombe, C. G. Power, W. Corbett, J. J. Reardigan, N. Sparrow, G. E. Gillies, E. M. Manning, J. F. Ryan, J. Vinicombe, (Coach), J. T. Vinicombe, (Mgr.)

1956 - M. Greene, H. C. Fardy, (Capt.) , N. C. Hutton, L. Coughlin, T. Murphy, N. Sparrow, E. Gillies, E. M. Manning, J. F. Ryan, J. J. McNamara, J. J. Reardigan, W. Organ, G. G. Gamberg, D. Sharpe, T. Manning, M. Woodford, (Coach), J. T. Vinicombe, (Mgr.)

1957 - G. G. Gamberg, M. Greene, H. C. Fardy, N. C. Hutton, L. Coughlin, D. Sharpe, W. Organ, G. E. Gillies, M. Woodford, N. Sparrow, F. J. Murphy, J. F. Ryan, R. Redmond, D. Barrett, T. Manning, D. Ryan, C. Doyle, (Coach), J. T. Vinicombe, (Mgr.), T. Woodford, (Prop.).

1958 - G. G. Gamberg, M. Greene, H. C. Fardy, (Coach), N. C. Hutton, L. Coughlin, D. Sharpe, D. Barrett, G. E. Gillies, M. Woodford, (Capt.), F. Power, R. Redmond, W. Gillies, D. Ryan, T. Murphy, J. F. Ryan, G. Lawlor, D. Sinnott, W. MacDonald, J. T. Vinicombe, (Mgr.), T. Woodford, (Prop.).

1959 - M. Greene, N. Hutton, L. Couglin, D. Sharpe, J. Slaney, E. Browne, E. Gillies, G. Gillies, B. Redmond, T. Murphy, D. Ryan, M. Woodford (playing coach), J. McNamara, E. St. George, N. Sparrow, G. Lawlor, D. Barrett, G. Gamberg, F. O'Grady (Mgr.) J. Walsh (Prop.).

INDEX